Dreamways of the Iroquois

"Moss's book reminds us of the spiritual magic awaiting each of us tonight when we cross the dreamgate to personal discovery. On the wings of his shamanic adventure, we follow Red-tailed Hawk, Dancing Bear, Silver Wolf, Wounded Stag, and his other guides to encounter the Ancient Mother who teaches him, and us, the 'way of the heart.' His practical tools help today's readers reclaim these ancient Dreamways for our own paths to healing and soul remembering."

PATRICIA GARFIELD, PH.D., author of *Creative Dreaming* and co-founder of The Association for the Study of Dreams

"In this remarkable book Robert Moss participates in Native American cultural knowledge directly—via his own dreams. His experiences delving into the Iroquois spiritual world along with his use of fascinating historical materials combine to make a rich literary feast. *Dreamways of the Iroquois* suggests that we profoundly coexist with those who live, or have lived, in our landscapes. It also offers valuable dreamwork techniques for understanding ourselves."

CHARLES STEWART, PH.D., Department of Anthropology, University College of London

"Before the European invasion of North America, advanced systems of knowledge had been amassed over the centuries by indigenous people. One of the most remarkable aspects of the Iroquois tradition was the process by which they worked with dreams. In this entertaining and informative book, Robert Moss has made these 'dreamways' available to contemporary readers, who will be inspired by the spiritual insight and practical advice that is still applicable today."

STANLEY KRIPPNER, PH.D., co-author of *Extraordinary Dreams and How to Work With Them*

Dreamways of the Iroquois

HONORING THE SECRET WISHES OF THE SOUL

Robert Moss

Destiny Books

Rochester, Vermont

Destiny Books
One Park Street
Rochester, Vermont 05767
www.InnerTraditions.com

Destiny Books is a division of Inner Traditions International

LIBRARY OF CONGRESS CATALOGING-IN-PUBLICATION DATA

Moss, Robert, 1946-
Dreamways of the Iroquois : honoring the secret wishes of the
soul / Robert Moss.
p. cm.
Includes bibliographical references and index.
ISBN 1-59477-034-4
1. Dreams. 2. Spiritual life. 3. Iroquois Indians—Religion—Miscellanea.
I. Title.
BF1091.M794 2005
299.7'855—dc22
2004021975

Printed and bound in the United States by Lake Book Manufacturing, Inc.

10   9   8   7   6   5   4   3   2

Text design by Mary Anne Hurhula
Text layout by Virginia Scott Bowman
This book was typeset in Sabon and Avenir with Gittani and
Skylark as the display typefaces

For Island Woman and her Sisters

The dreamworld is the Real World.

SENECA IROQUOIS SAYING

The soul has the ability to conform to her character the destiny that is allotted to her.

PLOTINUS

Magicam operare non est aliud quam maritare mundum

The work of the magus is none other than to marry the worlds.

PICO DELLA MIRANDOLA, CONCLUSIONES MAGICAE

Tohsa sasa nikon'hren—*Do not let your mind fall; do not forget.*

MOHAWK IROQUOIS SAYING

Contents

≋ Part Three ≋
THE TEACHINGS OF ISLAND WOMAN

≋ Part Four ≋
RECLAIMING THE ANCIENT DREAMWAYS

Acknowledgments

An adequate return of thanks to all of those who have encouraged, inspired, and supported me over the years since I started dreaming in Mohawk and embarked on the path of a dream teacher could easily occupy half the pages of this book. But I will keep this very short, in thanking four overlapping groups of friends and helpers: the Iroquois, the scholars, the dreamers, and the life supporters.

I begin by giving thanks to the Onkwehonwe, the Real People. I would never have presumed to write some of the most important passages in this book unless I had been given very strong reasons to believe that I had received blessing and direction from some of the "great ones"—above all, the arendiwanen I have identified as Island Woman. In my journeys among the Iroquois today, I was greatly helped and inspired by Ray Gonyea, Tom Porter, Peter Jemison, Hazel Dean-John, the late Chief Jake Thomas and Jan Longboat, among many others. I owe a great debt of gratitude to David R. Maracle of the Bay of Quinte band of the Mohawks for his pioneer *Mohawk Language Dictionary*, which helped me to decipher some of my dreams. At every turning, I have been conscious of the tremendous legacy—and sometimes the presence—of the great Tuscarora scholar of the Iroquois, J. N. B. Hewitt.

As I have noted in the book, the Iroquois have attracted the attention of some marvelously gifted scholars. I have benefited greatly from the generosity of William N. Fenton, Dean R. Snow, and George Hamell in sharing the fruits of their dedicated research over many decades. (None of them, of course, is to be held accountable for the use I have made of it!)

How can I begin to thank the dreamers? Over the years since I first encountered Island Woman, many thousands of dreamers have attended my workshops and shared their experiences with me, sometimes in shared adventures *inside* the dreamworlds. They are all my teachers. I was blessed, early on, to discover in Wanda Easter Burch a dream sister who was also a scholar of William Johnson and the Iroquois. I found a second dream sister in Carol Davis, and a wonderfully creative dream friend in Elizabeth Dimarco. For many years, I have benefitted greatly from the friendship and shared experience of a circle of Active Dreamers who gather with me twice a year on a mountain in Mohawk country in the Adirondacks where the Deer energy is strong (and Dragons are sometimes seen). At our private retreats we test-fly new techniques and embark on group dream travel, sacred drama, and spontaneous ritual.

I have gained many insights on contrasting approaches to dreaming and dreamwork from many delightful encounters with dream researchers and fellow-explorers in the International Association for the Study of Dreams, including Rita Dwyer, Stanley Krippner, Iain Edgar, Steve and Wewer Keohane, Robert Bosnack, Deirdre Barrett, Patricia Garfield, Wendy Pannier, Edward Bruce Bynum, Aad van Ouwerkerk, Alan Worsley, Richard Russo, and Bob and Lynn Hoss.

My understanding of how to adapt core shamanic techniques to modern society was enhanced by early trainings with Michael Harner, Sandra Ingerman, and the late Jessica Allen.

In my appreciation of how conscious dreaming techniques can facilitate imaginal healing, I was greatly inspired by the splendid work of Larry Dossey, Jean Achterberg, and Mary Watkins.

In the category of life supporters, I give thanks to the centers, sponsors and facilitators who have provided or created homes for my dream workshops over the years. The centers include the Kripalu Center for Yoga and Health in western Massachusetts, the Esalen Institute in Big Sur, the Still Point retreat center (near Saratoga, New York), East-West in Seattle, and the Ursuline Sophie Center in Cleveland. Among the hosts for the dreaming, my deepest debt is to my endlessly generous and dedicated volunteer Dream School facilitators, including Irene D'Alessio (who made good on her promise to create a modern "dream temple" in

Connecticut), Karen Silverstein, Donna Katsuranis, Susan Koenig, Elizabeth Dimarco, Susan Morgan, Liza Glazer and Ted Stefan, Karen Nell McKean, Carol Dombrose, Claire McKay, Lynda Jones, Josée DiSario and Joe Pincin, and Suzette Rios-Scheurer.

In my literary and historical research, I was supported by the dedicated staff of many libraries, museums and historic sites, including Johnson Hall, Fort Johnson, Ganondagan State Historic Site, Fort William Henry, Fort Ticonderoga, the Iroquois Indian Museum, the Albany Institute of History and Art, the New York State Library, the New York Historical Society, the New York State Historical Association, the Rochester Museum and Science Center, the Field Museum of Natural History, the National Museum of Man in Ottawa, the Woodland Indian Cultural Center in Brantford, Ontario, and the Albany Public Library.

In my quest for the Celtic ancestors who came stalking me in my dreams, I was inspired and guided by the excellent work of Count Nikolai Tolstoy (who put me on the trail of a Scottish Merlin in the landscape of my father's people), John and Caitlin Matthews, Miranda Green, Nigel Pennick, and Frank Henderson MacEowen.

On the way to turning many dreams and drafts into the present book, I was greatly helped and encouraged by Timothy White, the scholarly—as well as visionary—editor of *Shaman's Drum*, who goaded and guided me in shaping my early research into two articles that provide the meat for the chapter titled "Meeting the Dream People."

I have described in the introduction how Hawk guided me to a publisher whose nickname is "Hawk." I felt blessed to have found a new family in the extraordinary community of "farmers of the imagination" at Inner Traditions. I am especially grateful to Jon Graham, who knew at once that the old ones of the land were calling, to Jeanie Levitan, to my dedicated project editor, Vickie Trihy, to Susannah Noel, and of course to Ehud Sperling, a visionary publisher who sees (as the Iroquois say) "many looks away."

My work is sustained and strengthened every day by the loving support of my dream family and my home family. I am grateful, as always, for the love and understanding of my wife Marcia and my daughters.

My deepest debt is to my guides and teachers in the Real World, those who kept calling me to "remember the Sky" and follow the path with heart even when my little self found this risky or inconvenient. This is something all dreamers will understand.

Dreaming in Hawk

CALLED BY AN ANCIENT DREAMER

In the mid-1980s, I moved to a farm outside Chatham, in upstate New York, to get away from the hurry of big cities and the commercial fast track I had been on. I bought the farm because of an old white oak behind the house that had survived being struck by lightning. I felt an ancient kinship with this oak. When I first visited the property, I sat under her canopy, with my back against her broad trunk, and I let my awareness drift. I found myself watching scenes that might have been played out on this land in the centuries the oak had stood here. I felt I could slip deep into the earth through her roots. A deep earth energy rose up, strong and juicy, through the soles of my feet, through the base of my spine and my lower energy centers. I let my awareness float up, and I drank in the sunlight, like the tree. I flowed into the deep dream of the heartwood.

I opened my eyes and looked skyward. A red-tailed hawk hovered directly overhead, turning in slow circles. Its underfeathers flashed silver-bright, its wedge-shaped tail a deep russet red. It cried out several times, a sharp, slurring call. *Krrrrr, krrrr, krrrr.* As I walked back to the farmhouse, I found that the hawk had left me a wing feather. I took it as confirmation of what I had felt, sitting with the oak. I was being called to this land.

After I moved to the farm, the red-tailed hawk often appeared when I was walking the land, circling low over my head, speaking with gathering insistence in a language I felt I could understand, if only I could speak Hawk.

One night, the hawk lent me her wings. As the lightning bugs danced over the fields, I drifted in the twilight zone between waking and sleep. One of the images that rose spontaneously on my mental screen was a double spiral. I had studied one like it, carved in rock thousands of years ago, on a guardian stone at the great megalithic tomb at Newgrange during a recent trip to Ireland. I thought of it as the Eyes of the Goddess, containing the whirling patterns of creation and destruction. I was drawn into the double spiral. The shapes swirled and pulled me through. I found myself lifting effortlessly out of my body. I flowed toward a window, and its texture stretched like toffee to let me pass. I reveled in the sense of flight as I lifted above the tree line, traveling north over the villages in the direction of Lake George. The sense of flying was vividly physical, and, as I enjoyed it, I realized I was neither disembodied nor confined to my regular form. I had sprouted wings. They were those of a hawk, but scaled to my human proportions. I enjoyed the sensation of riding a thermal, and of swooping down to inspect the shoreline of the lake—and then the small stab of discomfort as one of my wings scraped the needles of an old dried-up spruce.

I noticed that the scenes below me seemed to be those of another time. There was no development around the lake, no modern roads, few signs of settlement. I flew over primal forests. I felt a tug of intention drawing me ever north. I chose to follow it, without any sense of compulsion. I was drawn down to a cabin in the woods, and I felt I might be somewhere near Montreal, though in this reality the modern city of Montreal did not exist.

I was welcomed by an ancient woman of great beauty and power. She held a wide, beaded belt. One end was draped over her shoulder. She stroked the belt as she spoke in a musical cadenced voice, wave after wave of sound lapping like lake water. I noticed that the beads were cylindrical and were mostly shining white, so bright they cast a glow between us. Human and animal figures—the silhouettes of a man and a woman holding hands, and a wolf—had been outlined in darker beads.

I was thrilled by this encounter, but mystified. The ancient woman's language was more foreign to me than the hawk's. In subsequent dreams and visions, I was drawn deeper into the world of the ancient woman. Though she spoke in a language I did not know, she spoke—like the hawk—as if I should understand her. I wrote down bits and pieces of her monologues, transcribing the words phonetically as best I could. Then, I sought out people in the ordinary world who might be able to decipher them for me. Native speakers eventually identified my dream language as an archaic form of the Mohawk Iroquois language—"the way we might have spoken three hundred years ago"—laced with some Huron words.

In time, I was helped to understand that the ancient woman who had called me was an *arendiwanen*, or woman of power, an *atetshents*, or dream shaman, and a clan mother of the Wolf Clan of the Mohawk nation, and that she was speaking to me from another time as well as another dimension. I came to call her Island Woman, partly because she was born among the Hurons, whom the Mohawks called the Island People.*

In contact with her, I became vividly aware of the possibility of time travel in dreaming. We can travel into the future to scout out challenges and opportunities that lie ahead on the road of life. We can also reach into the future—as Island Woman seemed to be doing—for solutions to problems that cannot be resolved with the tools available in our own time. Most exciting, as conscious dream travelers we can enter the now time of people living in other eras, past or future, and bring one another mutual support, guidance, and healing. The people we can visit through timefolding in this way may include our own younger or older selves.

THROUGH THE MOONGATE

These awakenings were thrilling, but not altogether exotic for me. I should explain that the dreamworld is my home base. While I was fascinated that the Iroquois say matter-of-factly that the dreamworld is the Real World (they call our waking existence the Shadow World or surface world), this is something I had known since my early childhood in Australia. Let me share a story about that by way of personal introduction. This episode is also an example of timefolding and transtemporal guidance and healing.

---

*The Jesuit missionary who compiled the first Mohawk lexicon reported in the seventeenth century that the Mohawks called the Hurons "Island People"—a term he rendered as *Hati'endogerha*—"because they used to live on an island." Jacques Bruyas, *Radices verborum iroquaeorum* [Root Words of the Iroquois], New York: Cramoisy Press, 1863, 22, 55, 69

When I was nine years old, I was rushed to a hospital in Melbourne, Australia, after complaining of a pain in my lower-right abdomen. The doctors found that my appendix was about to burst. They were worried about my ability to survive the operation, because I had just barely made it through the latest of many bouts of pneumonia. "You'd better give up on this one," one of the doctors told my mother. "He's never going to make it."

Under anesthesia on the operating table, I stepped out of my body, decided I did not care to watch the bloody work with the scalpel, and flowed through the door—which seemed to stretch before letting my energy body through—and along the corridor to where my mother sat hunched and weeping, my father's strong arm about her shoulders.

I moved to a window, to the brightness outside, to the colors of spring and the laughter of young lovers seated at a sidewalk table, drinking in each other's smiles. I felt the pull of the ocean. I could not see the beach from the hospital window, so I floated through the glass and out onto a ledge where a blackbird squalled at me and shot straight up into the air. I followed the bird and sailed over the rooftops.

Soaring over the city, I saw a huge moon face, its mouth opened wide to form the gateway to Luna Park, a popular amusement park on the water. I swooped down through the moongate—and plunged into darkness. I tried to reverse direction, but something sucked me downward. It was like tumbling into a mine shaft, miles beneath the surface of the earth.

I fell into a different world. It was hard to make out anything clearly because of smoke from a huge fire pit. A giant with skin the color of fine white ash lifted me high above the ground, singing. The people of this world welcomed me. They were tall and elongated and very pale, and they did not look like anyone I had seen in my nine years in the surface world. They told me they had dreamed my coming.

Years passed. These people raised me as their own. For the greater part of my schooling, I was required to dream—to dream alone, in an incubation cave, or to dream with others, lying around the banked ashes of the fire in the council house.

In the highest festival of the year, when the bonfires rose higher than the bird-headed finials of the council house, I was ritually joined to the favorite niece of the shaman-king of this people. As I grew older, my recollection of my life in the surface world faded and flickered out. I became a father and grandfather, a shaman and elder. When my body was played out, the people placed it on a funeral pyre.

As the smoke rose from the pyre, I traveled with it, looking for the path among the stars where the fires of the galaxies flow together like milk. As I spiraled upward out of my home below the earth's surface, I was entranced by the beauty of growing things. I plunged into the intoxication of green and burst through the earth's crust into a world of hot asphalt and cars and trains—and found myself shooting back into the tormented body of a nine-year-old boy in a Melbourne hospital bed.

From this and other experiences in early childhood, I have known, for as long as I can remember, that there are worlds beyond physical reality. But growing up in a military family in a conservative era, I found there were few people in waking life with whom I could safely share experiences of this kind. The first person I met who confirmed and validated my experiences was an Aboriginal boy, raised in a tradition that values dreaming and teaches that the dreamworld is a real world.

I met Jacko when I was living with my family in a rough suburb of Brisbane. We rode the trains and walked in the bush and told each other our dreams. Jacko confirmed that dreaming is traveling: we routinely get out of our bodies and can travel into the future, or into other dimensions, including realms of the ancestors and spiritual guides. Jacko's uncle, a popular artist, got the ideas for his most important work—the sacred paintings that were not for the tourists—by going into the Dreamtime.

In my dreams, other guides came to me. One of them was a radiant young Greek who insisted on using the difficult vocabulary of the neo-Platonic philosophers; he taught me that true knowledge comes through *anamnesis,* "remembering" the knowledge that belonged to us, on the level of soul and spirit, before we entered our current lives. One of my dream visitors was a dashing Royal Air Force pilot from the era of World War II. Another of my dream friends was a large man with white hair who seemed like a benign uncle. During my successive illnesses, he would turn up to promise me that despite everything, I was going to make it through. He would say, "This may seem strange, but a day will come when people will not only listen to your dreams, but will be eager to hear them." This avuncular man had an odd request. He wanted me to put salt and pepper on my crumpets when my mother took me to the café in Myer's department store for afternoon tea during her shopping expeditions. This was noted by my family as just one more of my boyhood oddities.

My Greek visitor showed me a serpent of living gold, wrapped around a staff, and told me that this sign would heal me. Walking home from school one day, I saw a stormy sky open to reveal the same image blown up to colossal proportions. After this, my series of life-threatening illnesses ceased.

As I followed my dreams in adult life, I found that it was possible to journey into multidimensional reality without undergoing the ordeals of my boyhood—that every night, in our dreams, gateways open into realms of limitless adventure and possibility. Many decades later, I returned to Australia from my new home in upstate New York to teach dreamwork techniques to large audiences. At an exhibition of Aboriginal art in a Sydney museum, I saw a wall of paintings that depicted, rather exactly, the beings I had encountered when I went flying through the moongate of Luna Park. They were the work of an Arnhem Land artist who called the pale elongated forms "mimi spirits." He said that when he gets sick, he goes to live among these spirits, and when he gets well, he returns to his regular world.

In Melbourne, I went to Myer's department store to eat crumpets with salt and pepper in the café. I discovered that crumpets were no longer on the menu. But as I glanced at myself in a mirror, I saw the big man with white hair who had visited me in my childhood. It was my adult self. I realized he had kept his promise.

HAWK GIVES ME THE GREEN LIGHT

After several years at the farm where I started dreaming in Island Woman's language, I was guided by a new cycle of dreams to move on, to places where I could pursue the big dream of midwifing the birth of a dreaming society in our times. On the day I drove away, I suddenly felt an urgent need to go back inside the house. There was no rational reason for doing this; I had checked and rechecked it repeatedly prior to leaving. But as I stepped into the kitchen, I heard an odd scuffling sound coming from the family room. I went in and saw something moving behind the screen of the huge fireplace. I found that a fledgling red-tailed hawk had somehow come down the chimney and was trapped. My last action—at the farm where Hawk had summoned me to explore new worlds—was to gently carry the fledgling outside, holding it near my heart, and release it. I watched joyously as it rose on shining wings and glided toward the old white oak that had shared my dreaming.

I continued to dream of Island Woman, and characters from her time, and Hawk continued to guide me. This brings me to the story of how I came to write and publish this book. I kept dreaming I had a new publisher, located in a pleasant rural setting far from the big city. I noticed around the same time that I had an increasing number of wonderful books on my shelves with logos of either Anubis, the Egyptian guide to the Otherworld, or Bear, the great Native American medicine animal. These were symbols of two imprints of Inner Traditions, an independent publishing house that, I now saw, was located in the village of Rochester, Vermont. They also happened to be important and favorite figures in the bestiary of my own visionary travels.

I decided to write to Ehud Sperling, the founder and publisher of Inner Traditions. He responded very quickly with a warm and spirited letter. We agreed that I would come to Rochester to meet the people at the company and see what dreams we might grow together.

Driving north from my new home on the Mohawk side of the Hudson River, I was alert for a signal from Hawk. I felt quite sure, given the genesis of my Iroquois connection, that if Inner Traditions was the right publisher for a book on that theme, Hawk would give me another sign.

On that glorious fall day, I saw not a single hawk along the drive. But as I approached the village, I noticed a beautiful sign with a painting of a red-tailed hawk with its wings outspread. The text on the sign read GREAT HAWK COLONY. Of course I made a sharp left, following the sign, looking for hawks. The side road wound up a hill. Handsome houses were set back among the trees on winding streets that had the names of raptors: Sparrowhawk Road, Osprey Road, Great Hawk Road. It took me a little time to realize that the Great Hawk Colony is an upscale development, not a bird sanctuary.

I stopped to ask a couple of workmen, through my car window, "Are there hawks here, or just people?"

"Mostly just people," one of them said, waving back. "Unfortunately."

I drove into the charming, quirky village of Rochester, Vermont, still hoping for a sign. Inner Traditions occupies a rambling Victorian Gothic with a steep gabled roof, right on the village green. Jon Graham, the scholarly and highly intuitive acquisitions editor, greeted me and led me through the building, introducing me to everyone. I was struck by how happy and alive the people seemed to be. There was magic crackling in the air.

As we walked around, I heard frequent references to the hawk. "Send it to Hawk." "Call Hawk." "I'm going to Hawk."

Jon answered my obvious question. Ehud Sperling, the publisher, lived on Great Hawk Road, and his home was referred to as "Hawk" by his coworkers. When he received me in his office, I saw that Ehud himself had the sharp, farsighted look of a desert hawk. He told me a dream from his boyhood in which he moved north to a community of artists, writers, creators—"farmers of the imagination," as he called them. He said he was happy to be living his dream now. I commented that, if it were my dream, I might reflect that it not only showed me a future path, but gave me the power of manifestation. We talked for a while about just that: how, as dreamers, we can be cocreators of our world.

When I told Ehud how I had been looking for a sign from Hawk, he said, "That was my nickname even before I moved to Great Hawk Road. People used to call me Hawk."

I guess Hawk did give me the green light.

FOUR ROADS OF DREAMING

Four is the sacred number of indigenous America. Accordingly, I've divided the book into four parts and four modes.

Journey to the Heart of Ancient Mother

Part 1 relates the personal odyssey that began when Island Woman called me. It reports on my forays—through books and colonial documents, through travel in Indian country today, and, above all, through dream travel to the ancient shamans and teachers—along the dreamways of the ancient Iroquois.

This section describes a tradition of shamanic dreaming that goes much deeper than Western psychology, deeper than the ordinary world. The Iroquois understand that dreams may be both experiences of the soul, and revelations of the soul's wishes and of our life's sacred purpose. In dreams, we routinely travel outside the body and the limits of time and space, and we receive visitations from other travelers who are also unbounded by physical laws. Our dreams also reveal what Island Woman's people called the *ondinnonk*, the secret wish of the soul. It is important to recognize what the soul wants, what the heart yearns for, as opposed to the petty agendas of our daily trivial mind, or the expectations we internalize from other people who constantly tell us who we are and what we can and cannot do. The Iroquois teach that it is the responsibility of caring people in a caring society to gather around dreamers and help them unfold their dreams and search them to identify the wishes of the soul and the soul's purpose—and then to take action to honor the soul's intent. This goes to the heart of healing, because if we are not living from our souls, our lives lose magic and vitality. Part of our soul may even go away, leaving a hole in our being.

The Iroquois believe that dreaming is one of the most important ways to acquire and accumulate authentic power. The Iroquoian term for this power is *orenda*. Those with unusual access to orenda—those who have the ability to harness and channel it—can accomplish extraordinary things as healers, creators, and leaders, because they can shape-shift the world.

The Iroquois also believe that beings from the spirit world are constantly seeking to communicate with us in the dreamspace, which offers an open frontier for contact between humans and the more than human, including the god/goddess we can talk to. Whether we are even comfortable with the word *spirits,* my own experiences suggest that—whatever we call them—there are two kinds of spirits we will encounter: the spirits of the place where we live, and our ancestral spirits going all the way back through the bloodlines to wherever our stock originated (Africa for sure, and maybe places before Africa).

The easiest and often the most comfortable way to interact with spirits is in dreaming. The connection between dreaming and visits with the departed is actually embedded in the English language. The English word *dream,* like the German *Traum,* the Dutch *droom,* and the corresponding Scandinavian terms, all preserve the Old Germanic root word *draugr,* which signifies one who is dead and returns to visit or haunt the living.[1]

We may discover, as we awaken to the deeper reality, that in addition to a connection with ancestral spirits and the spirits of the land, we are related to a spiritual family that transcends bloodlines and is not confined to linear time or three-dimensional space. Although this book focuses on a particular tradition, we are going to find that the great dream shamans of that way are in contact with the great ones of other traditions, and that any authentic way of knowing can take us back to the wells of memory that belong to all of us who are fully alive and ensouled.

The Iroquois Dream a World

Part 2 revisions and retells the great Iroquois Dreamtime stories of how a world is created and can be renewed.

The secret wisdom of the Iroquois, like that of so many ancient people, is encoded in sacred stories. The greatest of these stories belong to the Dreamtime, to a realm beyond linear time from which the events and situations of physical life are manifested. These stories describe the origin of our world and define the web of relationship between humans and the animate universe. They offer a detailed geography of multidimensional reality and paths for reclaiming the knowledge of higher worlds. In their dramas, we can find courage and moral purpose for our own journeys. We can also find practical guidance for healing ourselves and our world.

In the Iroquoian languages, to forget is to let your mind fall. *Tohsa sasa nikon'hren*, "do not forget," means literally "do not let your mind fall." The consequences of forgetting the origins and purpose of human existence are dramatized in the great Dreamtime stories of the Iroquois.

The Teachings of Island Woman

Part 3 enters the time and voice of Island Woman, the Iroquois dream shaman who called me on the wings of the hawk. It tells the story of the making of a great Iroquois woman of power and her extraordinary—and ultimately successful—attempt to reach across time and space, through dreaming, to find ways for her people to survive the irruption of the Europeans and their imported diseases, and the warfare generated by their greed and rivalries.

Just as Island Woman called to me across time, she has called, and continues to call, to others. I have come to believe she has sisters in other times and cultures who communicate with one another in dreaming, and who call selected men, as well as women, to champion their efforts to find a path for humanity through the Dark Times, to defend the Earth, and to open (or close, when necessary) gates between the worlds.

I was close to completing this book when Island Woman astonished me by stepping into my mind and telling me she belonged to a sisterhood of seers and priestesses who operate in various times and places—and who were taking an interest in *me*. The story of the Sisters of the Stones, as she refers to them, must be reserved for another book, but the sisters are introduced here because that is what Island Woman tells me she wants.

Reclaiming the Ancient Dreamways

Part 4 provides tools for reclaiming the ancient dreamways. For Island Woman, and for other messengers from the Dreamtime introduced in this book, this is a matter of supreme urgency. You will read why in the epilogue.

I must confess that I have a burning agenda: I want to do everything possible to help rebirth a dreaming culture, a society in which dreams are shared and celebrated everywhere, every when—in the workplace, in our families and schools, in our health-care facilities, in the line at the supermarket checkout, in a quiet moment in bed with a partner. If we honor dreams in our society as Island Woman honored dreams, we can heal and reenchant our world. Our relationships will be richer, more intimate and creative. Partners will remember how to honor and pleasure the god and goddess in each other. Parents will wake up to what their children *really* need and aspire to, and we will learn from our kids—who are wonderful dreamers until the "grown-up" world crushes their dreaming—what it truly means to dream.

In our dreaming culture, dream groups will be a vital part of every clinic, hospital, and treatment center, and doctors will begin their patient interviews by asking about dreams as well as physical symptoms. Health costs will plummet, because when we listen to our dreams, we receive keys to self-healing and we can detect—and sometimes avert—unwanted symptoms long before they manifest in the body. As a dreaming culture, we will remember that the sources of wellness and dis-ease are spiritual as well as physical. We will use dreams to monitor and rectify energy loss, psychic intrusions, and unhealthy relations between the living and the departed.

Like the ancient Iroquois dream scouts, we will track possible futures through dreaming and learn to tame the futures we do not want. We will help one another—and our leaders—to recognize the consequences of their actions, looking far beyond the pressures of current events and the calculations of expediency and profit-and-loss to the seventh generation beyond ourselves. We will reawaken to our obligations to the ancient ones and those (as the Iroquois say) whose "faces are still under the earth," and to all that shares life in our fragile bubble of oxygenated air.

In our dreaming society, we will heal our relationship with death and the departed. We will remember that our identity and destiny are not confined to our present personalities in a single lifetime.

The rebirth of a dreaming culture is not science fiction. It is a possible future that all dreamers can help bring into manifestation, because we all dream and because there are times when dreams will push through even the most hardened carapace of skepticism or materialism. We will need many dream teachers and dream ambassadors, but we do not need to preach or argue. Quietly, gently, all of us who value dreams and have mastered core techniques like the Lightning Dreamwork process (presented here in book form for the first time; see part 4, chapter 16, "The Shaman at the Breakfast Table") can give others a safe space in which to start sharing and honoring their sleep dreams and their life dreams. These encounters may come at a bus stop, in a supermarket, in line at the post office, or around the kitchen table, with a total stranger or a close relative who is opening up for the first time.

We can give those who are just beginning to share their dreams the gift of validation: confirmation that they are not alone, that they are not going crazy, that their dreams are not "only" dreams. We can be teachers at every turn of everyday life. We can encourage all dreamers to claim their own power, by recognizing them as the final authority on their own dreams. Without setting ourselves up as experts, we can offer the insights of frequent fliers. We can share what real dreamers know: we are born to fly, and in dreams we remember the soul has wings.

A brief note: Epigraphs and poems for which no source is indicated were written by me.

PART ONE

JOURNEY TO
THE HEART
OF
ANCIENT
MOTHER

The distinction between past, present and future is only an illusion, even if a stubborn one.

ALBERT EINSTEIN

In the end the only events of my life worth telling are those when the imperishable world irrupted into this transitory one. That is why I speak chiefly of inner experiences, amongst which I include my dreams and visions.

C. G. JUNG, MEMORIES, DREAMS, REFLECTIONS

When a person has an inborn genius for certain emotions, his life differs strangely from that of ordinary people, for none of their ordinary deterrents check him.

WILLIAM JAMES

The gods drink at the heart like a deer in a river.

MARTIN PRECHTEL, SECRETS OF THE TALKING JAGUAR

1

The Spirits Fall in Love

*A state of thoroughly conscious ignorance is the prelude to
any real advance of knowledge.*

JAMES CLERK MAXWELL

Go looking for the spirit world of the Indians, said an early traveler,
and you will find you are already inside it. I was not looking for that
world—not in my everyday understanding, at any rate—but I soon
found, after moving to the farm in Chatham, that I was deep inside it.

I cannot say that I had not been forewarned. Several years earlier,
in 1981, I had started looking quite intently for a path of soul, a path
beyond despair and the confusion of the daily trivial mind. I had just
achieved what for many people might have been a dream fulfilled, with
the precocious success of my first novel, a best-selling cold war thriller.
I was able to say good-bye to employers and buy a plane ticket to anywhere on the planet, and wherever I went people wanted to stroke me
and get my autograph. And I was miserably depressed. The Iroquois
term for my condition is *down-minded,* but I did not know that yet.

My dreams and my heart were telling me that I was wasting my
gifts, and when I watched myself showing off in front of studio audiences

15

and head waiters, I did not like what I saw. I was filling my bank account, but not a void I felt within. I was propelled by a rage for life, but I rushed at everything as if I hoped that by moving at the speed of a shooting star, I could avoid ever having to consider the choices I made or remember a deeper order of things.

Yet my dreams kept after me, mocking the agendas of my ravening ego, calling me back to a truer life. In one series of dreams—after my thrillers rose to the top of the *New York Times* Best Seller List—I found myself working in a forced-labor camp, presided over by strutting Kapos in comic-opera uniforms. I could walk out the gate at any time, but I chose to stay there because the camp commandant had given me the key to a private canteen where the refrigerators were stuffed with vast amounts of "American hamburger."

And I dreamed of the lion. He has been with me, in dreaming, since I was very small, though there have been phases in my life when I have not always been able to see him, like the children in the *Chronicles of Narnia* who can no longer see Aslan as they succumb to "grown-up" ways of looking at things. In this dream, I am watching a crowd of people who are gawking and jeering at a magnificent white lion through the bars of a cage. They are behaving like any crowd of careless Sunday idlers at a zoo, dropping trash on the ground, pulling silly faces. They think it is safe to mock the lion—until someone screams that the gate of his cage is open. The humans freak out and run for their lives. I walk, quite calmly, through the open gate. I feel no fear as the lion lopes toward me. He jumps up and rests his paws against my shoulders, like a huge and friendly dog. The lion wants me to look back, to understand the situation here. When I turn around, I see that it is the humans, not the lions, who are in a cage. The place of the lion is a place of nature, freedom, and limitless possibility. The white lion says to me in his deep, gravelly voice, "You see, humans are the only animals who *choose* to live in cages."

So I began looking for the way out of the cages I had constructed for myself for the sake of "American hamburger" and other self-limiting causes, back to the place of the lion.

On a muggy day when the rain came down as if someone at an upstairs window was emptying buckets at random intervals, my quest brought me to the house of an African divination priest in Old San Juan. In my earlier travels, I had come across practitioners of Santeria, the syncretic New World religion in which the spirits of Africa are worshipped under the masks of the Catholic saints. In Brazil, I had danced all night to the bata drums in Candomble ceremonies in which the masks of the saints were discarded and the orishas of the Yoruba and the ancestral spirits were invited to "ride" the celebrants and speak and heal through them. I had read that there was a higher path in the Yoruba tradition, a path involving the command of an immense body of knowledge encoded in poetic verses, and the cultivation of a direct relationship with a Higher Self. Though the talking drums excited me, it was this higher path that intrigued me most. In Puerto Rico, researching one of my novels, I learned that a Yoruba *babalao,* or "father of the mysteries" who was a master of the higher path of Ifa, was living in the capital and would be willing to talk with me.

Ade received me informally, in the midst of his family. A diploma on his wall revealed that he had a Ph.D. in electrical engineering. "I am a student of power in two senses," he quipped with gentle humor, "as a witch doctor and a doctor of philosophy."

He led me into his sacred space, into a profusion of colors and smells. We sat together on the floor on a rush mat, and he cast a set of bronze medallions, linked by a chain, to manifest the *odu*—the sacred patterns of Ifa divination. Each odu evoked a flow of poetic lore from a deep well of memory. From the babalao's lips spilled the names of gods and heroes. He spoke of the drama of an ancient king, depressed by the effects of his reckless actions and the constant strife between his women, who went to hang himself in a tree. But instead of killing himself, the ancient king became a god. In some way this story was relevant to my life. Ade explained that, according to his reading, I was the "son" of two West African deities (an unusual circumstance) who gifted me with their protection and their strongly contrasting personalities. It seemed there were rivalries and jealousies among the orishas, as among other gods. "The two defend you before the orishas," Ade told me.

Something was working with the babalao, I decided, as he proceeded to give me a highly accurate and specific description of my current circumstances and prospects—health, family, money, emotional life—that included a good deal of information that was not available to me at that time but checked out later. He told me, "Dreams will be very important in your life, more important than you understand. You must always follow your dreams, and the day will come when the world will hear them."

Ade's pace slowed as he sought guidance on my big question, about my life path. He frowned over the fall of the medallions, murmuring, "You were born with a box of mysteries." He cast again and closed his eyes, tracking forward and back through the forests of poetic memory.

Finally he stared at me and announced, with seeming reluctance, "Your path is the same as mine."

"What does that mean?" I demanded. Then it hit me. "You mean I am supposed to become an African witch doctor?"

This was no longer a joking matter. Ade reminded me that we were dealing with a universal tradition, though the path he was offering is specifically African. It would lead to a holy city of the Yoruba in Nigeria where I would be trained and eventually ordained as a high div-ination priest of Ifa, if I accepted the calling. The babalao was willing *that day* to admit me to two preliminary grades of initiation, and to make the initial contacts to speed my passage to Africa.

If the proposition had been less outrageous—and if Ade had been less evidently reluctant to voice it—my scam detector might now have been beeping, telling me something like, "Right, this guy knows I've got some money, and that I'm desperate for some kind of spiritual fix, and he's out to rip me off big-time." But my scam detector remained silent because what was going on was wholly authentic, and it was taking me deeper than the world I had been lost in.

I agreed to take the first grade of initiation on the path of Ifa that day, but I declined another initiation that would have carried ritual obligations. As a meat eater, I have no moral objection to animal sacri-fice, but in practical terms killing chickens or goats can be messy and is likely to trouble the neighbors in many parts of the world. I was relieved when Ade told me that, to his further surprise, the African powers did not require me to have any sacrifice performed on my behalf.

"The only sacrifice the orishas require of you is your love."

I promised they would have it. As for the invitation to Africa, I felt I would have to think it over.

"Go home and dream on it," Ade suggested. "There will be signs." He specified several. This is the one that is burned indelibly in my mind: "There is a fire growing close to you. You have not yet seen it, but very soon you will feel the heat of its flames."

I considered that prediction as I flew back to New York. I assumed that Ade was speaking metaphorically, sketching some new blowup in my life, perhaps an emotional storm in my love life. I did not yet fully appreciate how specific an earth-centered tradition can be.

Ten minutes after I walked into my seventh-floor apartment on East Eightieth Street, I heard a strange *whoosh* from outside the living room, whose windows faced a courtyard and a building on the other side. I rushed to the windows and saw a horizontal sheet of flame that had burst from the building opposite. The fire was licking at my windows; I could feel its heat through the glass.

Sirens, fire engines, cops, paramedics. I was told there was some kind of chemical explosion in an apartment in the building across the courtyard, and that the occupant was found dead on arrival by the emergency services.

This was the first sign. There were several more over the extraordinary days and nights that ensued, when I saw colors that have no names in our languages because they go beyond the spectrum of human color perception. I felt a deep soul connection with Africa, and the lion roamed with me there in my dreams. I was so hungry for a deeper life that it was not hard for me to contemplate leaving my Manhattan apartment, donating my fancy suits to the Salvation Army, and tearing up my lucrative publishing contracts and movie options. But the suggestion of such a radical life change was dismaying, even terrifying, to some of those I loved. And the thought also weighed on me that presumably I had been born a white Australian, with a lifelong connection to the Western mystery traditions, for a reason, and that perhaps this would not best be served by wedding myself to a culturally specific tradition from Africa, even if it was one my soul knew well.

I called the *santero* friend who had introduced me to Ade and told him my decision. I was not going to follow the path of a Yoruba priest, at least not in terms of formal training. The friend said to me, "Robert, there is something you should know. The spirits are like people. They fall in love. And because the spirits are in love with you, they are going to keep calling you. They will go on putting on different masks and costumes until you accept your relationship with them."

2

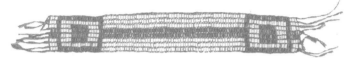

When the Ancestors Cross Into the Realm of the Living

The distance between the living and the dead is exactly as wide as the edge of a maple leaf.

HANDSOME LAKE, SENECA IROQUOIS PROPHET

ANUBIS IN THE BACKYARD

With one of the castings of the oracle of Ifa, the diviner may say, "The ancestors are crossing into the realm of the living." This is a time of danger and magic, when death is close and the veil of the spirit world thins or disappears. I entered this time when I moved to the farm where I met the white oak and the red-tailed hawk in 1986, and the spirits came in different masks.

We drove from Sag Harbor to the farm with two very large black dogs. They were Sag Harbor mutts, a cross between German shepherds and Labrador retrievers, but much bigger than the contributing breeds. I had named the elder dog Kipling in honor of the black dog owned by a boozy KGB philosopher in my thriller *Moscow Rules*. Kipling loved his human family with fierce devotion, and I loved him more than any other dog who had shared my life. When his ears stood up, he was a dead ringer for Anubis, the canine-headed Egyptian guardian of the roads to the Otherworld, an escort for the departing and a guide for all dream travelers. My fondest memories of the years at Sag Harbor were of splashing around with Kipling in summer, and of walking with him on snow-covered, deserted beaches at midwinter.

He loved our long walks through the wildwood near our new home. Often Kipling and his chubby sister Brandy and I would roam the property for hours. Kipling loved to chase woodchucks, and I let him catch them when he could, since the meat is clean and woodchuck holes are a peril for horses. But I never allowed him to chase the white-tailed deer who often drifted through the trees in great herds once I established a de facto wildlife sanctuary, or the family of red foxes whose earth was hidden under a stand of staghorn sumac.

The night before Halloween, that first year at the farm, Kipling got out on Route 66 and was struck and killed by a neighbor's car. Shaking with grief, I wrapped his huge body in an old blanket, got him into the back of the battered Jeep—where he had loved to ride—and drove, with a spade and mattock, up to the top of the hill on the north side of the house. I had often come here at night with Kipling to watch the rising of the moon. Sobbing, I dug a grave for my black dog just outside the bounds of the human burial ground where the headstones of the first white settlers leaned at crazy angles.

I felt as if something had been cut out of my heart.

But I soon noticed that although his body was in the ground, Kipling was still very much with us. Driving in the Jeep he loved, I once looked in the rearview mirror and saw him standing up, eager to see where we were. "Sit down, Kipling," I growled, before I realized that, in physical terms, my dog could not be there.

Others saw him, too. His presence was so palpable that when my elderly mother-in-law moved to a downtown street-level apartment, I asked Kipling to watch over her for the first few days, until we were able to get her a watchdog of her own. Late the first night, she heard people she considered to be ne'er-do-wells muttering on the sidewalk in front of her door. Then she heard a dog's deep-chested growl, rising to booming barks. Someone outside said, "Forget it, there's a dog." The curious thing, according to Mary, was that the barking seemed to come from inside the apartment.

My black dog's energy was with me in other ways, too, long after his death. I finally realized I needed to tell him it was okay to move on. I did this with an impromptu ceremony, barbecuing a steak for him on the deck, near the old loganberry tree. When I spoke words of love and releasing, the wind turned as quick as a kid on Rollerblades, and it sent the smoke skirring straight up the hill to Kipling's burial place.

Then my black dog started coming in my dreams. He appeared to me, running and hunting, on a mysterious island across a river. When I called to him, he turned but appeared not to be able to see me, as if he and his world were covered by some kind of shrink-wrap that was translucent only from my side.

Things moved along. His role in my dreams became one of a guide and ally, showing me things I needed to see but might not have noticed without his keen senses. Sometimes he came out of a hollow tree, slicked with something sticky, like honey or amniotic fluid. He escorted me on journeys across perilous country, sometimes into realms of the human dead. I began to understand why the Egyptians chose a black dog or jackal as a psychopomp, or guide of the soul on the roads between the worlds. Garbed in black, he moves easily through the dark places. His keen senses make him an excellent tracker and enable him to sniff out, and dispose of, dead meat and dead energy that the spirit is meant to leave behind. And of all animals the canids are those who are friendliest to humans.

TIMEGATE TO A CELTIC LION ON THE MOHAWK FRONTIER

By this point, I was dreaming of many other dead souls—mostly human, mostly people I knew nothing about, except for the dreams. I will now drop the misleading term *dead* and substitute *departed*. I am not much for theology, but one thing I know—something that anyone who truly dreams will learn very quickly—is that life continues after physical death, in other dimensions and in other vehicles of consciousness. One of the cruelest things our mainstream psychology—and often our mainstream Western religion—has done is to obfuscate or deny the simple fact that in dreams, we have natural access to our departed. Sometimes they come visiting us. Sometimes we travel into their realms. Sometimes they are in our dreams because they are in our space, having never moved on.

In sleep dreams, and in waking impressions—especially when I sat with the white oak or hiked through the woods up to the waterfalls—I often encountered people of an earlier time, both whites and Native Americans. I assumed these were the holographic residue, and maybe the lingering energies, of people who had lived and loved and suffered on that land, no doubt including the family of Moses Son, the first white landholder, whose sons had fought in the American Revolution and were buried on the hill just above Kipling's grave site.

I began to research the history of the area, and I discovered that this land was the first *real* American frontier, the border where many world-historical issues were decided, including how deep into the continent Europeans would be allowed to go, and whether France or Britain would be the dominant imperial power, and whether the colonies would continue to be ruled by a distant king or would gain independence under a constitution that would set fire to the imagination of people all over the world. I learned that the nearby city of Albany had been a kind of Casablanca in its heyday, with agents and undercover operatives vying for influence. I started to toy with the idea of writing another spy thriller in colonial drag.

I had not gotten very far with this plan when we decided to take a winter break with old friends, flying off to Cancun, which interested me less for the tan-and-margarita scene than for its access to the Mayan sites. On foreign soil, I found myself inside the first of the big dreams that were to bring me into the heart of the Iroquois story.

Below me, a shadow skims a primal landscape, mostly water, like an arrowhead. I come down in a clearing in a dense forest. I slip in and out of the perspective of an ancient speaker, dressed in skins. The scene shifts, and I seem to be in a Greek amphitheater. I move in and out of the minds and bodies of many players, spanning century after century. Now I am in the body of a powerful, broad-shouldered man in colonial garb. Sometimes he is dressed like a redcoat general, or a wealthy landowner; at other times, he wears skins and feathers and shells, like a woodland American Indian.

I wake from this last scene with a line like blank verse echoing through my mind:

> *I am from such as those by whom the worlds are*
> *shaken*

The sonorous words hung in the air. I blinked in the bright sunlight that spilled through the window of the hotel room, struggling to recall the details of my dream and to make sense of it. My dream took me into the thick of some ancient drama, played out across many centuries in many landscapes and many costumes. I felt that the scenes were all connected, and that the words reverberating in the room related to whatever was at the heart of this drama.

As soon as I got back to the United States, I confirmed a hunch about the identity of the man in colonial dress. Shortly before leaving for Cancun, my hand had fallen on a fat, blue-bound book in the local history section of a used bookstore in Albany. Opening it at random, I had been struck by the familiarity of the eighteenth-century voice that spoke to me from the pages, as he reported on a council with the Iroquois Indians. Checking the spine, I found I was holding a volume of the *Sir William Johnson Papers*. I had never heard of Johnson, but my curiosity led me to purchase the book.

When I studied portraits of Johnson, I became convinced he was the man in my dream who was and was not me. When I started reading his papers, and quickly expanded my reading to include a number of biographies, I learned that William Johnson (1715–74) was a giant of the first frontier who once ruled in Mohawk country like a tribal king, and—sharing his life and his bed with the Mohawks, becoming deeply versed in their language and customs—he probably came to know them better than any other white man in American history. As the King's Superintendent of Indians and an adopted Mohawk warchief, his influence with the Iroquois was the decisive factor in England's victory over France in the so-called French and Indian War, which paved the way for the American Revolution by removing the colonists' need to have one European army to defend them against another. He led a force of colonial militia and Iroquois warriors into victory over a professional French army led by one of Europe's most experienced generals in the Battle of Lake George in 1755.

The political history was interesting, but what was fascinating was the man, and his rage for life. He was credited with having fathered more than a hundred children by his numerous "temporary wives." The only woman who ever came close to taming him was Mohawk, known to history as Molly Brant—we will learn more about her in part 3.

Johnson's expansive, generous style was reminiscent of the high kings of Ireland. His flair for "going Native"—immersing himself in the culture of the American Indians—was all his own.

A shrewd French observer, Louis Antoine de Bougainville, described Johnson in his heyday as "raising the Celtic lion." Bougainville related a "fine scene" in which Johnson confronted a torpid British general near Lake George, a year or so after the Irishman's victory at the same site. Johnson appeared at the head of a Mohawk war party decorated in war paint and carrying a tomahawk, and he demanded that General Webb should march at once against the French who were then besieging Fort William Henry, the fort on the lake constructed by Johnson himself. When General Webb refused to move, Johnson "called up the Celtic lion," tore off one of his leggings, and flung it at the general's feet. "You won't do it?" "No." Johnson tore off the other legging. "You won't?" "No." This went on until Johnson had stripped himself virtually naked. Then, reports Bougainville, Johnson "galloped off with his troop who had imitated his actions entirely. Where is Homer to paint such scenes more than Greek?"[1]

This was colorful stuff, maybe the stuff of a lively novel. However, my initial research did not explain the huge reverberation from the dream, the sense of a transtemporal drama surpassing Johnson's story, or my own. There were things I needed to know, things that were not in the history books. For one, there was the personal question. Why was I confused, in my dream, about which player was Johnson and which was me? Why was I dreaming about Johnson at all?

The first time I drove out to Johnson Hall, an elegant manse flanked by stone blockhouses that was Sir William's last home in the Mohawk Valley, I went there without maps or directions, as if I were going home. I met a shy southern woman called Wanda Burch who had lived with the legacy of Johnson and his Iroquois friends, as curator of what was now a state historic site, for some twenty years. I soon discovered that she, too, was a powerful dreamer, and that we might have been connected in our dream lives long before a dream of Johnson brought me to his last home.

When I was nine years old, I slipped off the gangway of a boat on which I had gone fishing with my father and his friends. The water was pretty shallow, and I was a strong swimmer—most Australians are born with gills—so nobody could understand that I was drowning until most of my short life had flashed before my eyes and someone fished me out and thumped the water out of me. At around the same time, Wanda had dreamed of a boy her age with a round, freckly face who was drowning, inexplicably, in shallow waters. In her dream, she stuck in an arm and helped him out. We shared these experiences fairly early in what was to become a deep and extraordinary dream friendship. We had both grown up as only children, and had both longed for a sibling. As we grew our friendship, we decided we had found in each other the sister and brother that each had lacked during childhood.

So my dream of William Johnson had already brought me a precious gift: the gift of a soul sister. Wanda and I were soon sharing dreams almost daily, and we often found that our dreams overlapped. Together, we developed the practice of shared interactive dreaming, and we scouted the future, tracking forward to explore and choose among possible futures.

But the mystery of my connection with Johnson remained. He was born and bred in County Meath, Ireland, like my mother's family, and I soon decided I must go there to discover whether there were answers in our common roots.

EYES OF THE GODDESS

I flew to Dublin, on my dream quest, in 1987. On Easter Sunday, with two of my daughters, I sampled two masses on a cold, blowy, drizzling morning: the Anglican service in an almost deserted old church of St. Ann, where a plump vicar droned through the liturgy to empty pews, thrusting his hands against the sides of his nose to check his sneezing, and the Roman mass at St. Mary's pro-Cathedral. The pro-Cathedral is beautiful, classically Georgian—a perfect foil for the bustle and excitement on this great day of the Christian year, the day of the risen god-man. The sign at the door read: LADIES—WATCH YOUR HANDBAGS. There was some juice here—in the wild swoop of the organ music, the choir lifting the *alleluia*s, the bouncing walk of the priests—and it was possible to imagine how pagans could be drawn to a vision of a dying god reborn, the world renewed through symbolic cannibalism. I admired the pretty Irish girls with their swinging gait, flopping black or red hair, determined jaws, quick dark eyes, and rounded hips crowding in beside derelicts and drunks, the whole place astir with sibilants like the wind through rushes.

The next day, looking for Johnson (who was born in 1715), I began to enter an Ireland that was older than St. Patrick, let alone my dream alter ego, a time of turbulence belied by the surface placidity of the manicured lawns and neat hedgerows of the "West Britons" of Meath. We drove down a fierce back country road to Smithstown House, Johnson's birthplace. A bluff, rock-solid horse farmer showed me around the estate. The bluebells were just coming out, and I thrilled to my favorite combination of colors in nature: dreamy blues among soft greens. I walked through a fine stable with stone stalls, an apple orchard behind stone walls. And knew that what I was seeking was not here.

> *I am from such as those by whom the worlds are*
> *shaken*

I tried out the line on a scholar of Old Irish I met when we went on to Tara, a sacred hillside where ancient kings were crowned. "It has the ring of the bard in it," he told me. "The words are what a lordly one might say, landing among mortals. But I can't place it."

We drove through the Boyne River valley and on to Newgrange, the great mounded passage tomb and ritual site, old when the pyramids of Egypt were new. The tomb consists of a passage and chamber whose roof is built of large slabs without mortar, covered by a large circular cairn of loose rock, and ringed by guardian stones. On the day of my visit, Newgrange was flanked by bright yellow gorse that smelled like coconut oil in the sun.

I felt those shivers of recognition. *This is the place.* I did not know whether it was connected to my dream, but I knew that this was what I had come for. Truth comes with goose bumps. I shivered again when I saw the spirals on the guardian stones. Double spirals, treble spirals, whirling in and out of life. In the double spiral I saw, without thinking, the Eyes of the Goddess, holding the codes of creation and destruction.

Beyond the entrance, the passage to the central chamber was cool and dry. I entered the vaulted chamber and looked up at rings of stone corbeled to make the roof—circles within circles, like ripples in a pool. For some reason, men who had not had the use of the wheel had clambered up there, in darkness or guttering light, to lay the slabs with aching precision.

I looked at the sun gate, where the light shines through at the winter solstice, and at the hewn stone trough, hollowed on top to hold burned bones—and perhaps the blood of sacrifice. My vision flickered into something ancient. I saw an ancient queen, enthroned in this place. Actually, she was more than a queen. She opened her immortal body and projected the form of a lovely priestess who came to me, naked except for a strip of animal fur about her loins.

The Eyes of the Goddess are like whirlpools, like windstorms. They hold the birth and death of worlds.

What does this have to do with the Iroquois? More than I recognized, even when I embarked on this book.

I flew back from Ireland.

One night, on the cusp between waking and sleep—a wonderful sandlot for anyone who wants to play at conscious dreaming—I let images rise and fall. Quite quickly the stream of images resolved into a very strong and vivid sighting of the double spiral, as I had seen it carved on the stones in Ireland. It was the Eyes of the Goddess.

Without thinking about it, I found myself traveling through the double spiral, into a different landscape. I expected to find myself back in Ireland, but instead I was flying over a primal version of the landscape of the American Northeast, on the wings of a red-tailed hawk. I soon found I was flying to the ancient Iroquois woman of power I learned to call Island Woman. While I was writing this book, she reminded me that we first met when I found myself traveling through the double spiral from a place of my European ancestors, and that the double spiral might be a clue to mysteries that transcend time and space.

ISLAND WOMAN CONFIRMS HER CREDENTIALS

Just as I needed to know about Johnson, I needed to know about the meaning of the beaded belts that Island Woman had shown me, and the words she spoke over me, in our first visionary encounter.

I was fortunate to find my way to an Iroquois scholar working for the New York State Museum. Ray Gonyea was an Onondaga—friendly, learned, and deeply intuitive. The timing of our first meeting was interesting. Ray explained to me that the wampum records he was going to show me had been loaned to the New York State government for safekeeping almost a century before, but they were now to be returned to the Confederacy and would be preserved at Onondaga, the place of the central council fire.

I knew little about the Iroquois at that time, but had been excited to learn that they had created a federation that long predated the United States, and was believed by some to have inspired Ben Franklin and other framers of the American constitution. The traditional Iroquois homelands covered much of upstate New York, but the influence of the Confederacy spread far wider. From east to west, the original five nations of the Iroquois Confederacy, or League of the Longhouse, were: the Mohawk, the Oneida, the Onondaga, the Cayuga, and the Seneca.[2]

In the early eighteenth century, a sixth nation—the Tuscarora of the Carolinas—was invited to move north to join the Confederacy, and since then the Iroquois have been widely known as the Six Nations.[3] They call themselves the Onkwehonwe, the Real People, and the Haudenosonee, the People of the Longhouse.

Prior to European contact, they did not have written records, as the modern world understands them, but they did have their own remarkable system for holding memory. Island Woman had shown an example of it to me in my dream; now the wampum keeper at the State Museum was about to explain how it worked.

I had the vague idea that beads and shells were used by American Indians as money, and for personal decoration. This proved to be true enough,[4] but only part of the significance of wampum. As Ray Gonyea took belt after belt of wampum beads from the wide, shallow drawers of an immense steel cabinet, I was excited to realize that the symbolic and spiritual significance of wampum went very much deeper. I was being given my first tutorial in a rich visual language. Some of the belts held the memory of defining moments in the history of the Iroquois and their interaction with other people. The so-called Hiawatha Belt, with five linked symbols—the central one resembling both a heart and a tree—records the founding of the original Confederacy of Five Nations. The slanting shapes of rafters on another belt recollect and embody the moment when the People of the Longhouse spread the shelter of their alliance over the Tuscaroras, who had been devastated by war and land-grabbing in the Carolinas. A simple and beautiful two-row wampum, with two lines of dark purple beads running parallel along a shining white road, defines the hope that the peoples of two worlds— the Iroquois and the Europeans—could live in harmony, following the truth of their own ways. Some of the wampum was woven into messages: a summons to a council, a promise of hospitality, a call to arms.

As the belts proliferated, I had the feeling that their meaning and power extended far beyond the patterns of white and purple shells. *This belt contains my words.* This was the formula that turned up, over and over, in the records of Indian councils, in Johnson's time and before and after. There was mystery in that phrase, not easily fathomed. Was it possible that seashells—even shells milled and processed into tubular beads—that had been charged with intention and words of power could in themselves be data banks and energy containers?

Ray asked me to describe the belt that Island Woman had held up, and to mime how she had displayed it.

"The belt was white, with two human figures holding hands and a wolf depicted in a darker color," I told him. I moved my hands around, letting my body show me how Island Woman had displayed it. I felt her holding it with one end draped over her left shoulder, the patterns clearly visible over her heart, stroking the shells as she spoke in that cadenced, musical voice.

Ray held up a belt. "Something like this, maybe?"

I stared at him. He had conjured up the belt from my dreams, and he was holding it as Island Woman had done. There were the two human figures, holding hands. To their left was the large figure of a wolf.

"It's the belt I saw in my dream! What does it mean?"

Ray's face set, betraying no emotion. He said quietly, "These are the wampum credentials of a clan mother of the Wolf Clan. I guess you had a visit with a woman of power."

As he replaced the belt and locked the drawer, he gave me a sideways glance and remarked, "Power will come looking for you in dreams."

He turned back to the cabinet and took out one last belt. Against seven rows of dark beads, slanting lines and circles were defined in brilliant white. "Did she also show you something like this?"

"I'm not sure." There was something familiar about this belt, but I did not recall seeing it in Island Woman's cabin. "What does it mean?"

Ray gave a dry chuckle. "It's a ransom belt. It carries a woman's claim to adopt a captive to replace someone in her family that she lost. If she showed you that, she'd be saying you belong to us now."

MY FATHER BRINGS HEALING
FROM THE OTHER SIDE

In my dreams, and in waking, I was moving deeper and deeper into the realm of the ancestors, and they into mine. I dreamed of my father's passing and then, after his heart stopped in a hospital in Queensland, on the other side of the Pacific, I dreamed of him coming to visit, with helpful and loving guidance for me and other family members.

When I flew out to Australia for his funeral, his presence was so warm and joyous that my mother and I felt we were attending a celebration. Then one evening, as we sat on the balcony of her retirement home, some of the old rancor that had marred our relationship began to surface. She said some bitter words and slammed inside the apartment, upset.

I asked my father to intervene. My mother soon returned to the balcony like a leaf blown on the wind. She stood behind me for an hour, speaking words of love and mutual forgiveness, with her hand on my heart.

This was unprecedented. Since early childhood, my mother had never displayed physical affection. Though this confused and saddened me early in my life, I had come to understand that it was because she could not stand the pain of constantly being on the brink of losing her only child. I commented now on how touched I was that she had spoken while holding her hand to my heart.

"You know me, I would never do anything like that!" she protested.

"But maybe Dad would," I said gently.

We both felt him then.

3

Meeting the Dream People

The Iroquois have, properly speaking, only a single Divinity—the dream. To it they render their submission, and follow all its orders with the utmost exactness.

FATHER JACQUES FRÉMIN,
REPORTING FROM SENECA COUNTRY IN 1669

Through serendipity, as well as introductions from my new friends, I met several Iroquois scholars, grandmothers, and elders who offered to help me. "We will give you our best words," said Hazel Dean-John, a distinguished Seneca linguist, as she opened our first conversation. With her help and that of native Mohawk speakers on the Six Nations reserve, near Brantford, Ontario, and at Tiyendinaga on the Bay of Quinte in Ontario, and at Kahnawake, near Montreal, I began to decode some of the phrases from my dreams.

My Iroquois friends not only helped me identify and translate many key words, but also shed insights into the significance of my dream encounters with Island Woman. They explained that the Iroquois were traditionally a matriarchal society, and that Island Woman was almost certainly not only a clan mother but also an arendiwanen, or woman of power. Among the Iroquois people, as in many indigenous societies, the women are most frequently the spontaneous seers, the most brilliant storytellers, and the custodians of the web of life.

In our sharings, the idea drifted in the air that Island Woman might have called me from *her* now time, seeking information from *her* future that could help her family and her people. This suggestion gave me shivers of recognition. Yet I sensed there was an even deeper connection, something that joined my life to both Island Woman and William Johnson, and possibly to others in other times.

When I first spoke of my dream encounters to an elder at Onondaga, he said matter-of-factly, "I guess you had some visits." He counseled me to be careful when dealing with disincarnate spirits, and he suggested that it might be wise not to talk in public about the names and details of certain traditional rituals that had come to me in dreams. He explained, "Some of our great ones stay close to the Earth to watch over our people and to defend the Earth. They might talk to you, even though you are an outsider, because you dream the way we used to dream. You dream strong."

ON THE PATH OF THE DREAM SHAMANS

The call of the hawk and of Island Woman launched me on several parallel paths into the world of shamanic dreaming, and I eventually filled thousands of journal pages with detailed accounts of my experiences on these journeys.

One path led me to read everything I could about Iroquois dreamwork and healing. Under a strange moonlit evening at the farm, when twin white cloud lines—not vapor trails—made parallel roads across the sky, a bookseller friend turned up with several cardboard boxes in his trunk containing all seventy-three volumes of the *Jesuit Relations*, the reports of the black-robed missionaries on the first frontier in Northeast America in the seventeenth century. The books did not come cheap, but I had to have them. I already knew, from my secondary reading, that the Jesuit reports contained a treasury of information on the shamanic dreamways of the Iroquois and the Hurons from a time when the old practices were still intact. Blinkered by the iron certainties of their dogma, fearing Native dreams as the work of "demons" who had emigrated to the American wilderness after being driven out of the Old World by the soldiers of the new God, the Jesuits often misrepresented what they were encountering. Nonetheless, when read with a careful eye and some knowledge of what dreaming can be, the *Jesuit Relations* were an amazingly rich mine, one (I was to discover) that had scarcely begun to be tapped. For more than a year, these books became my favorite reading, sometimes confirming teachings coming from my dream visitors, and sometimes providing me with additional insights into Iroquois dreaming.

A second path led me to study directly with traditional Native dreamers and shamans. I studied with Tom Porter, a Mohawk Bear Clan elder and healer whose visions later inspired him to lead a band of his people from the Akwesasne reservation back to the Mohawk Valley, where they founded a spiritual community to revive the old ways of their ancestors. I also studied briefly with a Chippewa shaman and a Cayuga medicine man who taught me shamanic techniques for journeying to the spirit worlds and relocating lost souls.

A third path led me to study core shamanic journey techniques with Michael Harner. In my search to better understand my dream visitors, I had read Harner's book *The Way of the Shaman,* and I found his basic journeying techniques to be similar to visionary practices I had developed in childhood. When I heard that he was leading a workshop in my neighborhood, on a quartz mountain at the edge of the Berkshires, I decided to see what else he had to offer. Despite my initial reservations about whether traditional shamanic techniques should—or even could—be taught to anyone in a weekend retreat, I had a watershed experience in Harner's workshop. I traveled through many dimensions of the upper world, to the light—brighter than the sun—of the source of the god-forms, and through that black light to fly with winged beings over a world fresher than the first day of creation. Reluctant to come back, I at last saw my own lifeless corpse carried down in the talons of an immense eagle.

All of these explorations offered powerful insights into the world of shamanism and shamanic dreaming. However, as had been my experience since early childhood, I continued to receive my most important instruction directly from teachers inside the dreamworld itself.

GETTING LUCKY WITH DREAMING

My dreams were calling me to learn more about Island Woman's people, the early Iroquois and Huron. She made it plain that in order to understand what mattered, I would need to expand my vocabulary.

This would require the literal study of the languages of her people and time, not an easy undertaking, since Iroquoian languages work according to quite different principles than European ones, and Island Woman did not speak like a contemporary Mohawk, but in the archaic, complex, and poetic vocabulary of a shaman of another time.

While I struggled with Mohawk grammar and stem-words, I read the Jesuits and the anthropologists. I discovered that the Iroquois have drawn the dedicated interest, over the centuries, of a remarkable series of ethnographers. It might even be said that modern anthropology began, as a discipline, with the study of the Iroquois by the extraordinary Jesuit scholar, Joseph-François Lafitau, and several generations later by Lewis Henry Morgan.

The first Europeans to encounter the Iroquois were astonished—and sometimes terrified—by the depth of their respect for dreams, and the richness of their shamanic dream practices. I will briefly digress here from my personal narrative to explain the core elements in the ancient Iroquois way of dreaming, as I came to understand them.

Long before the first Europeans set foot on American soil, the Iroquois taught their children that dreams are the single most important source of both practical and spiritual guidance. The first business of the day in an Iroquois village was dream sharing, because it was assumed that dreams were messages from the spirits and the deeper self, and that they might contain guidance for the community as well as the individual.

The Jesuit missionaries marveled that the Iroquois would make life-or-death decisions on the basis of dream reports. Father Jacques Bruyas, who worked among the Oneida, complained about the powerful influence of one woman who was revered for her ability to dream future events. On one occasion, she announced that she had dreamed that a tribe to the south had taken the warpath against her nation, but she had also seen that they could be ambushed at a certain place. Because she had dreamed that the enemy war chief—whom she identified by name—would be captured and ceremonially put to death, the Oneida rallied and sent out a war party. Bruyas recorded that the people were so confident of the impending victory that they immediately fired up their kettles in preparation for the victory celebration.[1]

The Iroquois and their woodland neighbors relied regularly on dreams for guidance, not only in warfare but also in hunting and foraging. Father Paul LeJeune, wintering among the Montagnais in 1634, observed that these people believed that the success of a hunt depended on obtaining dreams of the animals. "If anyone, when asleep, sees the elder or progenitor of some animals, he will have a fortunate chase; if he sees the elder of the Beavers, he will take Beavers; if he sees the elder of the Elks, he will take Elks, possessing the juniors through the favor of their senior whom he has seen in the dream."[2]

Dreaming was prized as a survival tool. In the starving times, when supplies ran low in the depths of winter, the community looked to powerful dreamers to scout out the location of game, and to negotiate with the animal spirits to provide sustenance for the people.

The very words used by the Iroquois to describe dreaming reflect their view that dreaming is vital to bringing good fortune. The Iroquoian word *katera'swas* means "I dream," but it implies much more than the words suggest in English. It means that I dream as a habit, as a daily part of my way of being in the world. The phrase also carries the connotation that I am lucky in a proactive way—that I bring myself luck because I am able to manifest good fortune and prosperity through my dreaming. The Iroquoian term *watera'swo,* "dream," also means "it brings good luck."[3] The early Jesuit observers noted that the Iroquois believed that neglect of dreams brought bad luck. Father Jean de Quens noted, on a visit to Onondaga, that "men are told they will have ill luck if they disregard their dreams."[4]

It was easy for me to see why the Iroquois equated dreaming with good fortune. At many watersheds in my life, my dreams had helped me to overcome obstacles and find my path. On at least two occasions, my dream previews of my possible death in road accidents had prompted me to take evasive action that may have kept me alive. Now, thanks to my dream journeys and visitations, I was being propelled into the dreamworld of a Native people about which—in my surface mind—I had known virtually nothing.

The Iroquois not only believe that dreaming brings good luck; they also believe that dreaming is good medicine. The Mohawk word *atetshents,* which means "one who dreams," is also the term for a doctor, shaman, or healer. There, embedded in the language, is the recognition that dreaming is central to healing and is the heart of true shamanic practice.

HONORING THE WISHES OF THE SOUL

Again and again, my dreams put me on the track of the ancient dreamways. For example, there was one word that kept recurring in my dreams. I recorded it phonetically as *ondinnonk,* and I was perplexed when my new Iroquois friends could not decipher it for me. I eventually found the meaning of this word in a report by a Jesuit priest, Father Paul Ragueneau, who lived among Island Woman's birth people, the Hurons, in the winter of 1647–8. Here is Ragueneau, describing his discovery of the ondinnonk:

> In addition to conscious desires that arise from a previous knowledge of something we suppose to be good, the Hurons believe that our souls have other desires, which are, as it were, both natural and hidden. . . . They believe that our soul makes these natural desires known to us through dreams, which are its language. When these desires are accomplished, it is satisfied. But if, on the contrary, it is not granted what it desires, it becomes angry; not only does it fail to bring the body the health and well-being it might have wished to bring, but often it even revolts against the body, causing various diseases and even death. . . . Most of the Hurons are very careful to pay attention to their dreams, and to provide the soul with what it has represented to them during their sleep. If, for instance, they have seen a javelin in a dream, they try to get it; if they have dreamed that they gave a feast, they will give one on awakening. . . . They call this Ondinnonk, a secret desire of the soul expressed by a dream.[5]

I did not grasp right away that Island Woman had brought me to the heart of Iroquois dreaming and healing. I was simply delighted to have discovered the meaning of the mystery word and to find that several hundred years before Sigmund Freud developed his dream theories about the libido and Carl Jung popularized the concept of archetypes, the Iroquois had understood that there were conscious and unconscious parts of the mind.

As Ragueneau reported, the early Iroquois believed that certain dreams are messages from the soul, taking the dreamer beyond the limited perspectives of the daily trivial mind. Ignoring the "secret wishes" of the soul could make the soul disgusted or angry, prompting it to withdraw its energy, resulting in soul loss that could produce depression and disease. It was consequently regarded as a social duty—sometimes a duty of supreme importance—to help dreamers read the language of the soul, as revealed in their dreams, and take appropriate action. To quote Ragueneau again, "The Hurons believe that one of the most powerful remedies for rapidly restoring health is to grant the soul of the sick person its natural desires."[6]

With the help of my dream guides, I came to realize that dreams are at the heart of healing precisely because they connect us with the unfulfilled desires and ultimate purposes of the soul. As my understanding grew, the idea that we should help each other to honor our dreams as experiences of the soul became central to my development of the shamanic approach to dreamwork that I call Active Dreaming.

I learned that the early Iroquois had an excellent understanding of the dreaming mind and that they had developed powerful techniques and rituals for involving the whole community in sharing and honoring dreams and bringing their energy and insight into waking life. The early Iroquois believed that the community had an obligation to help the dreamer recognize and honor the secret wishes of the soul, as revealed in dreams. Communities would go to great lengths to help the dreamer satisfy the wishes of the soul.

Honoring the ondinnonk, Father Lalemant reported, often involved feasting, dancing, and dramatic performance. These people did not just sit around *talking* about dreams; they did something to bring the energy through. "When the Captains go about publishing the desires of the sick, or other persons who have dreamed, and when they say that it is the Ondinnonk of a certain person, each one immediately takes pains and applies himself with all his might to give pleasure and satisfaction to that one."[7] Lalemant described a three-hour dance ceremony, accompanied by the constant percussion of a large turtle rattle, performed to honor a sick woman's dream. The sick woman was very insistent that the performance must follow exact ritual forms, dictated by her dream, if she was to recover.[8]

Two centuries later, Iroquois elders told ethnologist Harriet Converse that you can lose your soul if you don't listen to what it's telling you in dreams. The punishment for failing to heed repeated dream warnings is that the "free soul" may abandon the dreamer, leaving him to live out his life as one of the walking dead, "bereft of his immortal soul."[9]

The early Iroquois regarded someone who was not in touch with their dreams as the victim of serious soul-loss. A specialist might be called on to bring the lost dreams, and the missing vital energy, to the sufferer. Father Ragueneau observed that among the Hurons, "there are certain persons, more enlightened than the common, whose sight penetrates into the depth of the soul and who see its natural and hidden desires even when the soul has not spoken through dreams—or the person who may have had dreams has completely forgotten them." In his opinion, these seers were usually guided by an *oki,* "a powerful genie who enters their bodies, or appears to them in dreams or after waking, and enables them to see these wonders. Some say that the genie appears to them in the form of an eagle, others say they see it as a raven, and in a thousand other shapes."[10]

Central to the Iroquois practice of honoring dreams as wishes of the soul is the recognition that *dreams require action.* Ragueneau is exceptionally interesting on the reason why feasting, performance, and gift giving are so often a part of dream enactment among the early Iroquois: "They say that these feasts are given to oblige the soul to keep its word. They believe the soul is pleased when it sees us take action to celebrate a favorable dream, and will move faster to help us manifest it. If we fail to honor a favorable dream, they think this can prevent the dream from being fulfilled, as if the angry soul revokes its promise."[11]

During the sacred midwinter rites of Ononhouroia (the Swirling of the Mind)—which are still celebrated in traditional Longhouse ceremonies on some reservations—the Iroquois engaged in dream-guessing contests that often turned into giveaways. To satisfy the dream wishes of others, individuals might give away their most treasured possessions. One Jesuit father indicated that the dream desires were most frequently satisfied by harmless giveaways of material items, but he lamented that, sometimes, "another will intimate that he desires an Andacwandet feast—that is to say, many fornications and adulteries."[12]

The Jesuit fathers specifically deplored the revelation of dreams involving sexual desires, because these dreams were not only discussed freely but were also sometimes acted out overtly in therapeutic orgies that took precedence over the Iroquois tendencies toward marital fidelity and public modesty. Father de Quens, attending the midwinter ceremony at Onondaga in 1656, reported that a warrior, returning from a successful war party, claimed that the deity Tharonhiawakon had appeared to him in a dream vision, announcing that the village needed to sacrifice ten dogs, a belt of wampum, and four measures each of sunflower seeds and beans. In addition, the man claimed the villagers had been directed to place two married women at his personal disposal for five days. On this occasion, all of the dreamer's desires were fulfilled—although not only Freudians might question whether, in the case of the final request, it was soul or libido talking.[13]

In one dream-guessing encounter described by de Quens, a Cayuga man, who had dreamed that he was giving a feast of human flesh, called together the chiefs of his nation and announced that he had dreamed an impossible dream that would end in the ruin of himself and his whole nation, and perhaps even the destruction of the earth. One man, guessing the nature of the dream, offered to donate his brother to be "cut up and put into the kettle." When the dreamer responded that his dream required a woman, the village chiefs reluctantly selected a young girl and offered her to the dreamer-executioner. Watching in disbelief, the Jesuit priest related what happened next: "He took her; they watched his actions, and pitied that innocent girl; but, when they thought him about to deal the death-blow, he cried out: 'I am satisfied; my dream requires nothing further.'"[14]

TRACKING THE FUTURE THROUGH DREAMING

From the earliest times, Iroquois dream practice has placed extraordinary emphasis on using dreams to scout out the future.

Many dreamwork traditions—modern and ancient—recognize that dreams can allow us to rehearse for events and situations that may unfold in our external lives. Some Western psychoanalysts operate on the assumption that a major function of dreams is to examine and pretest potential scenarios against our inner data banks of emotional experience. This may be valid, but recent research confirms what both ancient shamanic dreamers and contemporary active dreamers know: that dreams not only review the past and pretest alternative futures, but may also reveal future events.[15]

The best data on this subject come from dreamers who follow the practice of keeping detailed dream journals, scanning *all* dream material for possible precognitive elements, and monitoring the occasions when physical events replicate or catch up with the dream. My experience is that if we follow this practice over many years, we will find we have confirmation—scientific in the best sense—that dream precognition is not only possible, but even routine.

As I recorded and worked with thousands of my own dreams over the years, and studied thousands more that were shared with me, I came to the conclusion that there are three basic kinds of dreams involving the future that need to be clearly distinguished. These are (1) rehearsal dreams, (2) precognitive dreams, and (3) early-warning dreams. Rehearsal dreams help us to recognize alternatives, showing us the probable consequences of following our present course or taking a different turn. Precognitive dreams—which may be quite literal or highly symbolic—preview events that are later played out in waking life. Early-warning dreams show us events that may or may not be played out in the future, depending on what action we take, or fail to take, to head off an unwanted event or to manifest a desirable outcome. These types of dreams show us possible futures and give us the means to reshape the future for the better.

The following two dreams, shared with me by an Onondaga friend, at once confirm the mobility of consciousness in the dreamspace—which makes it possible for us to travel across time—and the challenge of distinguishing and acting on precognitive dreams.

Dream of a heart attack: "In my dream, I am under a blanket, with flickering lights around. It's like in a Lakota Yuwipi ceremony, when you go looking for something that's missing. My mother and father were both there; both of them have passed on, though I wasn't thinking about that in the dream. I felt something in my chest explode, pushing through. I was terrified I was going to have a heart attack. The next day, I found the body of a Lakota Indian beside the railroad tracks. He had died of heart attack."

Dream of a drowning: "I dreamed of an old guy in a snowsuit who was pushed into a creek. He'd been beaten bad, but he was still alive. I saw him carried along by the water, struggling to get out. Later, we heard that a family friend was killed that night near the reservation. He was mugged for thirty dollars in welfare money and pushed in the river. When they did the autopsy, they found he was alive when he hit the water but couldn't get up the banks of the creek."

It is not clear whether the above cases involved precognition of future events that could have been averted, or some type of remote viewing or empathic experience of the traumatic events when they were actually taking place. Theoretically, if the dreamer had been able to recognize the places and individuals involved, and realized that the dreams were precognitive, he might have been able to warn the individuals and perhaps helped prevent their deaths. However, one of the challenges of working with dream precognition is to disentangle transpersonal elements from personal themes. Often we fail to recognize specific precognitive elements until the event previewed in the dream begins to unfold in waking life. Sometimes, as in the case of my Onondaga friend's dreams, it is hard to tell—even after the fact—whether a specific dream is an instance of precognition, remote viewing, or telepathic communication.

For such reasons, when working with a potentially prophetic dream, the Iroquois often seek the help of other gifted dreamers to track—or travel inside—the original dream and verify details, or they might seek a "second opinion" through another form of divination. In earlier times, the most typical form of divination used by the Iroquois was pyromancy. Father Joseph-François Lafitau describes how Mohawks conducted divinations by lighting little pieces of cedarwood and noting which way the fire moved.[16] Today, it is popular on the Iroquois reservations for people to supplement their dreams with readings of tarot cards, tea leaves, or shreds of native tobacco bobbing in a simmering saucepan. I will discuss other techniques for getting a second opinion on a dream in part 4, chapter 16, "The Shaman at the Breakfast Table."

As shamanic dream journeyers, the Iroquois developed the practice of sending out dream scouts. The Jesuit missionaries were often astounded at the extraordinary foreknowledge and insight of the Iroquois "sorcerers" they encountered. They recorded accounts of dream trackers—typically shape-shifters who could assume the form of a power animal or bird ally—who would travel to locate an enemy war party, spy out an adversary's defense, or find where the deer were herding during hard times. In the starving times of midwinter, with supplies running low and game animals hard to find, they sent out their dream hunters to locate food. The dream hunters took flight—perhaps on the wings of a hawk or an owl—and ranged over the frozen landscape until they located the deer. When they returned from their dream flights, the village gathered around to listen. The skilled trackers asked questions to clarify which places the dream hunters had visited. Was the lightning-blasted oak the one on this side of the river, or the other side? When the details of the dream were clarified, hunting parties were sent out to follow an exact itinerary. There was not much leeway for wishful thinking or improving the story. The dream information had to produce results. If the dream information was wrong, the people lost respect for the atetshents, who might even be driven out of the village by public ridicule.

In an age of frequent wars and chaotic transformations, the Iroquois nations based their military strategy and their very survival on the power of gifted dreamers to scout out the future and observe things happening at a distance. The fact that the Iroquois were never defeated by their Native adversaries or by the European invaders suggests that their dream intelligence was quite reliable.

The *Jesuit Relations* indicate that gifted dreamers not only were skilled at seeing tomorrow's news today, but also were expected to look far into the future in order to guide their people. These dreamers were viewed as preceptors, in the original meaning of that word: "those who give counsel beforehand."

Father Jean Pierron, a missionary among the Mohawks, was astonished to find, on his return to one village that he had dismissed as hopelessly pagan, that a large cross had been set up in its center. His amazement deepened when he was told that the cross had been erected on the instructions of his staunchest adversary, a Mohawk shaman who he conceded was "the great prophet of his people." It turned out the shaman had dreamed that the cross was a genuine symbol of the master of life, and that his village would remain unconquered as long as the cross remained standing. With surprising candor, Father Pierron wrote, "I knew not at that time what to think of so extraordinary a dream."[17]

The early Iroquois were not fatalists about the futures perceived in dreams. They developed rituals and practices designed to divert—or reinforce—future episodes observed in dreams. They had a very interesting ritual approach for avoiding unwanted events. They believed that by playacting a dream under controlled circumstances, they might be able to prevent the dream from manifesting fully in the future. A dream of impending disaster or tragedy that felt close to fulfillment in physical reality might inspire quite radical enactment. A Mohawk warrior who dreamed that he was captured and fire-tortured to death by his enemies once arranged for his fellow villagers to bind him and burn him with red-hot knives and axes—but not to kill him.[18] Father Francesco Bressani observed a Huron man cutting off one of his fingers with a seashell because he had dreamed that his enemies had captured him and performed this amputation; it was assumed that severing the finger might at least prevent him from being taken captive by his enemies.[19] (Incidentally, poor Bressani later had a similar ritual performed on *him* by Iroquois captors who wanted to get the word out that they did not want Catholic priests in their country—primarily because it was noticed that wherever the missionaries went, white men's diseases quickly followed.)

The Iroquois not only recognize that dreams can give us life-supporting and even life-preserving information about the possible future; from early times, they have also seen that through dreaming, we can be present at the creation of the events that will manifest in physical life. There is a Jesuit account of a hunter who dreamed of a moose that said, "Come to me." The moose showed him an unusual stone inside its body. Guided by his dream, the warrior embarked on a hunting expedition. He found the location he had seen in his dream, and the moose was there. When he killed the moose and cut open its body, he found a stone in its gallbladder like the one he had dreamed.[20] This report is not only an example of how the Native dreamers of the Northeast scouted the future in dreams. It also suggests the belief and practice of *creating* the future inside the dreamspace.

BIG DREAMS

The Iroquois have long recognized that in much the same way that dreams reveal the desires of the soul, the spirits sometimes send certain individuals "big dreams" that provide major revelations about the soul's purpose and the environment. Big dreams may contain information of vital importance to the dreamer's personal health or physical survival, but many of these powerful dreams seem to be directed at benefiting the community as a whole. This is why, among Iroquois traditionalists, the first business of the day for the whole community was to share and tend to important dreams.

The Iroquois teach that big dreams can come about in two ways. During sleep, the dreaming mind or soul is released from the limitations of place and time, and it can range far and wide, into the future or the past, or into other dimensions of reality, where it may encounter spirit guides who may appear in the form of departed relatives, birds or other animals, or godlike beings. Or the dreamer may be visited by a being who may be another dreamer traveling in dream states, an ancestor or departed family member or friend, or an entity from dimensions of reality beyond the physical plane.

From a modern psychospiritual perspective, it seems that dreaming allows us to step into a world of cosmic consciousness that is outside linear time and space—where everything is happening *now*. To keep our limited memory banks from being overloaded by irrelevant miscellaneous information, the editor who becomes active as we surface from sleep may selectively focus or filter our precognitive searches, so that we recall a limited number of previews. But it is possible, as some Iroquois traditionalists believe, that we dream *everything* before it happens, even if we are amnesiac about what we experience in night dreams. By learning to maintain consciousness within the dreamworld, we may also be able to travel purposefully through the dreamgates of cosmic consciousness and communicate with other dreamers in either the past or the future. Conscious dreaming allows us to fold time and travel into the future or the past, as well as explore other life experiences. Beyond all of this, it may allow us to be present at the place of creation—the plane on which the events and circumstances of physical life are born.

DREAM ROADS TO THE AFTERLIFE

While mainstream Western psychology tends to ignore or deny the reality of communication with the departed, the traditional Iroquois, like other dreaming peoples, recognize that this goes on all the time. Handsome Lake, a Seneca prophet,[21] said that the dimension that separates the living and the dead is exactly as wide as the edge of a maple leaf. The traditional Iroquois acknowledge and work with several aspects of soul and spirit that survive death and may be encountered in dreams.

For the Iroquois, as for other Native American peoples, the practice of dreaming is the best preparation for dying. Iroquois tradition offers paths to the afterlife for different aspects of spirit—along a path lined with strawberries, across a narrow bridge with a ferocious guardian on the far side, through the Milky Way to the Earth-in-the-Sky where thought creates things. But the Real People have always been eager to update these itineraries, based on the experience of individual dream travelers.

Father Lalemant has a wonderful story about that. As he was struggling to convert the Hurons in 1639, he thought he had persuaded one of the most determined traditionalists to accept baptism on his deathbed. But . . .

this wretch, a little time before he died, fell into a swoon. Coming out of it, he said that he came from the other world, where he had seen nothing of what the French told. Rather, he had met there several of his own relatives, who had welcomed him warmly, assuring him that they had been waiting for him eagerly, and that they were going to hold many fine dances and celebrations to welcome him. He was so convinced of the truth of this that, in order to present himself in the same style as the people he had seen, he had his face painted and had brought and placed over him the finest articles he possessed, was given his dish and spoon, and then died.[22]

What happens after death is too important to be left to faith or opinion; we require firsthand information. The ancient Iroquois way encourages us to learn the soul's road beyond death through dreaming—in which we travel into the realms of the departed, and learn that there are many (possibly infinite) afterlife locales.

TIMEFOLDERS

While in the process of interacting with my Iroquois dream visitors, I realized that my own ability to dream true—to see things accurately at a distance across time and space—was growing very rapidly. I was being guided to many useful insights into ancient Iroquois dreaming and healing traditions that I found urgently relevant to healing our lives and our world today. These discoveries inspired me to revisit several paradigms that have been denied or suppressed by mainstream Western culture.

As I've said, the Iroquois believe that beings from the spirit world are constantly seeking to communicate with us in the dreamspace. Higher entities use costumes and vocabulary adjusted to our level of understanding, while pushing us—as in my dreams in a language I did not know—to go beyond our present understanding and expand our vocabularies. As I pursued a deepening dialogue with dream characters from other times by reentering my dreams and embarking on conscious dream journeys, I came to believe that we may be able to communicate with personalities living in the past or future in their own now time, for mutual benefit.

It seemed increasingly likely that Island Woman might be reaching across time intentionally, and that this might also be true of other characters from other times who were also appearing in my dreamspace. For example, as I deepened my studies of Native American shamanism, some of the shamans of my own ancestry—notably a Scottish druid in a cloak of raven feathers—stepped into my dreaming to encourage me to learn from and share with them. They offered me instruction in the practices of the *taibshear* (the Scots-Celtic seer) and songs for calling on spiritual allies. They asked me for information in return, and they suggested assignments to recover helpful rituals and practices for raising energy and opening and closing gateways between the worlds.

I came to believe that as I moved in and out of many parallel dream locales, I might actually be switching my awareness among many continuous realities involving life dramas being played out in both the past and the future. My experiences inspired me to develop the practice and teaching of techniques of conscious journeying for real-time communication with personalities in both the past and the future for mutual guidance.

DREAMS OF POWER

"Power is drawn to certain individuals," my Onondaga friend of the Beaver Clan instructed me. "It follows them and seeks them out, especially in dreams."

In those early years, after Island Woman called me, I discovered more and more ways in which this may be true. I had to fight psychic duels with a Native sorcerer, who manipulated mindless ghosts of the dead. I was helped, in these struggles, by animal guardians and by a wise Iroquois shaman who showed me—when our minds interlaced in vision—how to trap and relocate the lower energies of the dead and how to deflect intended harm without setting out to cause harm.

I had to pass a whole series of tests. One of them involved the temptation of a Faustian deal: tremendous wealth and power in return for pledging to serve a dark lord. On the night when I decisively rejected this offer, lightning bolt after lightning bolt shot down in a narrowing circle around the farm, like a distant gunner homing in on his target.

After the storm, I lifted out of my body. I found myself tugged by a benign intention—it felt like that of my father—and I floated down over an immense stone building, like a great cathedral open to the sky. I was uneasy when I saw giant figures below me, crowned with bird headdresses and arrayed in ancient armor, seated together at a vast table that glowed like purple fire. A voice like that of my father's walked through my mind, telling me that it was my time; I was welcome. I descended into that space and found a place set for me at the table. When I claimed my seat, I realized I was the same size as the ancient chiefs or kings, and dressed like them.

The events of that morning confirmed the reality of shared dreaming—our ability to enter the same space with another dreamer. In the morning, Wanda called me in high excitement to tell me she had seen me sitting in a circle of tribal elders or chiefs around a purple fire, beside a Native American who reminded her of our Mohawk friend Tom Porter.

The Iroquois believe that dreaming is one of the most important ways to accumulate authentic power, orenda. Those with unusual access to orenda—like the arendiwanen, the woman of power—can accomplish extraordinary things, as healers, creators, and leaders. Neighbors of the Iroquois, the Lenape or Delaware Indians, say that the most important thing to know about dreaming is that it directly increases one's access to *maskan*. According to Lee Irwin, a scholar of Lenape descent, maskan is "an enhanced ability to do things, an ability to do things considered well beyond the ordinary, something that is exceptional."[23] Here, in Native tradition, we find a fundamental understanding that is largely missing from Western analysis: that dreaming can be a source of vital energy, and that dreams can be transformers, allowing us to tap into a universal, inexhaustible source of authentic power.

Dreamwork, for me, is even more about channeling energy than about harvesting information. One gift of power that came to me through dreaming after my first encounters with Island Women is what might be called the shaman's inner light. On a summer night in 1988, I lay down on my bed and saw lights of many different colors shining through the dark, brighter than the fireflies that were dancing among the maples outside. I had the distinct impression that some power was seeking a common language in order to communicate with me. As if to confirm this thought, a series of childlike drawings flashed across my vision. Then, a powerful light came on in my head—not jolting and sporadic like the electric flashes that sometimes preface experiences of astral projection, but calm and steady. With this light, I could see very far, even friends living hundreds of miles away. I could also see into other dimensions. As I practiced seeing with this shaman light, a portal opened at the center of my vision, and

I reached through it into another world, where I found deep and wise intelligences waiting to instruct me.

SENECA SPIRITS

My forays into the world of the Iroquois led me into Seneca Indian landscapes in western New York. One night, at a motel on my way to a Seneca site near Rochester, New York, I had an interesting dream experience that reminded me that the spirits are always around.

I woke suddenly from a dream at about four AM. Remembering only a few fleeting images of some deer-hoof rattles and a little medicine pouch, I took a hot shower and then returned to bed, slipping into a conscious dream.

I was flying over some trees that turned into the form of huge bears and wolves moving toward cleared land—a formal garden. I landed near a greenhouse, and I opened a trapdoor and realized I was at a burial site. I saw two miniature masks inside a grave; then I saw a man hovering over the site and I instantly knew he was a Seneca medicine man. He spoke clearly and distinctly: "I will teach you about hon-wa-dee-oh."

The medicine man showed me some scenes from his life and several medicine objects. Then he said, "Burn tobacco for me." As we parted company, I saw some other people, including an animated red-haired woman and another Native figure who was wearing a magnificent circlet of bright orange feathers on his head. He looked like an Amazonian Indian, but there was something puzzling about his outfit.

I was amazed, but not altogether surprised, when the dream began to play out in waking life. I had an appointment that morning with G. Peter Jemison, a Seneca artist who was also the manager of Ganondagan State Historic Site, the site of a Seneca village burned by the French in the 1600s. When I arrived at his home, I found Peter at his kitchen table painting a picture of an Amazonian Indian replete with a sunburst of feathers around his head. It was clearly the figure in my dream, and I decided to see if he could explain the other clues in the dream.

As I described the formal garden I had seen, Peter suggested that it could be the Sonnenberg Gardens in nearby Canandaigua, and he confirmed there were almost certainly Seneca burials there. When I related my phonetic transcription of the Seneca medicine man's statement, Peter became very intent and he corrected my pronunciation: "Honondiho."

Intrigued, I asked him what the word meant, and he responded cautiously that the members of this society were in charge of some of the most powerful religious and healing ceremonies. Sensing that he was reluctant to talk more about the subject, I dropped it. However, as Peter walked me over to his office and introduced me to a redhead—similar to the one in my dream—I had no doubt that the dream was another visitation, probably from a deceased shaman who had lived in the area.

Later, I learned that the Honondiho are the keepers of the famous Little Water Medicine, the most powerful of the traditional medicines of the Seneca people, and their closely guarded secrets are passed from the keeper to his chosen successor.

REQUICKENING

When I had finally accepted an active engagement with the spirits, turned my back on past definitions of success and value, and learned enough of Island Woman's language to understand my dream teachers, they welcomed me into a sacred circle where I lay by the fire pit while they placed red-hot coals on my ears and eyes to change my senses, and on my tongue and over my heart to open it, "so that henceforth you will speak and act only from the heart." I felt I had literally died and been reborn.

I rose from this night vision charged with energy. I jumped in my car and drove out to Grafton Lakes State Park to a lake where I had walked with my black dogs. I stood by the water and made my pledge—to the lake, and the trees, and the red-tailed hawk who came knifing through the clouds: "Henceforth I will speak and act only from the heart."

I would later understand that I had undergone a requickening. In the ancient Iroquois way—as in that of my Celtic ancestors—requickening takes place when a space has been cleared in the body and the energy field of a living person so that it can be occupied by the spirit of a "great one." This may be the spirit of an ancestor, or a power of the Creator, or an aspect of the recipient's own Higher Self. The precondition is the cleansing and purging of heavy energy and negative emotions.

I did not understand, in my head, all that had happened to me among the dream people on the night when my senses were changed and my heart was opened. But my heart knew, and I had promised to follow the intelligence of the heart even when my head could not keep up.

DREAMING WITH THE ANIMAL POWERS

While sifting the Jesuit reports of the early Iroquois shamans, I found the transcription of another exotic word I had heard in my dreams: *oyaron*. It seemed that apprentice dreamers among the Hurons and the Iroquois courted the company of spirit guides known as oyaron. Powerful dreamers could shape-shift into the forms of their oyaron and even send them to perform missions while the shamans remained elsewhere. Father Lafitau, the superior at the Jesuit mission at Kahnawake and a pioneer anthropologist, observed that "by means of this oyaron, they can transform themselves, transport themselves, and do what they please."[24]

The oyaron is a spiritual guardian or ally that often appears in the form of an animal but is not necessarily confined to that form. Developing a relationship with an oyaron is far more than a matter of identifying with a personal symbol. If you have a strong working relationship with an oyaron, you can shape-shift into its form, at least in the energy body, and you can send it to perform missions for you while you are somewhere else.

I learned about this from Bear, a spirit guardian with whom I had formed a deep connection since he started calling on me in my dreams when I moved to the farm. In one early dream, an enormous standing bear caught me up in his embrace and danced with me. He showed me how we were joined at the heart, and how we could swap skins. He also showed me how to locate diseased points within the human energy field, and how to work on repairing them.

One day, I was up on a hill at the front of my property when I heard shots from the far side of our land, in the deep woods. I scanned to find out exactly what was going on, and I saw, with my inner sight, a couple of hunters who had come across the railroad tracks that bordered our land, ignoring the NO TRESPASSING signs, and were now trying to kill white-tailed deer in our woods. I was enraged and desperate to protect the deer. Since we had lived here, we had operated a de facto wildlife sanctuary, and we were often blessed with the sight of dozens of deer grazing in our fields or drifting among the trees. The hunters were a long way away, and far from our roads. It would take at least thirty minutes to get to them on foot. My rage and urgent concern for the deer rose stronger and stronger. In the bright sunlight, I was startled to see a cloud of vapor massing around my solar plexus. It took form as a bear. I watched the bear rush off into the woods at remarkable speed. With my inner sight, I saw it burst from the trees and strike fear into the hunters, who fled back across the railroad tracks. I heard no more shots. I felt rather light-headed until I was snacking inside the house and felt something join my energy field.

I was content to assume that my impression of a spirit bear chasing away the deer killers was just a pleasant fantasy—until the next day, when a carpenter who was doing some work for me arrived with some interesting news. "Did you know there's a bear on your land?" he asked in high excitement. "A big one, too. A couple of guys told me about it at breakfast in the Chatham Bakery. They were trespassing on your land when the bear came at them. They were so scared they ran off."

Today, whenever I am facilitating a healing circle in North America—and dreaming is always healing, as the Iroquois teach—I call on Bear to support our work.

4

Living in Two Worlds

We must assume our existence as broadly as we in any way
can; everything, even the unheard of, must be possible in it.
This is at bottom the only courage that is demanded of us;
to have courage for the most strange, the most inexplicable.

RAINER MARIA RILKE

My whole life began taking on the color of my dreams, and I sometimes
found my waking experience of time and space shifting. My dreamlife
spilled into my physical world, which was increasingly patterned by
shimmering webs of synchronicity.

My journey deepened, in both the Real World and the surface
world. I had extraordinary encounters with the animate forces of
nature. Lightning visited my house, skipping across the whole length of
a barn's tin roof to ground itself in the one place where that could happen safely.

I learned to talk to the elements. When a brush fire driven by a
fierce north wind almost took my house—after burning twenty acres of
dry grass—I spoke to the wind and it abruptly changed direction. I
watched as the wind hurled the blaze due east, away from the house

and towards the front of the property. Old pine and spruce trees exploded like fireworks. By the time the fire trucks rumbled up my drive, the danger had passed. The fire chief inspected the ruler-straight line of scorched grass a few feet from my door, and rubbed his forehead. "Something saved your house, but it sure wasn't us."

In a twisting limestone gorge alive with the figures of birds, animals, and spirits, and the voluminous shapes of a Great Mother giving birth, I found a passage into the Underworld. By a waterfall in a secret cave, I found an ancient place of mystery initiation and traveled there— in my physical body and in my dreambody—to commune with the wise ones of an earlier time.

In a clean mountain stream at the foot of Hart Fell, in the landscape of my Scottish ancestors, where the Scottish Merlin lived with the deer and shamanized, I met a beautiful spirit of the waters.

On a garnet mountain in Mohawk country, an antlered being appeared and showed me how to heal through his spirit antlers, directing subtle streams of energy where they were needed. I wrote a poem for him.

To the Deer of the Mountain
Deepheart, mountain guardian
who harries the hunter
who knows what belongs to us
and what does not:
Give us your speed,
your power to read the land
your ability to see what is around and behind us.
May we grow with the seasons
into your branching wisdom,
putting up antlers as taproots into the sky
to draw down the power of heaven,
walking as living candelabra
bearers of light
touching each other with tines of light
probing deep in the wounded places
to heal and make whole
crowned with light
crowning each other with light

THE SANTA FE BUG

Dreaming and waking became a seamless web through the play of synchronicity. This came home to me when I flew to Santa Fe in the summer of 1993 to attend a conference of the Association for the Study of Dreams, or ASD.

I reveled at being among several hundred wonderful people—not only academics and shrinks, but poets and artists and shamans and everyday dreamers—who enjoyed living and sharing the dream adventure. I made many friends, and I did not especially mind if some of these friends made their living, as tenured academics, writing papers on how dreams are only delusions generated by a chemical wash or random neuronal firings. I got to my feet to applaud the passionate address of the outgoing president, Rita Dwyer, who told us that her own spur to dream and to incite others to dream was the fact that her life had been saved by a friend's precognitive dream.

When they were both working in a rocket laboratory, the scientist-friend dreamed that there was a chemical explosion. Rita was engulfed in flames and might not have made it out had the friend not known, in the dream, exactly where to reach for her. He was embarrassed to share the dream, but subsequently it was played out exactly. When a chemical fire did break out in their laboratory, and no one else even noticed that Rita was missing when the alarms went off and toxic smoke rolled through the building, the friend knew just where to reach for Rita and pull her to safety.

I joined one of the morning dream-sharing groups but had to get out when I found that the leader was uncomfortable with precognitive or transpersonal dreams, such as dreams of the departed. Luckily for me, Rita had just launched a small dream circle of her own at the conference. An artist in the group shared a dream in which she was sitting in her private space when suddenly she became aware of a visitor. She turned to see a distinctly Native American man with long shiny black hair, sharp intent eyes, and a hollow in his solar plexus where a raven was perched, watching her with the same intent dark eyes.

We had fun discussing the raven dream, and I walked with the dreamer after the session to the Ark bookstore to look for books on ravens. I said to her, "If it were my dream, I would want to do more. I would want to go back inside the dream, talk to the raven man, and find out what he is doing in my personal space." We paused, because at that moment we were outside an art gallery with a sculpture in the window depicting a Native American with a hollow in the solar plexus and a bird perched in that cavernous space. Not a raven, but confirmation enough.

So I drummed for the artist on a new deerskin drum I had bought in a store on the plaza, and we journeyed together in our dreams to meet this shaman who identified himself as Menominee. He shared some of his healing and divinatory techniques and gave us a song. The artist kept in touch with him for a year or so, but he made her a little uncomfortable—Raven can be tricksterish—and she eventually moved on to other dream teachers.

The incident confirmed the importance of traveling into the dream-space, as opposed to simply talking about dreams as if they are finished "texts." It was also a vivid reminder that a deeper reality irrupts into our lives through "coincidence" as well as dreams and intuition.

I wandered a street market in the Santa Fe sun with new friends who included Steve and Wewer Keohane, wonderfully gifted artists and dreamers from Colorado. Steve had given up a high-paid corporate job to follow his heart's desire to become a sculptor and healer. I told him how strongly I had felt driven to make similar choices.

I was impelled to share the episode from twelve years earlier, when I had declined an invitation to become an African witch doctor and had been cautioned that because the spirits were in love with me, they would find me again. I explained that I had accepted only the first stage of initiation on the path of Ifa, which in the New World is called the *mano de Orunmila* and comes with sets of green-and-yellow beads, one of which is worn as a bracelet on the left wrist. To punctuate my tale, I tapped my bare left wrist. In that precise moment, a huge flying bug landed on my wrist, *exactly* where I was pointing. Its body was striped green and yellow in the same colors and pattern as the bracelet I was describing. I have never seen a bug like this before or since.

Our conversation was on pause until the bug took off. Then Steve said, "Do you think they might be sending you another message?"

I remembered what Ade, the African divination priest, had told me: that my dreams would be more important in my life, and the lives of others, than I had yet understood. This may have been the moment at which I began to understand that my path—the path that Ade had predicted and that Island Woman had opened for me—was going to be that of a dream teacher, something for which there is no obvious career track in modern Western society.

Another Santa Fe synchronicity put me firmly on that path. Stan Krippner was the president of the ASD that year. I was already familiar with some of his wide-ranging and brilliant research in the fields of shamanism and parapsychology. I greatly enjoyed his workshop on developing a personal mythology with the aid of dreams, and I resonated with his perception that one of the great healing gifts of dreaming is that it helps to put us in touch with our deeper stories. We had chatted briefly, but in the swirl of the conference we did not have occasion to talk at length—until I found myself on the wrong bus.

The Dream Ball was held on the last night of the conference. I went in my informal Johnson attire: colonial-style ruffled shirt, plenty of silver, a gorget, animal teeth and bones, and highly contemporary black jeans and boots. At a later conference, they gave me a ribbon for the Most Reincarnational Costume when I appeared in a similar outfit, this time with a *kahsto:wa,* a feathered Iroquois headdress.

I surfaced rather late the next morning and was told at the hotel desk that I had missed the airport shuttle and would need to get a cab if I wanted to make my plane. I decided that instead of springing for the taxi, I would wait for the next bus and see what turned up. When our plans get scrambled, the Trickster comes into play.

When I got on the "wrong" bus, I found Stan Krippner on board. We sat together and got to talk for the whole ninety-minute ride. I told him how I felt strongly that what was most notably missing from Western dreamwork and dream analysis was a simple, effective technique for traveling and operating inside the dreamspace. "Dreams are real experiences," I insisted, "and the best way to understand a dream is to go inside and recover the full depth of that experience, instead of simply talking about broken and garbled memories from the dream."

I tapped my new drum and suggested that heartbeat shamanic drumming was a very effective technology for shifting consciousness and entering the dreamspace, if accompanied by clear intention and a picture that could serve as a portal. Beyond helping an individual to go on a conscious dreaming, it could facilitate adventures in shared dreaming and even group dream travel to agreed destinations. I described how I put partners together as dreamers and trackers to enter each other's psychic space, with permission, for healing, adventure, and guidance. I explained that in the practice I had developed, the tracker is a person who makes a conscious journey into another person's dreamspace in order to gather information on their behalf, or support them in confronting terrors or claiming power—or simply to enjoy the experience of wide-awake interactive dreaming. As examples of dream reentry and tracking, I described how the raven dreamer and I had just entered her dreamspace together and interviewed a Menominee shaman who had lived in the nineteenth century, and how Wanda Burch and I had traveled together into other times, future and past, through the gateway of remembered dreams and visions.

Stan was quite familiar with shamanic journeying techniques, and he seemed intrigued by my proposal for a synthesis of the shaman's mode of travel with the personal maps and agendas that are the gifts of our dreams. When I got off the shuttle at my airline terminal, he jumped off after me to say that he intended to ensure that I was invited to be a presenter at the next ASD conference, which was to be held in the Netherlands.

Within the week, I was formally invited to lead a workshop on shamanic dreaming at the University of Leiden, a wonderful opportunity to introduce my approach to an international audience. After my workshop there, two shrinks from the Sigmund Freud Institute in Frankfurt came running after me across a pleasant courtyard, yelling, "*Schaman! Schaman!* Stop! You must tell us how you did that!"

"Did what?"

"During your workshop, we had the most vivid experience of telepathy we have ever had. But there was something more. It was as if we were really together in a different space."

"You did it for yourselves," I told them. "The dreamworld is a Real World, and we can go there as soon as we stop listening to our expensively educated left brains telling us that is not possible."

So the wrong bus got me to the right place. Oh yes—and my flight from Santa Fe to Albuquerque had been delayed that day, so in the end I took the plane I was scheduled to take.

THE PATH OF A DREAM TEACHER

In the months after that Santa Fe conference, I was in almost constant communication with teachers who operate from another reality, as the great teachers usually do. I continued to feel the presence of Island Woman and the ancient ones of the Iroquois, but the dominant teaching role in my dreams was now assumed by personalities, both male and female, who seemed to be connected with a Western mystery order; by personalities who seemed to be my counterparts in other times and dimensions; and by a deep, deep source of knowing I came to regard as my "witness in heaven," the Self of my self.

Almost every night, I trained for the work I now do through my Dream School. Some of the communications I recorded underscore the immense importance of this work and its ability to reopen our lines to higher intelligence, and to support the evolution of humanity into a more conscious and compassionate species.

The cusp of the turning year is always a good time to dream big. In the holiday season of 1993, lying on my back in the moonlight in a waking state of relaxed attention, I received and recorded this communication with a teacher on a different plane of existence:

> You were chosen to be a teacher and interpreter for your time. The choice, and its terms, were yours. The conditions were known to you before your descent into flesh. The miasmic conditions of the Earth plane have caused you to wander lost for significant periods. This is a frequent occurrence. It has affected many ambassadors of spirit. It has prepared you for the challenges of rescuing others from the fog of low desire and despair.

I was humbled, rather than inflated, by this communication. It stirred me to the depths of my being, and it gave me the courage to make a further and deeper break with some of the clutter of old habits and self-limiting beliefs that had been holding me back. It also brought a sense of urgency: the urgent need to serve a calling that may have been chosen a very long time ago.

Two days after Christmas that same year, I recorded a further communication with the same teacher, again in a waking state of relaxed attention:

Dreaming Is a Discipline

> This mode of being is provisional. The conditions of physical existence are narrowly circumscribed. You exist in your present form in a sheath of air, a bubble in space. Yet your consciousness is limitless. This is fact, the most basic knowing you possess.
>
> Out of consciousness proceeds physical form. What takes form

must be *thought* before it can manifest. You reenter this under-standing when you enter the larger attention, when you stretch beyond your ordinary faculties.

From the beginning, consciousness—*nous*—is the medium in which you exist. Let this be at the heart of your teaching.

Dreaming is a discipline, the most vital you possess.

Six months later, as I packed my bags to fly to Holland, my teacher rehearsed me in a conscious dream on what has become a core practice of Active Dreaming. He began by describing the substance of the dreamworld.

The Substance of Dreams

The stuff from which dreams are woven is supersensory but not supersensible. Though lighter and more malleable than matter, it is not without substance. This helps to explain the enduring charac-ter of dream geographies shared and maintained by different cul-tures and orders of practitioners.

My guide proceeded to clarify and confirm the techniques of Dream Reentry that I had been developing. I will discuss Dream Reentry in detail in part 4, chapter 16, "The Shaman at the Breakfast Table."

MASKING THE SPIRITS

I was feeling my way along a new path, the path of a dream teacher, for which, as I've said, there is no obvious career track in our society. I was also groping for a way to write about my experiences. I did not yet have the confidence to write en clair about what I knew to be going on—which was that I was having a series of encounters with beings from other times. So I decided to confine myself to writing the story of Johnson and Island Woman under the mask of fiction.

The dream people were watching, of course.

When I was working on the "fictional" story of Johnson and Island Woman that was published in 1995 as the novel *The Firekeeper,* I had some very vivid dialogues with William Johnson. He spelled out Mohawk names syllable by syllable, breaking them down so I could get to their root meanings. He also wanted to be sure I portrayed his rela-tions with women accurately. He gave me amazingly specific details about some of the women he knew and offered this apologia:

> Let me say something to the women. I have loved you better than
> my kingdom, without excess of discrimination, without stint or
> halt. I have gone full-tilt on the fields of love. I have spread myself
> as few men do—not only in the transports of the flesh, but in *soul*.[1]

And Island Woman appeared again. She came on a cold December
night, displaying her wampum credentials. She showed me scenes from
her time so I would write them correctly. "Let your mind be still. See
the lake. Focus on the sunlight on the water."

She showed me how her adopted people, the Mohawks, took captives and made them their own by putting a Mohawk spirit inside them.

She revealed the existence of a secret order of women of power who
called themselves by an unassuming name: burden straps. "There is an
order—forbidden to men, secret from ordinary women. To be a part of
it is to be other than ordinary people. You must be willing to carry the
burden of the people. If you are accepted, you will be poorer than any,
because the weight of their needs is your burden. If you are accepted,
you become the burden strap."

She explained how a woman related to Molly Brant had been
rejected by the order "because she did not think with her heart."[2]

I used all of this as material for *The Firekeeper,* a novel with foot-
notes. Since then, Island Woman has made it clear that she wants both
of us to drop the veil of fiction and speak directly. The result is part 3
of this book.

THINNING VEILS

Wherever I traveled, the spirits of the land continued to speak to me. I
flew back to Santa Fe and drove up to Bandelier National Monument,
an Anasazi site under the big sky where you can watch the weather
rolling in from fifty miles away.

At Bandelier, I had two encounters that would be the stuff of dream
archaeology, if more archaeologists were dreamers. On the trail to the
falls, beyond an area where I felt the mountain lion energy very
strongly, I lay down under ponderosa pines and immediately became
aware of the presence of a very short, very dark-skinned man who told
me his name was Patasihone (pah-tah-see-HO-nay). His name and

identity had something to do with the jackrabbit. I saw him hunting small animals a long time ago, living very close to the earth. I asked to enter his Dreamtime and I slipped inside the world of the animals. He and his people were (or are) more like animals than like city-dwelling humans. There was a simplicity, even an innocence here.

The veil thinned again in front of the petroglyphs at the "long-house" site—apartments built into the talus of a volcanic cliff—at the Anasazi village. The carved stone wall became a window rock: I could simply look through it into a scene on the other side. An ancient shaman appeared. He communicated to me, with some disgust, that white people know next to nothing about what really went on with the Anasazi, but that he would show me certain things, under certain con-ditions, "because you see the way we do." I was permitted to witness an ancient rainmaking ceremony, in which the priest held up and vibrated a large stuffed serpent while a helper made the sound of thun-der crashing with something resembling a mortar and pestle. I was shown methods for appealing directly to the animating forces of nature. Then I blew it by asking if the ancient rainmaker had a ritual for *stop-ping* the rain. He shut off our dialogue fast, beaming something like, "Stupid white man! Why would anyone want to *stop* the rain?"

On a hiking trip in the Cherokee National Forest, along the border of Tennessee and North Carolina, I had a powerful experience that took me deep into the spirit world of the southern Iroquois, or Cherokee. In this waking vision, I was tested. Before I was found worthy to receive sacred knowledge, I was required to enter into the pain and suffering of a Native people who had been cruelly dispossessed by the dominant culture.

My head could not keep up with all that was happening to me. This raw experience, recounted in the next chapter, connected me more deeply with the intelligence of the heart. It opened the way to the heart of Ancient Mother, who has many names and forms, but who is for me the deep nurturing power of the Earth Goddess.

5

Teachings of the Heart Shaman

A sacred being cannot be anticipated;
it must be encountered.

W. H. AUDEN

She smells like warm earth under rain. Her laughter is the gurgle of a cool mountain stream. Her tears are the overflow from her great heart, sliding down her bones where they show through her green raiment, making sudden cliffs and rock faces. She is garlanded with pearly dogwood blossoms and bright splashes of trillium. The trees are her numberless lovers and her children, and she opens herself to those who are willing to plunge deep into her mysteries.

Two immense poplars lean toward each other like lovers embracing. The hollow between them is a perfect triangle. From her deep-bosomed, limitless body, she projects a form in which I can honor and pleasure her. A lovely woman, gilded by the dappled light falling through the canopy of the forest, appears in the cleft of the giant poplars. She invites me eagerly into her embraces. Her eyes go dark and deep, and she calls me into the well of her memory. I feel the weight and curve of the living bones above my head. And my joy is tempered by grief. I remember an ancient wound, an ancient wrong, an ancient loss, in the cycles of a neverending story. . . .

After, I splash through the shallows of the creek, dive like a salmon into its deeps, and rush with the fast cold current, alarming the trout. I dry off in the morning sun for a bit, then pull on my shorts and hiking boots and start up an exiguous, winding trail into the mountains. Soon it's no more than a deer trail.

I notice a fleck of brilliant crimson among the soft greens. Then I see another. I stoop, expecting to find a small flashy wildflower, but instead I see what might be a spot of wet paint in another setting but here can only be blood. Something tugs at my heart. I feel urgent concern for a creature in the woods that is wounded and bleeding.

I need to find what is hurt and do what I can. Though I did not notice them until now, I see there are fresh tracks on the trail. Even to my city-fogged sight, they are not hard to follow now that I am looking for them. The runoff from recent rains has made the ground soft. When I come to a heap of fallen branches, I can make out the impress of a heavy body that recently hauled itself upward.

The slope is getting steeper and steeper, but the direction is always up. My breath comes in shallow, aching gasps as I struggle on. My chest is shiny with sweat, although it is getting notably cooler—and darker—as I climb. Mist rolls through the forest, settling like dense smoke, shutting out the sun. It's getting hard to see very far in any direction. I force the pace, heading straight up, and am rewarded by a glimpse of branching antlers moving high above me, where the ground cover thins and the poplars give way to mountain junipers and low scrub. Or am I deceiving myself? Can I really track a stag, even a wounded one, on my awkward legs, accustomed to mown grass and city sidewalks?

When I get to the place where I saw the antlers, I am bitterly disappointed. The branches of the sumacs all look like antlers. There is no sign of hoofprints here where the bedrock is exposed. Yet there, on the bark of a tree I cannot name, is a damp spot, dark and glistening. I test it with a forefinger, taking its stickiness onto my tongue. It might be blood. Or it could be the taste of my own mouth, desperate for water.

I see a stir of movement above me, close to the summit. The stag is there, I am sure of it, though the mist blots out my vision. I climb a few more yards. The mist parts, and I can see him clearly. He has turned to look at me. He stands immobile as I struggle toward him. I feel a stab of pain in my own heart when I see that he is bleeding from his chest.

He turns now, graceful as a ballet dancer performing a pirouette, and vanishes into the thick mist that is swirling above. I cannot see him, but he has given me my direction. I follow it without hesitation, hurling myself into the mist. The mountain smoke sucks me in. For a moment, all my senses are stilled. I have known this effect in nature only once before, when I was caught in a whiteout in a hurricane of snow in the Northeast. The mist wraps around me like wet cotton. I trip and go down. When I get up, I have no inkling of east or west. My cosmos has just two compass readings: up and down.

I climb up, always up. It is harder and harder to breathe. Then the mist opens a chink, like a curtain, and I see the stag's rump, rising and falling rhythmically as he bounds ahead of me. Now the mist thins and becomes opalescent. Everything is suffused by a sourceless, silvery light tinged with blue. There is a precipice ahead. The stag leaps into the air, and my heart aches for him, for he is plainly at the end of his powers. His leap is lopsided, and he is coming down in a ragged heap of splayed legs. I fear he will be terribly injured.

The blueness in the mist thickens and deepens as if a watercolor artist is infusing new color into a field of wet paint. The depth of the blue is beautiful. It is the blue you might find in a candle flame, or in the pure water of a limestone gorge. The blue depth seems to catch the stag and break his fall. His legs shoot forward, and paddle back, and plunge forward again. He is no longer falling, or leaping, or running. He is swimming in a blue lake that cannot possibly be there. And he has been healed.

It can only be a mirage, my left brain frets, a lake that color, at this barren height of the mountain. If this is really a lake, then where is the shore? Mist doesn't just become a blue lake, with no point of transition, in defiance of natural law. Am I dreaming? The soreness in my knees, and in my calves, tell me that—dreaming or hallucinating—I seem to be in a physical body.

The stag has vanished into the deeps of the blue lake. Something rises in me that is stronger than head-talk. As Pascal said, the heart has reasons of which reason knows nothing. It is my heart, not my head, that drives me to leap into that blue depth.

I plunge down and down, trying to hold my breath. Vague shapes float by. An immense eye, like that of a blue whale, contemplates me from very close. My lungs bursting, I head for the surface . . . and find there is no surface. Images from my life—and from lives both strange and familiar—spin around me. I know I am drowning, as I drink in that eerie blue. Yet as my lungs fill with the lake, I continue to breathe.

A wavelike movement carries me to land. I cannot say where this land is, in relation to where I came from. The mountainside looks as it did before, except that the mist has gone and there has been a time shift. Bright moonlight etches the trees and the things moving among them in sharp silhouette. I see the stag again. He tosses his antlers, proud and kingly and whole, and trots away down the slope.

Wood smoke is in the air and I follow the scent. As I approach the fire, I smell barbecue and my stomach rumbles. From the shelter of a rocky massif, I look down on a Native encampment. I am surprised to find Indians out in these woods; I thought the Cherokee of these parts had long gone on their Trail of Tears. I am astonished to see that these Indians live the old way—no pup tents and barbecue grills for them. They have constructed simple lean-tos from tree limbs and bark and skins, and they are roasting meat on a spit over an open fire, with a great pot of soup bubbling away on the coals. Some of the people gathered around the fire wear shirts and simple dresses, but they were not purchased in any department store; they are very old-fashioned in design and hung with brooches and medicine bags. There's no sign of denim. Some of the Indians are entirely clothed in skins and furs. There are only women and children in the camp, as far as I can see, apart from an old man who sits close to the fire with his pipe. The youngest of the children cluster tight around him as he points his pipestem at Taurus, talking the stars out of the sky.

I slowly become aware that I have traveled through a timegate. I am no longer in the twenty-first century. I watch white men in the clothes of an earlier time moving stealthily toward a Native village, and I am seized with the deep intuition that I am about to witness terrible crimes. The white men have come to kill Indians and rape their women.

I don't want to watch, but something intervenes to make me understand that I must bear witness. He shows himself in the shape of a man, but he's much larger than a regular human. His head rises almost to the treetops. Immense antlers sprout from his head. The antlers are not a headdress; they are part of him. I have met this being before, on a mountain in Mohawk country, and in the lands of my Celtic ancestors. I know the Antlered One, and I trust him more than I trust myself. The Antlered One is walking through my mind. He is making me understand that I must see and feel the suffering of the people who are native to this earth. This is the price of a deeper level of knowing.

Although I'm choking with grief and rage, I follow his intention and force myself to bear witness as a beautiful Native woman is raped and savaged by filthy, drunken white men and her family members are slain as they try to protect her. I continue to bear witness—gagging with revulsion—through scene after scene of sickening violence and violation. I watch as the remnants of a people who lived close to this earth, and close to the dreaming, are driven from their homes and herded on a long and bitter trail to the west, apart from a few who scatter like foxes and hide in the mountains where strangers cannot find them.

At last the Antlered One indicates that I have seen enough. Now that the tragic history of this people has streamed through me and been indelibly imprinted in my mind and energy field, I am considered ready to meet a new guide, a teacher who belongs to this land. The Antlered One withdraws into the forest, leaving me alone with the new teacher.

He shows himself first as a huge man with the head of a bird. The color of the bird head is smoky gray, but I can't identify the genus. He shows himself again with a human face surrounded by a solar disk, with rays projecting all around his head. His chest is enormous. He opens a window in his being and lets me look into the chamber of his heart. His heart is as large as that of two normal men. This is not the result of some cardiac condition; it is because his power and his mind are centered in the heart. He is a master of the heart.

He shows me how he heals—and how I may be able to heal—by opening the heart. He transfers his teachings through a kind of holographic movie that plays out around me. Inside it, I study ancient rituals. Some of these involve swallowing the hearts of animals, to take on their medicine and their sensory ability. I am shown how to do energy work to help people who have physical heart conditions. I am instructed in a method of soul healing in which a person who has opened his or her heart center fully transfers vital energy, courage (which is found only in the heart), and the truth of the heart to someone who is ready to receive.

I think of how so many of us, as we struggle through life, cover up our hearts, cutting ourselves off from the heart's wisdom. Sometimes we put a great boulder in front of our hearts, hoping that this way we'll never have to feel pain or grief or heartbreak again. Sometimes we put a veil or a covering over our heart center, so nobody can *see* us. When we cut ourselves off from the intelligence of the heart—which Native peoples rightly understand to be an organ of thought and perception as well as emotion, and above all the place where we are most likely to find personal truth—we no longer know what we want or who we are.

In scene after scene, this mountain master is reminding me how much deeper and wiser and juicier our lives can be if we can only reopen our hearts and reclaim the soul energy that should live in our heart center—starting with the bounding energy of our beautiful younger selves, when we still had our gift for wonder and an ability to experience the depth of joy and pain. I understand that an invitation is being renewed and deepened: the invitation that came in the ritual of requickening when the ancient ones opened my heart. I am being encouraged to bring an ancient practice of healing to many more people who are hungry to reclaim vital soul energy, and to remember and live from the truth of their hearts' desires.

The heart teacher is also a warrior. I am a little edgy when he reveals that he is a master of psychic warfare, because I have invested so much in trying to leave behind the war maker in myself, and I have made an unshakable commitment never to abuse spiritual power to harm or manipulate others. But the Heart Shaman patiently reminds me that we may be called upon to use psychic powers to defend those who cannot defend themselves. He shows me that there are psychic entities at work in the world that crave blood and violence and will drive humans to war and even self-destruction in their need to feed this appetite. He shows me how he has projected animal forms to scout and to strike at a distance in order to defend his people and deter their enemies. I remember how Bear once came from my solar plexus to protect the deer from wanton, disrespectful killers. I recall the cruel sufferings of the Native people of those mountains, and the reason I was shown these things. I watch and learn.

The mountain master communicated a personal name to me, and he also showed it to me written in a strange script that seemed to use the Cherokee alphabet. But I know it is not right to share his personal name in print, just as the Iroquois today prefer not to say the personal name of the Peacemaker out loud, except in sacred space. So I will refer to my Smoky Mountains teacher simply as the Heart Shaman.

The practical gifts he gave me were evident right away. Two days after our encounter, I had an appointment to do some healing work with a woman who had been suffering through a painful, protracted divorce. The woman indicated that she felt an energy intrusion—something like an "arrowhead"—embedded in her lower back that was contributing to the burning pain she was experiencing in that area. During a walk across a meadow that day, I was suddenly inspired to perform an extraction on her. To my surprise, I sucked out something that felt like a barbed bullet, and I ended up retching and puking the bad stuff onto the ground.

The Heart Shaman stepped into my mind and told me to open my heart and let the energy flowing from him pour through me into the woman's heart. The image seemed to bring a powerful and deeply healing energy transfer. I was also guided to encourage the woman to construct a personal shield, decorated with the outline of an open human hand, with the outline of a bear's paw inside. After this session, I felt charged with energy, even though this kind of extraction work is often exhausting. The woman told me later that she was no longer experiencing the lower-back pain.

After my return to New York from North Carolina, I continued to wonder about that mysterious blue lake where the wounded stag had been healed. I began to do some research on Cherokee traditions. In a recent collection of traditional Cherokee stories collected from elders, I was thrilled to discover that my powerful experience seemed to have unfolded within a mythic landscape well known to the First Peoples of the Smoky Mountains.

In the Cherokee story, a boy is out walking in the mountains when he notices drops of blood among the fallen leaves. He tracks the wounded animal—which in this version proves to be a bear cub with a wounded leg—high up the mountain, where it vanishes into fog that transforms into a clear blue lake. The bear swims in the lake and comes out healed, just like my stag. Other wounded animals get in the lake and are healed the same way. My Heart Shaman is not in this story, but there is an interesting exchange between the protagonist and the Great Spirit of the Cherokee, who instructs him to tell his people that "if you are good to animals, and good to each other, then you may be able to come here, too."[1]

It seems that I slipped into the same well of vision, and the same lake of healing, that were known to the Native people of the land I was visiting. This echoed my experience in Mohawk country, and in other landscapes in both the New World and the Old. This has become so familiar that I have come to believe that the gates to the Otherworld are everywhere, and that entering them is essentially a matter of shifting perception and energy signatures. Certainly there are places of power and sacred sites on this Earth where the veil is especially thin and interdimensional travel is faster and easier than at other places. But wherever we are is, in practical terms, the center of our own multidimensional universe. And we can share; we can build and maintain places of power in the imaginal realm and invite others to share them for healing, initiation, training, and adventure.

I wanted to know, right away, whether I could invite others to bathe in that blue lake of healing that the deer had opened to me. I decided to experiment by inviting a circle of dreamers to travel into that space together, with the aid of focused intention and heartbeat drumming.

I wove the portal with words spun from my own vision. With my voice, I guided them out of our physical room into the clean, fresh air of the woods.

"Among the greens and wildflower pastels of the forest, you notice a tiny splash of bright red, then another. You bend to see what this is and realize you are looking at drops of fresh blood. You know there is something wounded that needs help. And you want to give that help, if you can. So you start following the trail of blood. The fresh bloodstains lead you deeper and higher into the woods. Your way becomes steeper and steeper until you are gasping for breath.

"Now you can see the wounded animal ahead of you. It stumbles and falls and gets up again, climbing the mountain. You are awed and amazed by its determination to get to the top.

"Finally you are approaching the summit. The wounded animal is just ahead of you. But now a thick blanketing fog is coming down and the animal vanishes into the mist. You will yourself to follow it. For a moment, you are blinded. But now the mist begins to lift and, amazingly, it is becoming a clear blue lake. As you gaze into the blue depth, you see the animal, swimming underwater. It swims on and on, then makes a loop and swims back toward you. As it steps from the blue water, you see that the animal is completely healed.

"While you are trying to puzzle out how this can be, a bird with a broken wing drops clumsily into the lake. You look into the water and see the bird diving and swimming. When it bursts through the surface, it takes flight on shining wings, healed and complete.

"More injured animals and birds come to the lake, and each time they immerse themselves in the healing blue waters, they emerge whole and intact. In your head, something is telling you this can't be real, that it's just a fantasy. But in your heart, you know that healing is here for *you*, in the depths of that blue lake.

"Lie back now. Let your body go soft and comfy. You are ready to flow into a different landscape, to dive into the blue lake and receive its healing. You are going on a dream. Let the drum make it easy to enter the blue lake of healing."

We shared tremendous, overlapping experiences that evening, and several participants believed they received spontaneous healing. When I guided them into the journey I was careful not to tell them what wounded animal to expect. As I had hoped, this resulted in different people tracking different animals. The animals and birds they identified reflected their own energy conditions and connections, and sometimes specific health or emotional challenges closely related to their chakras. One dreamer saw a beloved puppy half-garroted by a vicious choke collar. When the puppy was healed in the lake, she felt blessedly released from something that had been stealing her own power to speak and contributing to physical challenges in her throat area. After the journey, she delighted our circle by singing to us—something she said she would never have done previously—to celebrate her healing at the throat center.

When our journeyers followed the animals and birds into the blue lake in their dreambodies, they had marvelous adventures in a shared reality far beyond our physical space. Some of our divers entered a realm where deeper levels of healing appear to be available. Here is an excerpt from one journey report:

I dive into the lake and find myself in a blue depth that is vast and oceanic. I see many sea creatures swim by: dolphins, whales, sharks, schools of fish, squid, and octopus. The blue whale is very close to me, and I swim with it for a while. It is surprisingly elegant.

When I join the blue whale, I am no longer aware of any difference in size between us.

I go deeper. Far, far down I have a strong sense of contact with a different kind of being—a being that produces its own light, a soft glow. These beings have bodies that resemble a soft, mobile coral. They can shape-shift and grow new digits—or organs?— very easily. I have the impression that what they know and what they are can be very helpful in mending and strengthening bones, including generating new cartilage and releasing pain from joints. I have an impression of myself laid out on a smooth surface on the ocean floor, receiving a treatment to release the pain in my knees and elbows and strengthen my joints.

This traveler had complained of quite severe pain immediately before the journey. After the journey, the pain was gone.

I believed I was following the path of teaching and healing the Heart Shaman had shown me, the path I was called to by the Antlered One.

But Island Woman and the ancient ones of her people were not done with me. They wanted more. I was not altogether surprised to make a connection with an ancient shaman in Cherokee country, because I knew that the Cherokee are cousins—though distant ones— of the Iroquois, and that they speak a related language. But I did not expect the Iroquois to find me in California and call me to stand in the place of the lion and open my heart to the world.

Tree Gate
to Ancient Mother

*Since it has been said that you are my twin and true
companion, examine yourself so that you may
understand who you are.*

JESUS TO THOMAS IN *THE BOOK OF THOMAS THE CONTENDER*

The adventure continued to deepen. Dozing in bed in the dappled light
of a crisp, early-fall morning in 2002, I found myself drawn to another
bedroom, a boy's room with a single bed against the wall and a window looking out on the muddy browns and gum-tree greens of the
Australian bush. Could this be my room when I was living with my
family in Queensland, at the age of six?

The Australian space became more real, more solid. I maintained
some awareness of my body under the covers in New York, but I let
that scene fade and become dormant. Now I was lying in my
Queensland boy's bed. I wanted to explore the scene outside the window. I left the body and flowed through the window. I delighted in the

sights and sounds of the bush, of the she-oaks sighing and singing in the breeze, of the call of rainbirds, of the smell of wattle under sunlight. Quite soon I was drawn to the mouth of a passage leading down into the earth. I became conscious of human figures moving through the scrub. The men were naked, or nearly naked, and their skin was slate gray. They were armed with primitive weapons; one was shaped like a large hook and looked very fierce. I slipped back into my family home and my six-year-old body in the bed.

I spent a little time in his mind, checking how he was thinking and feeling. I was glad to find that he was relatively well and happy. His time in the Queensland sunshine was a rare interval of reasonable good health and connectedness with other people in a childhood marred by tremendous pain, recurring near-fatal illnesses, and isolation. He did not yet know, in his boy's mind, that his father was about to be transferred to Melbourne, and that in Melbourne he was going to die for a second time, and a third, losing vital signs in the hospital during bouts of double pneumonia. I focused my intention of being the mentor and counselor he so desperately needed.

"Robert," I told him, "you are going to make it through. You are going to survive everything, and come out stronger, and be able to teach and help others. Always listen to your dreams. Your dreams will get you through.

"You will be a writer and storyteller," I promised him. "And people will love your stories. You'll find your sister. You'll love girls, and they will love you, even if you're shy about them now. Remember your dreams, Robert," I repeated. "Your dreams will get you through."

When I returned from this Australian outing to my grown-up body in my room in New York and inspected the digital face of the bedside clock, I saw that only a couple of minutes had passed. The curtains to the alcove were vibrating a little, as if someone has just brushed through them. I remembered a Seneca legend of a duel between dream shamans in which the old witch challenges the young hero to perform a series of seemingly impossible tasks before the skin flap of the doorway through which he must exit has stopped vibrating.

My visit to my six-year-old self made me vividly aware of one of the great gifts of dreaming. Once we wake up to the fact that in dreaming we are not confined to time and space, we can have conscious encounters with our own younger and older selves. We can provide the mentoring and reassurance our younger self may have needed desperately and lacked altogether, in waking life, in a time of pain or shame or betrayal. Through contact with an older and hopefully wiser self, we can in turn receive guidance at the crossroads of our present lives. In my workshops, I led more and more journeys in which people traveled to their younger and older selves to offer and receive guidance and blessing in just this way. And to honor my own encounters, I stationed the toy soldiers my six-year-old loved around my desk, along with a marble shooter that looks like a blue world, and a picture of a black dog.[1]

HEART JOURNEYS

The Heart Shaman had reminded me that we must go to the heart, not the head, for true wisdom and courage. As my work as a dream teacher evolved and deepened, I led more and more journeys that centered on the heart.

I invited a circle of dreamers in the gentle woods of western Connecticut to open their hearts and let the light of their heart's longing carry them into the presence of a spiritual teacher, a friend of the soul on the highest level accessible to them in that moment in their lives.

I borrowed words from Suhrawardi, a Persian master of the heart journey to the soul of the soul, and a frequent flier in the imaginal realms.

> *Lift the veils of darkness from my heart*
> *Show me the radiance of your dazzling face*[2]

I told the group, "Let your longing for the beloved of your soul, the friend who will not leave you, stream as a ray of light from your heart and rise toward the highest. Follow the light from your heart. If you travel far enough, you will find an answering flame from heaven reaching down to you like a long finger of light. At the place where your heart light meets the fire from heaven, you may meet the teacher of your life."

As soon as I began drumming, I entered a spacious state of multiple consciousness. I was aware of my body, keeping the rhythms with the beater as I circled the space, moving around outstretched legs, avoiding the forest of candles and power objects on the quilted altar cloth I had spread at the center. I was monitoring our psychic space, checking in with our guardian spirits and watching the movements of energy within and around the circle. I was helping to hold open a tunnel of vision that soared up into cosmic space; standing within it was like standing inside an immense crystal shaft ablaze with myriad lights. I was sticking my head into the dreams of individual participants to see how they were doing, and to offer a little encouragement or added fuel where required.

And of course I was journeying for myself. In that part of my awareness, I was floating high above an active volcano, with a whole island visible around it. I realized this might be what Mount Etna, and the island of Sicily, looked like in ancient times. A great tongue of fire leaped up from the mouth of the volcano, and I found myself rising at tremendous speed on the power of the flame. High, high above—above multiple layers of reality tiered like layers of a wedding cake, solid *and* transparent to my sight, all at once—I saw the darkness at the core of the blazing light from which the god-forms are endlessly projected. From this source, a beam of strong golden light descended toward me.

I continued to soar upward at incalculable speed, while still drumming and tending to the group. When I reached the junction with the descending light, I saw a beautiful winged being, a being of living gold. The face distantly resembled my own, but in a perfect form, radiant in its beauty. I knew at once that I was meeting what the Yoruba call your double in heaven. I felt the stab of longing, yearning to leave with him and fly over worlds as fresh as the first day.

He was gentle with me. "We are sending strength and healing to you," he told me, to enable me to move beyond some physical problems I had been experiencing and to go on with the tasks I had accepted in this lifetime. He invited me to carry back as much of his energy as I could take. "You are an angel, after all."

I was embarrassed by this, even though I remembered that in Greek *angelos* means "messenger," and that in some sense all of us humans can be angels for one another.

"A fallen angel?" I quipped.

"No, not a fallen angel. You are an angel that fell down."

A fell-down angel. I rather liked that.[3]

MOUNTAIN LION PULLS ME UP TO
THE PLACE OF THE HEART

Two weeks later, I was teaching at the Esalen Institute at Big Sur, California, one of the most beautiful locations on the planet. The Big House, where I taught and dreamed, overhangs the Pacific. On one side, a cool stream flows down through a rocky ravine, over waterfalls, to splash into the ocean. A short hike away, along the breathtaking curves of Highway One, the redwood forests begin.

The participants and I shared deep adventures at Esalen that week, traveling together as a flight of dreamers to locations in the afterlife, and the realm of the moon, and deep within the earth, and in other times and cultures. But my biggest adventure began in a quite ordinary way.

I was walking from the Big House to my rental car, grumbling a little because I was carrying a lot of stuff and had had to leave the car up the hill because the nearby parking lot was full. The sun was hot, and I was sweating lightly as the slope of the hill rose steeper. My companion offered to carry some of my things, and I was grateful to lighten the load.

The slope continued to get steeper, and I decided to put down my suitcase and computer bag. I could come back for them later. Now I was carrying just one item, a small white cardboard box. Ahead of me, the slope had become a towering cliff. I knew I must go up this cliff, but there were precious few handholds or footholds, and it was very difficult going, even without all the luggage. My companion was no longer with me; I had to face this climb alone.

I struggled with the cliff face. Then I saw that I had help from above: something like a lifeline was being lowered to me. As I gratefully grabbed hold of the end, I noticed that it was actually a beaded belt of distinctly Iroquois design.

I did not puzzle over the motifs, or the unexpected reappearance of an Iroquois connection on the other side of the continent. I gripped the belt and used it to haul myself up the cliff. My climb now became very easy, because my helper was pulling me up with immense strength.

As I neared the top, I saw my benefactor for the first time. She was a mountain lion, gripping the other end of the strap in her paws. She was wildly beautiful and highly focused. When she had helped me all the way to the top, she licked me and nuzzled me, rubbing herself against the whole length of my body. Then she came prowling through my mind. Her message did not come in human speech, but it came with absolute clarity and fierce love. It was time to open the box I had been carrying.

I did so. I found that inside the white box was a living heart—a fleshy, juicy human heart, throbbing with life.

The lioness made me know what I must do next. I must set up the beating heart on the highest point of land and let the heartbeat sound out in all directions. When I did this, I felt waves of healing energy vibrating outward, across the wide bay, across mountains and forests and deserts and spaghetti highways and fortified golfers' ghettoes and inner-city neighborhoods, bringing healing and reopening the pathways of soul.

When I woke from this dream, light was shining in my face. It was the bright light of the full moon, shining across the ocean through the open window of my room. My heart was beating strongly, flowing into the rhythm of the waves breaking against the rocks.

In the early dawn, I walked down to the ravine. Crossing the plank bridge over the gorge, among billowing mists rolling in from the sea, I experienced a moment of fierce joy, the kind that brings tears to your eyes and drops you down to your knees. Swaying and kneeling on the narrow bridge, I felt the presence of the ancient ones, thick around me. They were scanning me, searching to confirm my intentions.

"I will help people to reclaim the paths of soul," I promised. "I will help them to dream with the Peacemaker. I will give you my best words."

I felt an immense surge of supportive energy, radiant and heart-stirring. I crossed the bridge and burned tobacco for the Real People at the Gatekeeper Tree where previous visitors had left little offerings of coins and candy and flowers. As the smoke swirled across the ravine, words of the old tongue, Island Woman's language, streamed through my mind. "You will be as we are, a walking stick and a burden strap for the people. You will help people everywhere to see the consequences of their actions, down to the seventh generation after themselves."

The rolling mist seemed to tighten and solidify, revealing the shapes of Native figures, of elders and grandmothers. Above them, as tall as the redwoods, loomed a huge figure crowned with antlers.[4]

FINDING TRUE NORTH

This book was conceived in the place of the lion. It grew inside a creative womb that was opened to me during another powerful encounter with the ancient dreamers. This took place in the darkening time the same year Mountain Lion reached out to me, when any sensible bear in snow country should have been snuggling down in some soft, warm place for a long winter's dream.

I am walking with Carol, another of my dream sisters and a gifted healer and dream teacher in her own right, in a very pleasant sunlit setting. As we amble along, I'm improvising a chant in praise of Mother Earth. The last verse has six lines. I'm repeating and playing with the lines, humming when I do not quite have the words. I notice that we've come to a beautiful place. There's a steep descent to a cove where an ancient tree grows close to the water.

I go down to the ancient tree. The roots are exposed to a height of a couple of feet, and I am fascinated by the patterns they make. I *know* there is something of immense value within the roots of the tree, and that it can bring guidance and healing to many, many people. I picture the people who are waiting for gifts from this deep space, and see families of all kinds, in many different settings.

There is a price of admission to the treasure-house inside the ancient tree. I must come with a song, the song I am composing for Ancient Mother.

I woke from this dream excited, but also frustrated, because I had not completed the song. I had the simple tune, but even the few words I had managed to compose inside the dream were fading away as I returned to the surface world. I called my friend Carol. After all, she was part of the dream.

"I'm like Winnie the Pooh," I told her. "I have a little hum. But I need the *words*." When I explained that I needed to go back inside my dream to complete the song and open the tree gates, she did not waste a second. She grabbed her drum, jumped in her car, and drove over to my house.

Within minutes of her arrival, I was lying on the floor of my cave—

the basement apartment in my townhouse where I write and sometimes lead smaller groups—with my eyes covered by a bandanna, enjoying the luxury of being able to give myself single-mindedly to a journey while someone else drummed for me.

When the drumming began, I was transported, deeply and vividly, back into my dreamscape. I could smell the earth and enjoy that bouncy, deep-pile sensation of tall, soft grass flattened out and springing back underfoot. Looking down, I saw the imprint of bear paws in the earth, the heels and five toes clearly defined. I felt the way the bear comes down on its heels, like a human. I looked again and noticed, without any real surprise, that the bear prints were my own.

I needed the song. As I moved, its wordless rhythms moved with me. Now the words flowed through my mind, without calculation.

> *I am walking with the Mother*
> *I am sailing on her skin*
> *I become her child and lover*
> *From the outside enter in*

And the next verse:

> *I will praise the sky above her*
> *I will praise her in the deep*
> *I am dreaming with the Mother*
> *She awakens me from sleep*

And a third, opening into a chorus:

> *Walk lightly on the Mother*
> *And let her grace unfold*
> *Praise and serve the Mother*
> *And reenchant the world*
> *Praise and serve the Mother*
> *And reenchant the world*

Singing my dreamsong, I returned to the ancient tree. A gateway opened among the roots, and I found myself in a different realm. A large family of bears had gathered around a cozy fire. I was welcomed into their midst. My heart swelled with joy at the depth of their welcome and recognition.

This world is ruled by the Mother. She showed herself now as *ohk-wari,* the Mother Bear. She offered me healing.

She asked me to take off my skin. As I did so, I noticed it was a very shaggy bearskin, looking creamy gray rather than pure white. She wanted me to lie over the fire, like a carcass on spits. I agreed to do this. I expected the bear family to devour me. Instead, they licked different organs and cleansed me with moist green herbs.

Then Mama Bear guided me to put on my white bearskin again and she took me on her lap. I was only a quarter her size. She nursed me like a baby, and I sobbed as the milk of her healing and compassion coursed through my being. I was strengthened, full of inspiration. She laid her paws over my hand to reinforce my connection with the healing gifts of Bear, and my ability to sense and heal through my own hands.

She invited me to go deeper into her realm. She showed me a kind of creative cave, a pleasant chamber whose walls were part earth and part shaped stones; it was well lit by a roundish opening to the upper air. I saw a simple table of untreated wood, cheerfully messy with toys and art supplies as well as writing materials. I thought that I should come here to write what most needs to be written through me.[5]

I have guided many others through that tree gate—to receive healing in the realm of Ancient Mother; to connect with animal guardians; to open a creative space; and to find "True North," the flawless compass direction that becomes clear to us when we live with heart and ground ourselves in the deep wisdom of Earth.

I have written this book from that space that Ancient Mother opened, through the roots of the ancient tree. If you are looking for a passage to the Otherworld, look at a tree. It may be one in your backyard, one in your neighborhood, or one you remember from childhood or while on vacation in a foreign country. It may be a tree you know from dreaming. Any tree may prove to be the axis mundi, the ladder between the worlds. A tree gate can always take us from the Shadow World to the Real World.

We are going to learn much more about this as we plunge through the tree gates of the Iroquois Dreamtime and learn how worlds are created and renewed.

PART TWO

THE
IROQUOIS
DREAM
A WORLD

In my breast the wound opens again
when the stars descend and become kin to my body.
GEORGE SEFERIS, *MYTHISTOREMA* 20

There are fairy stories to be written for adults, stories that
are still in a green state.
ANDRE BRETON, *SURREALIST MANIFESTO*

Dreaming is the source of all metaphysics; it is the source
of the gods.
NIETZSCHE, *MENSCHLICHES, ALLZUMENSCHICHES*

Say my name in the bushes, and I will stand here again.
PROMISE OF THE PEACEMAKER (IROQUOIS)

7

Story Codes and Inner Songs

Such a price the gods exact for song:
to become what we sing.

PYTHAGORAS

It has been said that a story is the shortest route between a human and the truth. The pre-Socratic Greek philosophers defined *truth,* in the context of a human life, as what we remember and act upon. Truth, *alethia,* is literally "not-forgetting," not being overwhelmed by the draught of forgetfulness from the river Lethe, from which all human souls are required to drink on the way to embodied life on this Earth. A powerful story that stirs our minds and our hearts can give us the kind of truth we remember and enact. Something we have to look up in a book or solicit from other people is not yet *living* truth.

As I've explained, in the Iroquoian languages, to forget is to let your mind fall. The consequences of forgetting the origins and purpose of human existence are vividly dramatized in the great Dreamtime stories of the Iroquois.

Rather than calling them myths or legends, I would like to call them mythistories, anglicizing the Greek term *mythistorema,* which the poet George Seferis used for his first great cycle of mythic poems.[1] They are interdimensional dramas, weaving between worlds. They unfold in a time that sometimes coincides with human time lines, but the engine of events is in a deeper reality, as we come to notice in our own lives when we tap into our dreams and navigate by synchronicity. They chart the interplay between humans and beings other than human, including extraterrestrial gods who initiated the often embattled experiment in developing consciousness in a life form on this planet.

The primal struggle between creation and destruction, light and dark, the heroic ordeals and the fabulous bestiaries of the Iroquois mythistories lend them the quality of the epics *Lord of the Rings* or *Mahabharata.* The breathtaking Iroquois mythistory of the Peacemaker—a god-man who is sent to this Earth from a higher world to save humans from themselves, is born without a mortal father, travels in a vehicle that defies human understanding, and finds his first apostle in a woman who services men—is not an indigenous copy of the story of Jesus and Mary Magdalene, but an independent collective vision of equal power, opening into universal wisdom. As codes for calling in sacred power, tapping into the akashic information field, and gaining experiential access to realms beyond the physical, the Iroquois mythistories rank with the most important of the lost books, not only of the Americas, but of the world.

Lost books may seem an odd term in this context, for two reasons. First, because many people have heard of the stories of the Woman Who Fell from the Sky, the Battle of the Twins, and Hiawatha. These stories have been told and retold and published in formats ranging from popular children's stories to almost unobtainable transcriptions of oral tellings by the old wisdomkeepers with interlinear translations by ethnographers and linguists. Second, despite the many published versions, the Iroquois mythistories are not books in the sense that we generally understand them. At the time of their first contact with Europeans, the Iroquois were nonliterate, a term that should not be confused with illiterate or preliterate, as Sam Gill has argued eloquently.[2] In other words, they knew how to store and access the knowledge that matters, but they did not do this by recording on skin or clay or paper with an alphabet. The knowledge of the first and last things was encoded in stories that were half-sung, half-spoken, over the wampum shells that held their inner resonance. The stories were unfolded, along with the strings and belts of wampum, in sacred gatherings when the telling of one of the great mythistories by a great memory-keeper might continue for many days. Holding and delivering one of these sacred teachings was a tremendous feat of memory—but it was far more than a memory exercise. It was an act of soul remembering.

To deliver the story correctly, the Speaker had to reach into the realm from which it came. The Speaker had to put his or her head into the Sky World and look into the mirror with Hiawatha to see the radiant face of the guide. To share one of these story codes, it was necessary to shift consciousness and *become* what was being told. It was understood that, when a story of gods and humans is told, the gods may draw near. Telling the story right may actually requicken the play of sacred powers in our world and reassert the proper rules of engagement for interdimensional encounters. What was *not* desirable was to rattle off a version of the big stories by rote. For a start, this might bore or irritate the spirits, who like to be entertained by "fresh words" (as the Inuit say). Also, unless the tellers make the stories their own by dreaming their way deep inside them, freshly and authentically, they are not truly attuned to the story codes. Woven into the Iroquois mythistories is the understanding that everything is in flux, everything is ideoplastic—shaped and reformed by thought and intention—and the world is endlessly in play between the forces of creation and destruction.

So while these stories are sacred, they are *not* scriptures. There is no standard, let alone canonical, text of any of them. Listen to any two Speakers and you will notice huge discrepancies between their accounts. This is sometimes because a Speaker has adapted a tale to suit the audience. For example, a Mohawk teller will say that Hiawatha was a Mohawk, whereas an Onondaga might make him an Onondaga. Also, there will be a PG version and an R version of some critical details. The humongous penis-snake of the sorcerer-tyrant in the Peacemaker story has been censored out of public tellings not only because it might be deemed unsuitable for children, but also because it contains a clue to the vital importance of sexual energy in real magic. Where a lineage of Speakers has been broken—as happened to a devastating extent quite early after contact with the Europeans, through the spread of warfare and imported disease—there may be serious gaps, and confusing garbles, in the recitations.

The most complete narrations of the great Iroquois mythistories recorded from native Speakers are long recitations in the Onondaga language by John Arthur Gibson, a revered memorykeeper and ritualist who held the Confederacy title of a Seneca chief. In 1900, he dictated a remarkable version of the creation story to the Tuscarora ethnographer Jonathan Napoleon Brinton Hewitt, a fascinating figure who epitomized the Iroquois ability to live in two worlds.[3] Hewitt sat patiently with the old Speakers on the reservations, married a Washington socialite, attended a Unitarian church, and, without a relevant diploma, awed droves of newly minted anthropology Ph.D.s at the Smithsonian with his inexhaustible scholarship and command of languages. He appeared to me in a dream while I was writing this book, in Edwardian wing collar and frock coat, to urge me to read his essay on Tawiskaron (one of the great Iroquois deities), an important source previously unknown to me that I was eventually able to locate in a rare 1910 volume.[4]

In 1912, shortly before his death, the same Chief Gibson who sat with Hewitt dictated a lengthy account of the Peacemaker story, and associated rituals of condolence, to an ethnographer named Alexander Goldenweiser, another colorful and enterprising character.[5] In his last retelling of the Peacemaker story, Gibson notably changed many critical details he had included in a previous version dictated to Hewitt.

Even the most meticulous and painstaking transcriptions are suspect. Memory lapses, mood swings, deliberate obfuscation or concealment of the keys to sacred power, and the play of the sacred powers themselves may all be at work. Then there is the "anthropology effect" summarized by the statement—attributed to Australian Aborigines, but reflecting a near-universal feeling among indigenous peoples—that "when the anthropologists arrive, the spirits leave."

But there is a deeper challenge in reclaiming the inner meaning of the sacred stories. British anthropologist Graham Townsley discusses how Amazonian shamans in Peru use "twisting-twisting words," a complex, opaque, metaphorical vocabulary that enables them to open and travel into an interactive space with the spirits, into places of healing and creation. A Yaminahua shaman explains that if you try to fly in nonordinary reality with only ordinary words, you'll "crash."[6] In all cultures, including the Iroquois, the poets of consciousness—those born and dreamed to be our shamans and Speakers—understand this. We'll never be able to travel the song lines and story lines into the space where worlds are made and can be re-created until we come up with our own fresh words.

So I think it is valid to describe the mythistories I am about to retell as lost books of the Americas—"lost" in the sense that the inner meaning and power of these stories must be reclaimed by dreaming our way into them, "books" in the sense that the Book of Thoth or the Book of Raziel or the I Ching are books of the first and last things—although not necessarily embodied in human writing—for which humans have hungered from generation to generation. These books contain what William Blake called the lost originals. As Blake knew so well, reclaiming the lost originals is the common act of the dreamer and the creative mind. It involves reaching beyond the limits of culture and text to dip into a primal source.[7]

Mary Austin, in justifying her fresh and free renditions of Paiute songs and stories—including a song to call back dreams to heal depression—wrote of the poet's responsibility to go beyond texts and literalist interpretations and deliver the "inner song."[8] This is what I have tried to do here. I have sat with Iroquois memorykeepers, including Mohawk Bear Clan elder and visionary Tom Porter. I have spent many nights deep in the ethnographers' transcriptions of the older tellings, with photocopies of Mohawk and Onondaga typescript dictionaries and word lists at my elbow, puzzling over alternative decodings of the stem meanings of mystery words. I have led groups into ritual dramas in which we have acted out and improvised on key scenes from these mythistories on a sacred mountain in Mohawk land, and I have had the thrilling pleasure of witnessing Sky Woman and Hiawatha and the Entangled One and the crow-men speak and act in changing forms and voices, and of watching a whole flight of brave spirits throw themselves down a rocky mountain slope to embody their willingness to make a new world. Above all, I have dreamed my way deeply into these stories and have received spontaneous insights, including an ancient personal name for the Peacemaker that is to be found nowhere in the written records.*

---

*I am not referring to the D-name, often translated as He Has Two Rows of Teeth, which is in many secondary sources but that the Iroquois now prefer not to voice or to see transcribed, or to the Peacemaker's Mohawk name, which means He Who Raises Up the House. The name I was given, in Old Mohawk, may mean He Is Two People in One Body, or One Being in Two Bodies.

8

Falling Woman Creates a World

"Come to the edge."
"No, we will fall."
"Come to the edge."
"No, we will fall."
They came to the edge.
He pushed them, and they flew.

APOLLINAIRE

There is a world before this one, above this world, deeper than this world. Call it Earth-in-the-Sky. The beings who made humans come from this other world. They are called Onkwe, the People. They are not human, but they contain the seed and spirit of what can become human. They do things by the power of thought. We talk about them as if they are men and women, but they are gods in relation to us. As with all gods, we see ourselves in them and find them in us. They know pain and rage and love and ecstasy, as we do. But their emotions, when fully aroused, are strong enough to make or unmake a world.

There is a sky woman who lives in this Sky World. Some call her Ataensic.[1] She is young and beautiful and has never been touched by a sky man. She has dreams and longings, and she talks about them at night with her father, who, being dead, is wise and farsighted beyond others. It is said that he was the first of the People to undergo death, and that his body was placed in the upper branches of a tree because his daughter dreamed this should be done. Night after night, Ataensic climbs the tree on a ladder to commune with her father, until we come to know that now he lives in the tree, more than in the body he used up. The tree has become his spirit home and his voice box. Ataensic hears him whispering in the leaves, singing through the branches. She finds his smile and his streaming hair in the folds of the bark.

The tree-father tells Ataensic that she must prepare for a long and dangerous journey. She must prepare food as an offering to the man she will marry; this is the custom of the People. Her husband—known to her only through her father's sight—is a being of power. His magic is very old, and the land that he rules is itself magical. There is no need for a sun there, because the country is illuminated and nourished by the pearly glow of a flowering tree whose blossoms shine like radiant spheres.* Ataensic will know the house of the mage she is to marry by this Tree of Light, or Tree of Life, which stands near it. The powerful being has a powerful name: Earth Holder. Ataensic can only guess at its meaning. If Ataensic is disappointed that the being she is to wed is very old, she does not complain about that to her father. She prepares for her journey, taking care to memorize the road map he gives her in their night conversations.

To reach the house of the mage, she must cross a raging river on a floating log, brave mountain passes, and avoid the many beings—alternately seductive, distracting, and terrifying—who will try various ruses to induce her to abandon her mission. Her father cautions her that nothing will get easier when she finds the guardian of the Tree of Life. The one called Earth Holder is proud and fierce. He has known many wives and may feel no need for another. He will surely put Ataensic through many tests. Tree-father's joints creak and his fingers sway as he rehearses the young woman for the ordeals that lie ahead. She must stand her ground if Earth Holder tries to send her away. She must carry out his orders

---

*Although in many contemporary accounts there is no sun in the Sky World, only the Tree of Light, it is quite clear in the Newhouse (Mohawk) version that a sun shines on some of the territory. Indeed, Ataensic is instructed by her father to travel in the direction of the sunrise.

without hesitation or complaint, even if he sets her impossible tasks, even if he subjects her to unbearable pain, even if he abandons her to monsters. "If you do not lose your courage," her father tells her, "you will bring great gifts to the People, and you will be a worthy bride."

With her mother's help, Ataensic makes bread—a perfect loaf—as her marriage offering, and then sets off along the trail her father described to her. Her family and friends think she has lost her mind. The road is full of perils, and she is going in quest of a being she has never met, on the advice of a dead man. She swings her legs from the hips, covering the distance from her village to the first line of foothills at an amazing speed. She continues to pick up speed, leaving forests and hills and wetlands behind her in a blur of green. She is at the raging river in no time.

It looks exactly as her father described it, with its riffs of white water, the strong currents as muscular and changeable as water snakes. She sees the floating log she is supposed to catch and ride to the farther shore. But here Ataensic has her first moment of doubt. Her heart is strong enough for the crossing, but her head is telling her that she has already screwed things up. Her father had detailed a long, arduous journey to this river. She got here quicker than it used to take her to get to the berry patch behind her village. *This can't be the right place,* she tells herself. *I got here too fast.*

She might ask someone for advice, but her father warned her to trust no one for directions. So she retraces her steps and returns to her father's tree. He tells her right away she made no mistake; she was exactly on track. "You are coming into your power," her father tells her. "Time and space will work differently now." He does not tell her— it is something we must find out for ourselves—that if she were to put her mind to it fully, she could travel from the Talking Tree to the Tree of Life in a single bound. What you can see in your mind is where you can go, in that instant, in the Earth-in-the-Sky. But if Ataensic did that, she would miss out on some tests and trials. And there is no quest without an ordeal, no coming-into-knowing without suffering.

So Ataensic takes the road again. She catches the floating log and rides it like a bucking horse over the white water. On the far side of the river, her trials come in the shapes of a handsome charmer whose presence makes her long for a vigorous lover, the Trickster-guides who turn up again and again, offering shortcuts and side entertainments, and the frighteners who try to scare her back with evil gossip and naked threats.

She goes on until the sun is gone and, beyond the dark mists, she sees the lovely twilight of Earth Holder's realm. The Tree of Life is beautiful beyond words, which has never stopped a good storyteller from trying to put words on it. The old ones say it is something like a dogwood, or a wild cherry, in full flower.[2] You could see it that way. You could also see it as the Tree of the Sephiroth, hung with all the codes and patterns of manifestation, shining through the Four Worlds.

Ataensic stands at the threshold of Earth Holder, the keeper of the Tree of Light, under the opalescent blossoms. She is achingly beautiful, sweet and ripe and unplucked, her great shining eyes full of faith and promise. But Earth Holder is unimpressed, or pretends to be. He's not interested in getting married again. He's been around for so long he may be beyond male and female. When she offers him the wedding loaf, he is surly. He challenges her to fix him a *real* meal. It turns out this will involve fetching and preparing enough food to supply a medium-sized human town. Because the old ones like corn soup, they say that Earth Holder wanted her to fix him a great big pot of that. This is a bit like the Europeans picturing their gods and dead heroes getting tipsy, or roaring drunk, on wine and beer. We all *know* that food and drink in the Otherworld is different from on Earth, but it helps us and our taste buds to picture the People (and others who enter their realms) eating and drinking things we understand. So in the old Longhouse tellings, Ataensic sets out to make corn soup.

She has to pound a great quantity of corn into mush and boil it up. She now discovers that her power to speed things up and operate outside consensus reality extends beyond fast walking. Pounding a barn load of corn is no great challenge for her; when she puts her mind to it, she just leans on that pounder and the job is done.

Earth Holder is getting interested now. He tells the girl to take off her clothes. He wants her to get naked before she approaches the great cauldron where his food is going to be cooked over the fire. There is a glint in his eye as he watches the dance of firelight and shadow over Ataensic's lithe, ripe body working the stirrer in the pot. The heat in the place is rising, rising. Whatever is in that cauldron—corn soup, or a magic potion, or both—is bubbling and seething. The boiling liquid hisses and lashes at the girl. Gobbets of red-hot mush fly out and spatter her, burning deep through her skin. She remembers her father's warning: she must show no pain, voice no complaint. If she can see it through, she will come into extraordinary power. She will be Sky Woman, ruling with Earth Holder under the Tree of Life.

At last the food is ready. The master of the house announces he will call his slaves to heal the girl's wounds. Ataensic knows what is going to happen next—her tree-father told her everything—but she still gasps when she sees them. Earth Holder's slaves are more like dogs than People, but they are not exactly dogs either. With slavering, great jaws snapping, they jump her, pull her down, straddle her as if they are going to mount her. She is glad it is their huge hot tongues, not their hard penises, that come into play. But the play is rough. Being licked by those *erhar-onkwe,* those dog-men, is like being rubbed down with sandpaper. The pain transferred to her brain from her cracking, tortured skin brings her close to fainting. She gasps again as the dog-beings tongue her secret places. They roll her over and she lies splayed under their panting attentions, for the old wizard to enjoy. She sees a sheen of blood flowering across her breasts, across her belly. She thinks, *I might almost have given birth*. She does not cry out. The dog-men are gentler now, but their drool gushes over her. The slobber is healing. When they leave off, she is glowing. Her skin is fresh and flawless. She is embarrassed to see that her nipples are erect.

Earth Holder finishes his dinner and invites her to bed—not *his* bed, but a bed he has laid for her on the other side of the fire. Either voyeurism was enough, or her intended really is not too interested in sex, or he is in firm control of his libido. He does not go near her during the night. The only part of him that has touched the beautiful naked girl is his breath. When they tell the story, the old ones like you to notice that.

In the morning, Earth Holder makes a return of gifts. She brought him the marriage bread; he will give her the means to feed her whole community. The tools are a simple bag for provisions, a burden strap, and the message she is to take back to her extended family. Like nested worlds, like subatomic space, the bag is much bigger inside than outside. It can hold whatever you choose to put into it. For today, its load is venison. Earth Holder brings deer after deer inside the lodge, nicely quartered and dried for the journey. He tells Ataensic to fill up the bag and make sure she fills it up tight. She stuffs in that venison and when the bag is bursting, he tells her to give its contents a good hard push. As soon as she does this, it feels like the bag is almost empty. Herds of deer enter the bag in this way, as Ataensic fills and opens, fills and opens, until Earth Holder is satisfied she has enough of a load to make the trip worthwhile.

Next, he gives her the burden strap she will use to haul her load. A burden strap is a sling that is looped around the forehead. The old mage shows Ataensic where she must place the strap to sustain the weight of the impossible load.

Earth Holder also entrusts her with a message for the folks in her village: "Tell them to take the roofs off their houses tonight." He hints at a gift greater than the bag that is bigger inside than out. To receive it, the People must be open to the sky.

Ataensic sets off on the journey home. She tries not to think about the weight she is carrying, a weight heavy enough to crush a hunting party of strong warriors. As long as she does not put her mind on it, she travels nearly as fast and easily as before. Then she gets to thinking about what she is bringing back, and her burden weighs on her like a mountain. She is dropping with fatigue when her kinsfolk find her at the edge of the woods and help her back into her family's lodge. Tired as she is, she remembers the message and tells the People: "We must all remove the roofs of our houses tonight."

They do it, just like that. They have seen what she brought in the bag. They are open to possibility.

That night, the stars come down close, looking in at the People through their open roofs. Then the sky starts falling like feathery snow, sometimes like soft hail. It is manna, of course, a gift from on high. The old ones (for whom corn is life) say it was the finest white corn that came down like the dust of stars, turning the houses into grain silos.

After these marvels of the sky food and the bottomless bag, Ataensic sets off again to join her new husband in the twilight glow of the Tree of Life. He is welcoming now, yet still quite reserved, treating her more like a second father, or a priest, than a husband. They do not jump into bed together. Their intimacy goes exactly this far: they lie by the fire with the soles of their feet touching.

They still have not had sex—as we know sex—when Ataensic finds she is carrying a child. The fathering of this child is one of the great mysteries, a mystery repeated later in the story, as in other cultures. With a virgin birth, there is always plenty of room for rumor. Some might wonder whether Ataensic dallied on her way back with that handsome charmer. Those dog-men could be suspects. Is it possible that something passed between the old mage and Ataensic when they were lying sole to sole? To fit a crazy situation, go for the craziest explanation. It's one the grandmothers favor. They say that the sky woman became pregnant when the old mage breathed on her the first night. Earth Holder was so powerful that he could put a new life inside you with his breath.*

This makes crazy sense, and good sense. When we hear about a virgin birth in a sacred story, we know that something is coming straight from spirit. It could be an avatar, a god-man, a goddess-woman. It could be the mother of a new world. That's where this story is going.

The making of our world begins with a fall.

As life quickens in Ataensic's womb, Earth Holder sickens. Maybe orenda—the life force—has slipped from him to she who is coming, borne on his breath. Maybe it is jealousy that is making him sick. When Ataensic's daughter is born, brimming with life, Earth Holder's spirit wanders far away, into the dreamlands, leaving his body like a discarded robe.

The People are troubled. If Earth Holder leaves them, a blight will come into their world. Already it seems that the shining flowers of the Tree of Life are beginning to dull. What if the flowers should fall? The People gather around, seeking the way of healing.

At this point, we are going to learn about the deep connection between dreaming and healing. Earth Holder announces that he has dreamed a dream. He tells the assembled People, "I want you to seek my word. The reason is that what my soul has visioned should become manifest. My soul has shown me this dream."[3]

Earth Holder will not speak the dream. He will mime part of it, giving them clues. Let the People catch his "dreamword" if they can. How can you trust anyone to understand a dream unless they can put themselves inside it?

So they follow Earth Holder around as he leads them on a strange dance, always returning to the Tree of Light. They can't guess what he is miming even when he starts digging among the roots of the tree like a dog after a bone, and the erhar-onkwe, the dog-men, come panting to join him, tearing up dirt and rocks. It's hard to guess because what Earth Holder wants is unthinkable.

In an old Onondaga version, it is only a being that is always capa-

---

*Hewitt notes that "a great fact of life, attested by all human experience [is] that breath (spirit, air, wind, atmos, atman) is the principle of life and feeling, and that without it there can be no manifestation of life. This is the key to the riddle of the virgin, or parthenogenetic, conception." Hewitt, "Iroquoian Cosmology, Part 1," 138. The role of the breath in transferring life and spirit is especially clear in the Gibson (Onondaga) version.

ble of the unthinkable that can guess the dreamer's unthinkable desire. This being is identified as the Fire Dragon of the White Body. The Hurons call him White Lion. He moves through the sky like a shooting star, and his Mohawk name, Kahaseri'nes, means Light Traveling Constantly. He tends to show himself at the coming of a new aeon, at the moment when a world may be born or destroyed. He burns with such a bright flame that when he comes down from the sky, he must live deep, deep underwater, so he does not set a world on fire.[4]

The Fire Dragon knows what Earth Holder is dreaming. He wants the Tree of Light to be uprooted. The People are horrified. No one has ever presumed to root around under the Tree of Life. The consequences are beyond knowing—except, perhaps, for Ataensic, whose tree-father has prepared her for everything.

The People confer. They agree that the dream of their Sky chief must be honored, because it has revealed the wish of his soul.[5] With her baby on her back, Ataensic helps the People dig among the roots of the Tree of Life. The dog-men are pretty good at this, but they soon lose interest and run off to play other games. The roots go deeper than deep. Soon mountains of soil are heaped around the excavation site. Then Ataensic remembers how things change when you put your mind on them. She leans on her digging stick the way she leaned on the corn pounder and finds the moist earth willing. The soil responds by rushing inward and downward. With a sound no less disturbing than the last grains of sand slipping through an hourglass, a hole opens in the world. Ataensic looks into an unfathomable depth of blue.

Earth Holder stands above her, approving. This is the dream. Waves of colors stream in his eyes. Through the sea foam, Ataensic reads the birth and death of worlds.

Does she fall or does she jump? It is often said that she was pushed, because the old man was jealous of whoever had fathered that bouncing baby girl. There's no harm in putting a little soap in the solemnest of sacred tales, and it's the way of a Native storyteller to use any trick to hold an audience. Why should the gods be any different from us, anyway?

But maybe it's like this: there is no creation without a leap into the raw unknown. If we are not ready to make that jump, something will push us—if we are lucky. Like Ataensic, primed by her know-it-all father, we may *know* what lies ahead. We may have chosen every step of the way. All the same, when we come to that drop into the wild blue, we may just freeze and stand shaking in front of the open hatch, like a virgin skydiver who suddenly can't believe the parachute will open.

Earth Holder might grab Ataensic's shoulders and hurl her down through the hole. He might give her a rough push in the back. But he has other ways. Can you feel the wind of his breath rising, fanning Ataensic until she is airborne, drifting beyond the gravity that keeps our feet on the ground and blocks us from playing the divine game? Now she is falling, falling, from Earth-in-the-Sky toward a world she will spin from inside herself, like a spider; we can call her Falling Woman.

The baby is at the heart of this. Falling Woman's beautiful bouncing girl is no longer strapped to her back. The child is inside her again, safe and warm and dreaming in the amniotic lake. Not all the old ones will tell you this mystery, but it is to be found in the rarest and truest tellings. Falling Woman has her child inside her again, as she falls toward a world in the making. We'll never understand this until we remember how our souls came into the body—the origin of our personal world—and the times our own beautiful children left and came home, or just left. When she looks back, Falling Woman can no longer see any hole in the indigo immensity of space. She is falling among the stars, through an airy wilderness of midnight blue.

At this point, the Fire Dragon, or White Lion, reappears as her ally. In one version, he "seizes her body in flight"—to protect her, not to harm her. We can picture her traveling part of the way within his brilliant nimbus of light, dancing across the abyss in the coils of a cosmic serpent. He promises to help her in all the ways he can. Like a booster rocket, he will power and escort her for only part of the way—precisely half the distance she must travel to a destiny still undefined.[6] In some of the tellings, the Fire Dragon gives her food and tools for life. What does the Fire Dragon look like? Intriguingly, in a drawing by an early-twentieth-century Seneca, he is a maned lion who strongly resembles Aslan from C. S. Lewis's *Chronicles of Narnia*.[7] He is even less confined to specific forms than other sacred beings. He can show himself as a man the color of the sky. We may dream him as a living sphinx, or a griffin, or a composite lion-dragon, or something quite beyond familiar forms. Whatever shapes he chooses, there is a lot of energy here.

The Fire Dragon must leave Ataensic to complete her journey alone, though he turns up again after she has made a world, appearing at times of maximum danger and opportunity in the life of a person of power, or of the planet.

Far below Falling Woman is a blue black ocean, formless and fearful to landsmen who do not know the promise of water. She is no longer sure whether she is falling down or falling up. This goes on even longer than it takes us to decide, in our own dreams, that it is better to fly than to fall. When Falling Woman decides she would rather be flying, the birds fly up to give her wings. They are birds who can swim through the air and fly through the water. They could be ducks, cranes, or cormorants. But probably they are most like the great blue heron, the bird in whose shape other ancient minds found the power of the phoenix. The birds catch Sky Woman (this is her simplest name, and she has earned it) and the *anima mundi*, the world-soul that is with her, and waft them down gently, nestled on the magic carpet of their great wings.

The primal ocean below them is no desert of water. The ancestors of animals we can name are already living there. Of course, they are all animals who are at home in water. Beaver is one the elders like to mention, making the *thwack* of a beaver tail hitting the water as they say his name. And there is Great Turtle. This story is going nowhere without Turtle.

The woman from the sky is a mystery to the animals, but they know that they must tend this mystery and give it space to unfold. Now all of this is happening in the time before time when beings of different shapes, and creatures who take on many shapes, have no trouble communicating with one another. The great chain of being has not yet been sliced and diced into little fixities of species differentiation and mutual distrust and incomprehension. The animals gather in a council and ask Sky Woman what they can do to help. She thinks about it, and then she lets them know that what might help is a place to land, a place where she can feel earth beneath her soles, a place where the daughter of a tree-father can take root and raise a child.

The animals can understand her well enough, except they don't know what she means by this thing called earth. Sky Woman has to show them what earth is like. She makes the motions of scooping and molding wet clay. She runs her hands lavishly over her earth mother's gravid body, patting her belly, cupping her swollen breasts.

This gets the animal council astir with excitement. They have a live one here. Beaver remembers a story passed down from the Mother of All Beavers. In the story, a great deep-sea diver found mucky stuff at the bottom of the ocean. Being Beaver, he naturally tried to build a lodge with it, but he could not stay down long enough to enjoy it and there was nowhere to build it up top. Otter and Muskrat will not be outdone. They speak up for their own ancestors, who also found something on the ocean floor. Beaver thwacks his tail, angry at this attempt to upstage him. He volunteers to go down first and look for this thing called earth.

But wait a bit. There's the old problem of where to put it. Great Turtle rises from the waves like an island and offers his broad back. (I always think of Turtle as she, but the old ones say that this turtle is a he. And though, in this watery realm, we might picture Turtle as a sea turtle, for the Iroquois it is most definitely a snapping turtle, another amazing swimmer.)

Beaver makes the dive. He is a long time coming back, and when he floats up his breath is gone, his paws empty. Otter tries next, with the same results. Little Muskrat is not deterred. After an aching age, Muskrat floats up, seemingly dead. But there is a warm spot over his heart, and between his tiny paws are a few scrapings of something brownish and clayey that must be earth.

Woman Who Fell from the Sky is no longer falling, or flying. Standing with her feet firmly planted on Turtle's back, she smears that little bit of earth over the shell. You might think it's not enough for a worm to live in. But Sky Woman has orenda, the juice and spirit of life, and the power of shaping and growing. And she is a dancer. She is dancing now, magnificent in her swollen body. She is in an expanding spiral. Under her dancing feet, the scrapings of earth from the seafloor thicken and spread until they become a new Earth, a new world to live in. Call it Turtle Island, the world on Turtle's back. It's where we are, when we are not in the dreamlands.

Sky Woman gives birth to her baby girl again, in the world she has made. Her daughter grows fast and strong. Call her Earth Woman. Soon Earth Woman is dreaming of harvests streaming from her ripening body. A cloud comes out of the west and leans over her hills and valleys. The cloud-being tries out many shapes, seeking the one that will please her best. It becomes a beautiful man. Earth Woman loves him on sight, as the parched soil loves the rain. She is eager to take him inside her.

The cloud-being's approach to mating is as strange as Earth Holder's, but perhaps more fun. He spreads Earth Woman, reaching deep into her folds. His cloud-form cannot be confined to one set of limbs. He touches her in many places, with many hands and tendrils and suckers. He awakens all her nerve endings, and waves of pleasure crash through her. She feels the organ of completion, long and hard as an arrow, across the golden slope of her belly. She trembles with delight when she realizes that her lover has two of these organs. One is straight and hard as a maple sapling, the other wild and quick and sharp and cunning as a water darter. They thrust and slide over and under and around each other. She cries out, feeling her body must explode, but it explodes instead into rapture.

When she surfaces from her swoon of satiation, her lover has gone, but she feels his arrows inside her. It does not take long for Sky Woman and her daughter to realize that she is carrying twins, and that those boys are going to be trouble. Soon they are kicking and fighting inside the womb, contending for the best place. Their wrestling sets off tremors in their mother's body. Fooling around in the amniotic lake is no fun anymore. The twins want out.

The one who is straight as a sapling finds a way. There is a river that flows from the warm lake through a narrowing gorge to a water-fall. The gorge is so narrow it will be hard for the boys to get their heads and shoulders through, even with the help of the current, but this feels like the natural way to Sapling, the Straight Man. Tawiskaron, the edgy guy, the Twisty Man, thinks you would need to be soft in the head to go that way and do all that work to get out. He's not softheaded at all. "I'll go first," Sapling encourages him, pushing off downriver. "Nice and slow," Sapling calls back. But Twisty Man does not like nice and slow, and he never wants to be second.

Tawiskaron thinks he knows a quicker way out. He has seen some light filtering down from somewhere high above the cavern where he and his brother have been living like lungfish. The edgy guy has a tough, comblike ridge along his skull—some say it is flint, others crystal—and he uses this to force his way up toward that distant light. He bulls a passage like a mineshaft through his mother's body and bursts out, triumphant, into the dawning world.

Tawiskaron's haste does not benefit him. His brother is born first nonetheless, and he will be known as the elder of the Twins. But Tawiskaron's impatience has killed his mother. Earth Woman is bleeding to death from the gaping wound he has made in her body. Some say he burst from her armpit, others from her navel (the version that feels right to me). Let's remember that her geography is not exactly that of a human body. Humans have not yet been created.

The Light Twin—Sapling—is seized with grief and remorse when he sees what has happened to his mother. Maybe he could have saved her if he had taken charge of his impetuous, pointy-headed brother.

Sky Woman, now a grandmother, missed the birth scene. Maybe she was dancing up an extension to her property. She arrives now and when she sees her daughter torn up and dead, she demands to know who is responsible. Tawiskaron, the Dark Twin, is never at a loss for words, even this early in his career. Dabbing at a nonexistent tear, he tells Sky Woman, "My brother did it."

"Is it true?" Sky Woman demands of Sapling. Elder Brother can't say a word. Maybe he is struck dumb by the enormity of Tawiskaron's lie.

Sky Woman chooses to believe Tawiskaron. She takes an active dislike to the Light Twin, withholding food and favors from him until eventually he goes away into the wilderness to fend for himself. Can this be Woman Who Fell from the Sky, the one who always knew what was going to happen? Maybe she lost her gift with the fall. Maybe she is the victim of love at first sight. Oh, he can be a charming devil, that Tawiskaron. His eyes are shining now. He is weeping tears of exultation as his grandmother presses him between her breasts, kissing and caressing. Never underestimate the glamour of the dark side.

Sky Woman's daughter enters the womb of earth. This is an exact, not a cute, way of saying she is buried. In Mohawk, the same word, *kia'tat,* means both "I am buried" and "I enter the womb."

We'll be lost now in what we will wrongly suppose to be the illogical mishmash of the "primitive" mind, unless we recognize a sacred code. Before she came down from Earth-in-the-Sky, Ataensic's daughter had already exited and reentered the womb. Now that she has given birth to the Twins, she goes inside her own womb. She is, after all, the original Earth Mother. Take off your shoes, walk barefoot on the grass, feel her under your feet. From the womb of earth comes yet another birth. The Three Sisters—corn, beans, and squash, the life supporters of the Longhouse people—sprout from the breasts and belly of Sky Woman's daughter.

With the birth of the primal Twins, a battle has started that will go on until the end of the world. There is no creation without contraries, says the poet. Without struggle, we stagnate. If the struggle is won or lost for all time, then time and the world are wound up. Round One goes to the Twisty Man, the charmer, Granny's boy. See how his crooked shadow flits everywhere in the world under the sky.

9

The Battle of the Twins

If either wins, the game is over.
Without contraries, nothing is created.
It is through your unending battle
and its lack of resolution
that the game goes on.

"THE STAND"

The one becomes two, and we are ready to play the multiplication game. In all the Iroquois tellings, the primal Twins are both male, but this does not impede them from birthing all manner of things. The Light Twin, in particular, is full of procreative power. Being more than human, of course, the Twins are not confined to human sexual divisions or limitations.

The one becomes two, and we are set for a fight, if the divided halves no longer recognize themselves in each other. Humans who identify exclusively with one of the Twins—or are entered and possessed by a split archetype, which lodges inside them like a crystal shard or a dagger of ice—will turn the world into a war zone. Partisans of the light, if it blinds them, may demonize the dark side and crusade against perceived forces of evil, making enemies of half the world and tending to become what they hate, even as they fight against it. On the other hand, those possessed by the dark side are consumed by the ravening jealousy of the Dark Twin, writhing against the light wherever it manifests, simply because it is the light.

We can find all manner of polarities in the struggle of the Twins: creation and destruction, order and chaos, summer and winter, healing and wounding, the power to fructify and the power to blight, day and night, life and death. But we should refrain from identifying them as good and evil in any absolute way, even if followers of the Iroquois religion inspired by Handsome Lake (and possibly influenced by church conceptions of the devil) call them the Good-Minded and the Evil-Minded. Mohawk wisdomkeeper Tom Porter is lucid on this: "The power over the world is divided fifty-fifty between them. Mohawks don't see it as good versus evil. It would be a terrible mistake to see Tawiskaron as a kind of Satan, as Christians may have done. You would be pitting yourself against half the power of creation. And you are just a little human."[1]

In the deeper Iroquois mythistory of the Battle of the Twins, we will find that each contains something of the other. The Light Twin is capable of deception and killing; the Dark Twin has creative as well as destructive gifts, and a wicked sense of humor. We will find the deep wisdom that the two are actually one. As the battle is played out over the centuries on different fields and in different bodies, we will also find the practical understanding that to bring true healing and balance to our world, we must make friends with chaos as well as order.

To understand what is at issue in the Iroquois Battle of the Twins, we need to look, once again, at the names.

Let's start with the Dark Twin, because—perhaps moved by his impatience?—I have already given his name of power, Tawiskaron. His name is essentially the same in Huron, Mohawk, and Cherokee (Tawiskala). The nominal stem, *wiskar,* can refer to ice, rock crystal, or something that has the properties of being cold, slick, and slippery. It reminds me of a real northeastern ice storm, and in the Iroquois imagination an ice storm is unequivocally a gift of Tawiskaron.

Hewitt was fascinated by the strange, archaic word *Tawiskaron,* and he made repeated efforts to decode it. Because the *t* prefix refers to duality, or doubling, Hewitt translated *Tawiskaron* as "he is arrayed in ice in a double degree."[2]

Tawiskaron is a changer who won't be boxed in to any single shape or definition. I feel the following meanings in his name: Ice Man, Ice Double, Stone Mirror, Slippery Guy, Twisty Man, Slick, Cold Cold Heart. He has a strong connection with sharp stones, such as flint and chert; in fact, he is called Flint by the Onondaga and the Seneca.

Ruffling my hair with his fingers, Tom Porter told me he had a vision that Tawiskaron's true identity is Whirlwind. Though the power of Whirlwind is not in the etymology, it is there in the way the Dark Twin manifests in the natural world, turning things around, lifting you off your foundations.

As a personified power of nature, Tawiskaron is very much a winter god, or frost king. Hewitt described him as "the personification of the winter power transformed into a man-being, a god of winter, whose functions and activities constitute him the mighty frost king, whose breath and magic power blight the verdure of plants and trees and lock lakes and rivers in bonds of ice."[3] The Seneca artist Jesse Cornplanter depicted a frost god wearing a long white robe and a hood pointed like a stalagmite, or up-pointing icicle, and this is certainly a way of seeing and understanding Tawiskaron. His contest with his brother clearly involves the annual struggle between the forces in nature that fructify and blight. But he is more than a seasonal deity. He is half of *everything* that is at play in the world.

I have been calling the Elder Brother Sapling, which is a favorite Mohawk name for him and evokes the way that as a Creator god and indigenous Green Man—a fertile and inseminating masculine power— he brings plants and trees and fruits and flowers bursting from the earth. But the Light Twin has a deeper name, and the story of how he received this name takes us to the heart of the difference between the Twins, a difference we must understand if we are to accept their struggle in ourselves and our world.

After their birth contest, the Twins develop fast. Within a few days, Sky Woman asks them, "Do you know where you have come from? And do you two know where you will go when the time comes for you to leave this world?"

The Elder Brother says, "I know where we have come from. We

have come from the sky, from the world above the sky. I will never forget this. I will continue to hold on with both hands to the place I have come from. When the time comes for me to leave here I will simply return to the place of our origin."

His grandmother says, "You know this matter. Your mind has not fallen. Therefore I shall name you Sky Holder, Tharonhiawakon. The reason is that you remember what you knew before you left the Sky World to come here. You hold on to the sky with both hands."

Then she asks Tawiskaron what's on his mind.

He thinks Sky Holder's attitude is a drag. "Why do I need to think about where I come from, or where I might go if I ever leave this world? Don't give me a headache talking about some other world. I'm in this one now, and I'm ready to party. I am hard and strong, and pretty soon it's going to be a lot of fun fooling around in this world."[4]

It's hard not to feel sympathy for both attitudes, and we are probably in trouble if we cannot acknowledge and make room for both of them in our lives. But here an edge of warning slips in. We are going to see that in the Iroquois worldview, the Dark Times come, and come again, when humans let their minds fall and they cease to remember the Sky. This is why Sky Holder, under various names and masks, will become so important as a god of dreams and visions. Through dreaming, he will reach to humans—and reach *through* humans who become his Speakers—to recall us to the memory of the soul's origin and destiny in the Sky World.

In the naming story, Sky Woman seems to be praising the Light Twin. How does this consort with the fact that, in all versions I have seen or heard, Tawiskaron is his grandmother's favorite, and that she bought his big lie about how Earth Mother died? Let's remember that while we are describing the goings-on within a strange family as if they were humans, there are still no humans on the Earth that is still being formed. We are dealing with multidimensional beings who can pull the sun and moon out of the sky and give life with their breath. Why should they conform to our notions of sequence and consistency, when they can step in and out of shape and time faster than we can get in and out of the shower?

As the story unfolds, Sky Holder emerges as a Creator who sees his primary function as preparing a welcoming environment for a species that has not yet been designed, a species that will, if he has his way, be linked to the higher consciousness for which he stands. Tawiskaron has no interest in humans until his brother makes some, at which point he wants a set of his own to play with, just like a boy who is envious of a playmate's new action figures. Meanwhile, Sky Woman's attitude toward humans is ambiguous. The way she sides with Tawiskaron, as he meddles with Sky Holder's arrangements, suggests that she believes that this new species should not have it too easy; they should have to undergo challenges and trials, just as she did on her way to making a world. There is another important player: the father of the Twins, who sides unequivocally with Sky Holder and supports all his efforts to make a world where humans can thrive. If we dream our way into the story, we are listening to a family feud among gods divided not only by their own jealousies, but also by rival opinions about how to conduct an experiment with a new species, and whether that experiment is worth conducting at all. Their conflicts evoke the feuds among other gods who come from other worlds, such as the contendings of the Annunaki of Mesopotamia and the Neteru of Egypt.

Let's follow the Battle of the Twins as if it is unfolding as a wide-screen epic, with a beginning, a middle, and a cliff-hanger before the credits that makes a sequel inevitable.

Sky Holder stands straight and sturdy as a world tree, spreading its limbs to create a sheltering space for life. He has the power of his grandfather, Earth Holder, to breathe life into being.

When Ataensic drives him into the wilderness, he finds a mentor. This happens after he has made himself a bow and arrow. He shoots an arrow that falls into a lake. He decides to go out into the water to find his arrow. But when he plunges in, he finds himself in an underwater realm where he can breathe and move as easily as on the surface. In this realm, there is a lodge, and a man-being who is waiting for him. The master of this realm tells Sky Holder, "I sent for you."

We are now let in on a big secret: Sapling's father is also Great Turtle, who rose up from the primal ocean to give Falling Woman a home.[5] Great Turtle has many forms, but first and last, he is a power and a teacher from the deep. Under his father's guidance, Sapling learns that he is a Maker. He runs along a lakeshore and everywhere his feet come down, saplings and shoots burst from the ground. He shouts and sings, "Let the Earth keep on growing." Wherever he runs, the earth expands and sprouts new life. He keeps calling out, "Let the Earth keep growing!" and "They call me Sapling!"[6] These are magic words. Each time he repeats the phrases, the world bursts into fruit and flower. He first makes the sunflower, as a welcome sign for the humans who are coming. Then he makes the willow, the medicine tree that is the origin of aspirin. Then he makes the strawberry plant.

He plucks a handful of soil from the ground and aims it skyward, and flocks of geese rise, beating pinions.

He makes animals to sustain and protect the humans who are coming. He gathers red clay and black loam and sea foam and makes gentle animals, starting with the deer, who the old ones say is the chief of all animals.

There are two kinds of deep magic: making and changing. Sky Holder is a Maker; Tawiskaron is a Changer.

Tawiskaron is basking in his grandmother's favor, but basking can be boring, so he amuses himself by tracking and spying on his brother. He watches how Sky Holder takes some of that clay, molds it into a deer or a rabbit, and blows life into it. He watches the new animals as they munch and graze their way through the woods, and he decides it would be fun to give them something more to think about than the next stand of young evergreens. Tawiskaron shapes something lean and fast and hungry, with long jaws full of teeth and the close-set eyes of a predator. He breathes on his clay-person, copying Sky Holder. The clay-thing snuffles and yelps and tries to stand up, but it is weak and off balance. Tawiskaron has to trick his brother into giving it some of *his* breath—the real wind of spirit—before Wolf comes, hungry, into the new world.

The old ones say that the surface world, the one we can see and touch and smell without using our inner and deeper senses, is the work of the Twins and their ancient conflict. Sky Holder made rivers that flowed straight and smooth, with currents moving in two directions, like a freeway, so travelers could cross from one side to the other for an effortless round trip. Then Tawiskaron, just for the hell of it, made the courses run crooked, and put in rapids and dangerous rocks, and fixed the flow so it always takes you down and there is never an easy way up. Sky Holder made the rose; Tawiskaron gave it thorns. The Light Twin made trees that give shade and sugar, and plants that heal; the Dark Twin made briars and poison oak and plants that can be medicine as well as poison, but only when you learn how to handle them.

Humans started out as Sky Holder's experiment. Maybe the idea came from Great Turtle, or from minds in the world up top. It's a radical project, and a risky one: to mold a species that will be more like the People than anything that walks or creeps or flies down here, a species that can think and choose and remember a deeper world. Sapling tries out many styles and colors and sexes before he settles on a prototype that stands upright and, with limbs extended, resembles a star. He mixes ash with the dust of stars, so the earliest humans come out black. He tries yellow ochre in the next mix. He uses sea foam, and his manikins come out white as ghosts. Then he puts in red clay, and he likes the creatures who come out coppery red so well he decides to give human making a rest.

The Dark Twin is missing none of this, and he knows a dominant species when he sees one, even if it is puny in proportion to him. He is keen to make some human creatures according to his own tastes. But, whatever he tries, his progeny won't stand up without the breath of life Tawiskaron cannot give. Once again, he borrows it from his brother. It's hard to understand why Sky Holder gives his breath to make monsters and killers, except that he is into sharing and is clearly playing a deeper game. Tawiskaron's set of villains and vampires come alive and caper about in a danse macabre. And Twisty Man returns his brother's gift by twisting something in all the creatures Sky Holder made. So there is the breath of the Light Twin in the darkest person, and a twisty bit of the Dark Twin in the saintliest sister or brother.

The Twins are emerging as corulers of this new world. Daytime is Sapling's, as is summer and the deer and broad, fertile plains. Night and winter and the wolf and high stony mountains are Tawiskaron's. Go on with the list, and you'll fill an encyclopedia. There are no fixed boundaries between their kingdoms. Even in their inner keeps and citadels, you will find the mark of the other.

We find straight and twisty in our own bodies and souls as well. Oh, you can *say* you only believe in the Straight Guy, under one of his manifold names, and reject all the works and designs of the Dark One as the spawn of Satan. And you'll haunt yourself with a shadow half as heavy as the world. Or, like Sky Woman, you could be charmed and deceived by the Dark One; you might even set him up as your master, until light energy leaks out of you like water from a sieve and you stumble through lust and appetency and the rage for power into things for

which there is no forgiveness. The wise ones say you can't have one
without the other, and to act otherwise is to set out to kill something in
yourself, and the world.

There is a killing in the story. Because the victim is one of the Twins, it's
a temporary death; these People have a way of coming back. But it is a
killing nonetheless. Using lies and deception, one of the Twins finds the
means to overpower and kill the other. Which one would do that? If
you guessed the Twisty Man, you are wrong. On this occasion, it is the
Straight Guy who cheats and deceives. Dark within light, light within
dark, yin and yang with stabbing horns.

The father, Great Turtle, warns Sapling in one of their underwater
seminars that Tawiskaron Man is planning to kill him. Neither of the
Twins can be killed in an ordinary way, but each has a weak spot.
Tawiskaron would very much like to know his brother's vulnerability.
On some of those rare evenings when they have been relaxing—or pre-
tending to relax—together, shooting the breeze, Twisty Man has even
come out and asked, "What would it take to kill you?" Here is Turtle's
advice: "Next time Tawiskaron asks what would kill you, tell him it is
only the cattail plant."

The Twins have the conversation, and Tawiskaron buys it. He goes
and gathers some cattails and challenges his brother to a duel. On his
side, Sky Holder is armed with deer antlers. Again on his father's
advice, he has been walking close to Deer from the beginning. For seven
winters, they say, Sky Holder followed Deer to where he dropped his
antlers, and then he gathered the living bones and learned the power
that is in them—to reach above the head, into the spirit world. To die
and grow back.

Sky Woman watches the big fight. The cattails are useless against
Sky Holder. The down spraying from them blurs Tawiskaron's sight as
he tries to defend himself against the thrusting antlers. The deer horns,
applied again and again, crack Tawiskaron's stony hide and he fractures
into myriad flints. Spirit streams out of him like a pack of fleeing wind
wolves.

Sky Woman screams and attacks her surviving grandson. Sky
Holder is so enraged he grabs his grandmother and throws her up into
the sky. Her trajectory stops somewhere between Earth and Earth-in-
the-Sky. An old one points a long bony finger at the moon and whispers

that she is there, and you can draw her down if you watch the rising of the moon and say the right words.

Mysteries within mysteries. How could a flinty fellow like Tawiskaron be duped into believing that cattail rushes could damage his twin? If Sky Holder is good, how could he deceive and kill his brother in a rigged fight? If Tawiskaron is an immortal, how could he be killed?

With the help of thirty gifted dreamers, I explored these questions in a sacred drama we improvised over a whole weekend on a mountain in Mohawk country where the deer energy is strong and the ancient ones—and the Fire Dragon—are sometimes seen. Bending genders, we cast a sharp, quirky, beautiful dark-haired woman—a belly dancer and world traveler—to play the Dark Twin.

We brought a bunch of dried cattails, and we were amused as we watched the actor playing Tawiskaron trying to tickle Sky Holder to death, launching an all-out assault on the soles of his feet. Our thespian playing the Dark Twin went deeply into the role, and later contributed the following insights: "I really did not believe Sky Holder would kill me. I expected he would use his light to make things right between us so we can contribute to humanity. There is something wrong with this story. The good, pure Light Twin would not do this. It has to be the dark energy in the Light Twin who did the killing. So I think that maybe I won after all."[7]

There is another battle in the story of Sky Woman and her grandchildren. It reminds us not only that duality is a condition of the created world, but also that we can, with evolving consciousness, move beyond the clash of contraries to healing. We grow our gods, just as they grow us.

Sky Holder is wandering the world, checking on the beings he has made, possibly feeling a little ennui now that there is no one his own size to contend with. At an outer edge of the world, he comes upon a strange being with a masklike face who challenges him to a contest. "It is said you are a Maker," the Mask-man says mockingly. "I challenge you to prove the strength of your orenda."

"Name the test."

Mask points to a towering mountain range in the distance. "We will take turns to make the mountains move. The one who brings them closest will be honored as the greater."

The nature of the test is a clue to the identity of the mysterious rim dweller. Tawiskaron made the mountains, the old ones say. Surely some part of him has returned in this ungainly body.

Mask tries first, sitting with his back to the mountains. With the force of his will, he brings the mountains halfway to where the magicians are stationed. Now it is Sky Holder's turn. As he bends his orenda to his purpose, the Mask hears a noise and swings round, startled. As he turns, he breaks his great beak of a nose on a mountain that now rises right behind him. Mask concedes to Sky Holder, though if we reflect on the performance, we might conclude that the powers of the two players are rather evenly matched.

Mask makes a very interesting proposal. He will now use his orenda to help heal the human creatures Sky Holder has made, provided that humans honor him by wearing masks of his face, broken nose and all, over their own. They will know it is time to do this when he comes to them in their dreams. They will make the faces by carving them out of a living tree trunk.

The great dream shamans of the Iroquois know that it is sometimes necessary to reach into the dark and claim its powers. The trick is to do this without being mastered and commanded by those powers. When the Iroquois don these masks, they take on the power of a diseased spirit, or the Dark Twin himself, in the hopes of harnessing and directing that energy for healing and the preservation of life.

I learned about this through dreaming. In my original dream, I was with a group of stocky Native American men in work clothes. They were kicking a ball around in a clearing near the woods. I knew they had important information for me but that I would need to be patient and respectful to let it come through. After a while, they told me they were Seneca Indians and gave me their names. The elder's name was Chauncey Johnny John. They told me to look closer at the woods, and I saw that the woods were full of spirits. There were living faces in the trees, and wild things—including flying heads—whirling among the shadows.

The Seneca men told me, "We go to the dark side to bring back the faces, so we can control the dark powers. They come to kidnap our best people and win them to their purpose."

They explained that they reach into the darkness for power and control of chaos. The dark side reaches into the light to steal or destroy the best minds. The ball in their game is actually the mind, *o'nikon:ra*. The flying heads I saw rushing through the woods are "those who have lost their minds. They stray to the dark side and do not know where they belong."[8]

I found this dream in one of my old dream journals when I was writing this book, and I realized I had failed to follow its research lead: that odd and hard-to-forget name, Chauncey Johnny John. After some digging, I found Chauncey in William Fenton's book *The False Faces of the Iroquois* and in his earlier book on the eagle dance. In the 1930s, Chauncey (long since departed) was a proficient mask maker who carved "models" for Fenton, which are now in the Smithsonian. I found photos of him carving a mask in a tree on a Seneca reservation. He dictated his own version of the origin of the faces in the duel between the Creator and Mask.[9]

Whether my dream was a literal encounter with Chauncey and his friends (as some Native dreamers believe) or a movie production by my inner producer (the preferred explanation of Western psychology), it underscored the wisdom of the Iroquois teaching that we must work with both sides of power, and make room for disorder.

After our sacred drama on the mountain, our theatrical Twins staged a surprise. They announced that they wanted to be joined together in a sacred marriage. Though our players did not know this, their gravitation matched a deeper level of the Iroquois story. In the Sky World to which they both eventually return, the two are one. Behind the great lodge of Ataensic is a being whose name means He Whose Body Is Divided in Two. Half of him is crystal ice, the other warm flesh. He comes to the door of his lodge twice a year. When he shows the side that is ice, winter comes on Earth. When he shows his warm side, summer begins.[10]

Today, one of the Iroquois masks, or false faces—the mask of the Divided One, half red and half black—recalls both the separation of the Twins and the possibility of union. But in the world below the sky, their contest is continual. It plays out toward a radically different ending, and a model for world healing, in the mythistory of the real Hiawatha.

10

Hiawatha's Mirror

It is from the Sky he comes with his mission.
ATTRIBUTED TO THE FIRST IROQUOIS CHIEF
WHO RECOGNIZED THE PEACEMAKER

The shining one comes from a land across the water, from the True North. He does not enter this world in an ordinary way. He comes through a young woman who has never known the touch of a man. She has been chosen by an extraterrestrial god as the landing place for an envoy who is being sent to save humans from themselves. His human grandmother dreams his identity and his mission.

He comes down from his Earth-in-the-Sky in a time of terror when the minds of men are darkened and confused. An immense power of darkness has occupied the twisted body and diseased mind of a sorcerer-tyrant called Thadodaho, the Entangled One, and his hydra-shadow falls everywhere across the land. Humans have fallen lower than any beast, killing and raping and eating one another. The god-man grows up fast; fast is essential, because he is needed urgently. He flies into the killing fields across an inland sea in a vehicle humans cannot understand. He spreads the good word that we are all related and should treat one another as kin. He announces himself as the Peacemaker. His first apostle is a fallen woman who feeds and fucks with the killers but is transformed by the shining one's radiant light, weeping tears of cleansing joy and recognition.

But the Peacemaker is hard for most people to understand. He needs a Speaker. He goes to the house of a fallen man who has lost every vestige of his once-noble self and now devours his own kind. The Peacemaker shows the cannibal his own shining face in a mirror. The fallen man becomes Hiawatha, the Awakened One. Together, Hiawatha and the Peacemaker survive many ordeals and spread the word that we are all kin. They gather a gentle host, and bird-men fly ahead, scouting the way. They confront the dark sorcerer and break his power. Instead of killing the Entangled One, they cleanse and renew his mind, and raise him up to be the first of the men of good minds, the lords of the new-born Confederacy. The chiefs are crowned by the woman who has become the Mother of Nations, the Queen of Peace. She places deer antlers on their heads.

One of the world's greatest experiments in enlightened government and federation has begun. It will shame and awe divided American colonists into dreaming up their own plan that evolves into the Constitution of the United States. But the story is bigger. It teaches us that psychic forces are at the root of hatred and violence, and that resolving our conflicts requires us to reach out to cleanse and heal those whose minds have become darkened and confused. It reminds us that, even in the darkest moments of human history, there are saving powers that seek to rescue us from ourselves and recall us to the soul's purpose.

The Peacemaker's mission is for all people, and it is for now as well as then. There is still a Hiawatha in the roll call of the Iroquois chiefs. Though the Peacemaker returned to the Real World above the sky when his work in the Shadow World was done, he promised us that he will return when he is called by people of good minds: "Say my name in the bushes, and I will stand here again."[1]

In a time of blood and tears, when every man's hand is turned against his neighbor, a mother and daughter decide to make a new life by traveling deep into a northern forest, far from their village and the violence of men. The mother's name is Kanetokhta, which means End of the Field. The daughter's name is Kahetehsuk, which means She Walks Ahead. Call her Forward Woman.[2]

They live quietly for years, gathering wild foods in the woods and tilling their modest field of corn, beans, and squash. Then Forward Woman's belly starts to swell. Her mother demands to know who is the father of the baby that is obviously on its way. Forward Woman protests that she has not been forward at all; she has not had contact, let alone congress, with any man in all the time they have been living out here. She cannot explain her condition.

The mother, End of the Field, is soon at the end of her wits. She is convinced—as we might be—that Forward Woman is lying to hide the identity of a secret lover. Believing that her daughter has shamed and betrayed her, Kanetokhta becomes down-minded, falling into a deep depression, refusing food and spending much of the day on her sleeping mat, face turned to the wall.

The women are being closely observed by powers beyond the human realm. The mother's despair is troubling; her mind is so burdened she could do harm to herself or her daughter. She might even try to get rid of the baby. This cannot be allowed to happen, because this family is part of a sacred plan.

A messenger is sent to Kanetokhta, the grandmother-to-be. He visits her in a dream. He appears as a man, and he tells the dreamer that he has come with a message from the Maker, Sky Holder. The dream visitor reveals that the child who is coming is a boy, that his name is Deganawidah, and that the Maker has sent him from "a land above the sky" to bring peace among men. "A great thing has happened. The one you call the Maker has chosen your daughter to be the place where a man-child from a land in the sky will come to earth."[3] The dream visitor instructs Kanetokhta that the child will grow amazingly fast, and that he will be called to travel far from their home on a mission for all humanity.

The baby boy is born radiantly beautiful and strong, with only one defect: he has two rows of teeth. This is the meaning of his personal name, a name the Iroquois today prefer not to say aloud. We'll call him the Peacemaker from now on. His Mohawk title is Ranonshonniton, He Lifts Up the House. His two rows of teeth are a speech impediment; when he is ready to talk, it is very hard for most people to understand him. To get his message across, he is going to need an interpreter, a Speaker who grasps what he is about and is able to convey it to others with the necessary force and eloquence.

His mother and grandmother are his first translators. They return to their village to introduce him and explain his mission. Not everyone is convinced. When he is still in his infancy, the Peacemaker survives several efforts to kill him. On one occasion, his would-be murderer thrusts him down through a hole in the ice. He suffers no harm at all, swimming about under the ice as easily as a turtle and turning up later in his family's cabin.[4] Maybe he actually *becomes* a turtle to survive this ordeal. We are still in a time when full-body shape-shifting is common, even among ordinary people.

He is driven by his mission, which will take him south, across a great lake, deep into the shadow of Thadodaho, the Entangled One, the sorcerer-tyrant who enslaves souls and embodies an active evil that possesses humans' minds and drives them to devour their own kind. The Peacemaker works alone to assemble the vessel he will use for the crossing. When it is ready, he asks his mother and grandmother to help him launch it. He wants them to bear witness to what he has done.

Before he shows them his ship, he takes them up on a hill and introduces them to a great white pine. He explains that however far he may travel, the women can keep in touch with him through this tree. If they are anxious to know his fate, they can cut a notch in the pine, as he then does with an ax. If the pine delivers sweet sap, they will know he is well. He offers them the resin on his finger; it is sweet as honey. If the Peacemaker is wounded or killed, however, the tree will bleed like a human, dripping red blood. We understand, in this moment, that some part of the Peacemaker's identity is in that tree. We will find the great white pine recurring in different landscapes throughout the story. There is a pine on that hill, and another on the edge of a falls, and another that is planted at the heart of the Confederacy that is about to be born. Beyond the individual pines, there is an Evergrowing Tree that travels everywhere with the Peacemaker, as Merlin's apple orchard traveled with him.

After demonstrating the oracular tree, the Peacemaker shows the women his means of transportation. In this time and place, normal people peel birch bark or elm bark to make canoes—but the Peacemaker's boat seems to be made of white stone. It gleams like white quartzite, and it is hard and smooth to the touch. The design is not like any regular canoe. The women are incredulous; this thing cannot possibly float. "You'll see," he tells them. "Help me get it into the water."

They slide the vessel down the slope, and the Peacemaker steps in as it slips into the water. The women marvel at his latest wonder. The stone canoe not only floats; the Peacemaker has only to touch the paddle—if it *is* a paddle, because it is certainly not made of wood—and the vessel goes skimming away across the lake, folding the distance. Maybe it does not even touch the surface. On the other side of the lake, where the very air seems clotted by evil, the Peacemaker sets up his unlikely vessel as a surety and a place of rendezvous.

The first person he meets is a man who is dipping for water at the edge of the lake. This man is edgy, scared of any stranger, and amazed by the Peacemaker's ship. But his fear ebbs away in the presence of the shining one. The water dipper explains that he is a fugitive; he and his family have fled from Mohawk country to escape the constant feuding and killing. The strange being who is hard to understand amazes the Mohawk by telling him, "We are related." The Peacemaker does not give a lengthy sermon by the lake. He instructs the Mohawk to gather his family and return to his own settlement. "Tell them I am coming, and that peace is in my word."

"They are not ready."

"Tell them to get ready."

"You look after yourself," the refugee warns. "*Nobody* is ready for you. They'll kill you sooner than look at you."

The Peacemaker has announced his coming, but he needs stronger allies, and he needs a Speaker, and he must win them from the heart of darkness. So he embarks on two dangerous journeys.

He goes first to the House on the Warpath. This house is visited day and night by warriors moving back and forth along the great trail, their faces and chests painted black for death and red for blood, scalps dangling from their belts, cruel ball-headed clubs in their hands. The mistress of the house has generous cooking pots forever on the boil, and she is a generous pot herself, according to her name and reputation. Her name is Jigonsahsen, which means Fat Face. She is plump and lusty, and she boasts that she never lets a warrior go hungry. Shaking her mounds of flesh, she promises, "There's plenty of me to go around." In the starving times, when the warriors are short of supplies, her cooking pots and storage bins keep them going, and her voluptuous body reassures them they are heroes. Until the Peacemaker gets into her house and into her mind, she is part of the darkness that has fallen over the land.

Unseen by the roaring killers who are feasting and lounging around Fat Face's cooking fires, the Peacemaker gets her alone and starts working the change. He talks funny, but the energy that is with him wraps itself around her, squeezing and pushing in ways different from the men who have rolled with her on her sleeping mat. She feels something raking, gently but firmly, through her energy field, like a brushwood broom. It is stripping away all the psychic litter and the hungry ghosts that have been traveling with her. Something hisses and rears inside her, resisting the cleansing. As she moves to put her tongue in the stranger's mouth, it strikes at him like a rattlesnake. But the Peacemaker is stronger. He rips the psychic intruder from Fat Face's body and sends it back where it came from. From the house of the sorcerer-tyrant, many looks away, a mad howl of thwarted lust and ambition rises with the black fumes from the smoke hole.

Fat Face is sobbing. Her tears are a salt waterfall of cleansing and joy. She feels light and beautiful, and she is. She has undergone a kind of shamanic exfoliation. She will be known from now on as New Face. She wants to reward her visitor in her accustomed way, but he has come for things other than food and sex. The easy woman is the first to hear the full nature of his plan. It is contained in three magic words that have multiple layers of meaning: peace, power, and the good word. Peace, as he describes it, is a vital, sexy process. Peace is how you feel when your mind is untroubled and you are in glowing good health and all the parts of your body are working together well. The power he invokes is not the sorcerer's mania for control or the killer's muscle in the field; it is the energy that flows when we are serving the spirit and are hooked up to the life force of the universe. The good word is that we are all related, and we must treat everyone and everything as our kin. Instead of fighting and killing, the warring tribes are to settle down as one extended family, sharing an extended house, or longhouse, with plenty of room for all.*

New Face is the first person to receive and grasp the full nature of the Peacemaker's message. She is his first apostle. So it is not surprising that in the Peacemaker's scheme of things, it is the women who will hold the power to raise up or remove the chiefs. New Face, acting for all women, is going to take the men in hand in a new way. The Peacemaker makes a date with her: at a certain time she is to meet him, and those who will have joined him, in a confrontation with the Entangled One that will either mend the world or hurl it into unrelieved darkness.

---

*An unpublished note by Hewitt explains that each of the three words of the Peacemaker has a double meaning. *Ne'skennon,* "peace," is both (1) tranquility, rest in body politic; and (2) health and soundness, normal functioning in human body. *Ga'shasdenhsen,* "power," is (1) force, including war power; and (2) orenda, magic potency, authentic power. *Ne'gai'hwiyo,* "the good word" or "Great Law," is (1) good doctrine, gospel, ethics; and (2) justice, right. Hewitt Papers, National Anthropological Archives, Smithsonian. Cited in William N. Fenton, *The Great Law and the Longhouse* (Norman, OK: University of Oklahoma Press, 1998) 86, note 3.

The Peacemaker is now on the trail of the man who will be his Speaker. The trail leads him to the house of a cannibal who is engaged, right now, in dragging the corpse of a victim home for his dinner. The Peacemaker climbs up on the roof of the cannibal's lodge, unobserved, and watches covertly through the smoke hole.

The man-eater proceeds to dismember his victim's body and throw body parts into a cooking pot over the fire to boil. He goes back and forth, trimming his choice cuts, checking on his meal. When he is ready to eat, he looks into the pot and is startled to see a face looking back at him.

The cannibal mutters spells and grabs at his amulets, fearing he is being bewitched. Maybe it's the ghost of his victim come to haunt him, or something sent by an enemy sorcerer.

He looks in the pot again. The shining one who looks back at him is unlike the man the cannibal killed and butchered. He is unlike anyone. The face glows with extraordinary, unearthly beauty. The cannibal stares wildly around, but he can find no explanation. He slumps down on his bench, trying to figure out what is going on.

"It has to be me," he concludes. He looks down into the mirror of the water again, and the face seems even more beautiful than before. As he looks at the shining face, a fog begins to lift from his mind. He remembers a time before he fell into this wallow and began preying on his fellow humans. Once he walked in beauty between earth and sky. Once he loved a good woman, and raised beautiful children. Then a shadow fell upon him. He was beaten and humiliated, lost everything he loved . . . and sought to blot out the memory of a time when he was at home in the sunlit world of growing things.

"That is not the face of a man who destroys his fellow men," he mumbles over the mirror water. "That is not the face of a man who lives as I do."

In this moment, he decides to change his life. He begins by getting rid of his dinner. He collects the body parts and carries them to a place of burial—a hole in the ground where a tree was uprooted.

But he knows that changing his dinner plans is not enough. Somehow, he must make amends for the evil things he has done. If only he had a friend who could counsel him. He wishes fervently for such a friend, an adviser who will help him make things right without judging him—the friend we all need but do not always welcome.

As he stumbles back to his cabin, thinking such thoughts, the reforming cannibal meets the Peacemaker, who has slipped down off the roof. There is something reassuring, even familiar, about this person, though the ex-cannibal does not recognize him. "I was just wishing for a friend," he tells the shining one. "Come inside."

They sit next to the fire, across from each other, and, following Iroquois custom, the host speaks first. The man describes his vision of beauty and tells how he buried the body parts.

The Peacemaker tells him, "What has happened is wonderful. You have changed the pattern of your life. Now you have a new mind. I will tell you what to do. I am seeking a friend to work with me in the cause of peace and good minds.

"First we will prepare food. You will go for fresh water, and be sure to go with the flow of the water, dipping into the stream and letting the current fill the container. I will bring a game animal. As we cook the meat together, we will merge our two minds."

When they meet back at the house, the Peacemaker has brought a deer with huge antlers. He explains that the Maker—Sky Holder—intends venison as food for humans.

As they skin the deer, the cannibal asks what use they should make of the antlers. The Peacemaker taps the top of his head and says, "They shall be placed here upon humans. When this is done, it will be possible for all humankind to continue to live by them."

When they have cooked the meat and removed the pot from the fire, the shining one asks the man, "Show me exactly where you were standing when the thought came to you that you had seen yourself as you truly are. Stand there now."

The man stands at the place where he had his vision of beauty.

The Peacemaker tells him, "This is the place of your wisdom. You must always think and act from this place."

The shining one places his hands on the man's head, and then he passes them down over his own face. "The Maker has brought you good mind. Now you and I will look into the pot." When they look together, they see that their faces and bodies appear to be identical in the water.

The man exclaims, "It is amazing that we look the same."

They are not different, and not the same, the fallen man and the shining one. In this moment of epiphany, the fallen man becomes Hiawatha, the Awakened One.

The shining one says, "The Maker has given us the same mind. Now we can eat."[5]

Hiawatha and the Peacemaker become a double act. Their stories interweave so closely, and so often in defiance of the supposed rules of physical reality, that we may suspect that they were always two-in-one, or two-split-from-one. People cannot tell them apart. In fact, it is by no means certain that anyone except Hiawatha actually sees the Peacemaker as a separate being. It is possible that the whole of the Peacemaker story up to the moment when Hiawatha awakens is Hiawatha's dream of a deeper and parallel life, something that goes on—as in our dreams—even when we are lost in the miasma of everyday existence.

The Peacemaker instructs Hiawatha in his plan for peace, and Hiawatha picks up the details so fast that we can clearly see he is being reminded of things he knew before his fall. Humans are animals that remember and forget, forget and remember.

The first part of the joint mission of Hiawatha and the Peacemaker is the conversion of the Mohawks. The Peacemaker will go ahead to the strongest of the Mohawk castles, where he is expected, because of the messenger he sent after he crossed the big lake. Hiawatha will meet him there later.

The Mohawk castle is defended by great ramparts of sharpened logs. Hawk-eyed sentinels perch up high, ready to screech the alarm, or the croaking death cry, *kwaa-kwaaa*. The Peacemaker proceeds cautiously. He makes camp at the woods' edge, and he lights a fire to announce his presence in an unobtrusive way. This will become a model in Iroquois diplomacy. The guards at the Mohawk castle see the smoke and alert the chief. He has been expecting an unusual visitor; since the returning fugitive brought him word of the Peacemaker, he has dreamed every night of a light brighter than the sun.

The Mohawk chief is ready for the Peacemaker, but the men of war are not. The war captains circle and sniff the Peacemaker like hungry wolves. He says they are all related, but he is definitely from out of town. A hulking warrior with a necklace of human bones and a black mask painted above and below his flinty eyes feints at the Peacemaker with his war club. Another takes a sharpened flint and affects to start flaying the skin from the Peacemaker's body. The Peacemaker does not flinch, but that proves nothing; Mohawks are trained not to express fear or pain even under fire torture, even when their guts or sinews are being unwrapped, with exquisite care, from their living bodies.

The warriors demand proof of the Peacemaker's identity. If he has come from Earth-in-the-Sky, then he must prove it by submitting to a test that would kill an ordinary man. The Peacemaker says that he will be happy to prove himself.

They make a plan. The Peacemaker will climb to the top of a great white pine that towers above the falls. The Mohawks will cut down the tree, toppling man and pine into the gorge. If the Peacemaker survives, this will be evidence that he carries real magic—maybe strong enough magic to match that of the Entangled One, who is watching all of this in his looking bowl, and probing for weakness and opportunity with his hydra-shadow, which darts everywhere in the country of the Mohawks.

Once again, the Peacemaker's fate is linked to a tree. Does the oracular tree in his mother's country start to bleed a little as he climbs its counterpart over the gorge? As he climbs, the great pine sways and complains, attacked at its base by warriors wielding axes and flaming torches. A final blow sends the man on the tree toppling into the gorge. He is lost to sight in the churning waters of the falls. The Mohawks wait to see if he comes bobbing up downstream. When he fails to surface, they conclude that the peace man was, after all, just a man.

But in the morning, the lookouts at the Mohawk castle see a twist of smoke coming from somewhere downriver. They send out scouts who return with Hiawatha, who looks exactly like the Peacemaker and is greeted by his title. Hiawatha kept his date with the Peacemaker, helped him at the foot of the falls, and stands in for him while the Peacemaker goes off to carry the good word to other tribes.

Hiawatha must now face trials of his own. The Entangled One is watching and probing, and he does not miss the fact that a significant challenge to his power is taking form. Inspired by the change in Hiawatha and the light of the Peacemaker, Mohawks are leaving the warpath and putting out peace feelers to other nations. The sorcerer's thoughts hiss from his mind like venomous snakes, seeking to maim and taint, to confuse and make mad. Master of things that creep and sting, he sends out poisonous bugs and swarms of mosquitoes and no-see-ums. Herder of captive souls, he directs wave after wave of psychic confusers against those who are struggling toward the light.

Where people gather to hear the Peacemaker's word, the confusers disrupt and divide. When Hiawatha is speaking, some people in his audience collapse in hysterical laughter or violent fits of sneezing.

Others flee from assaults of paper wasps and burrowing ticks, or freak out and set fire to the lodges.

The Awakened One is allowed no peace. At night, mocking birds assail him with doubts, inviting him to divert his mission into a guilt trip, haunting him with his past crimes and omissions, telling him he can never change, never be forgiven, never carry the light. But Hiawatha stands by the place of his wisdom, holding to the vision of the shining one, feeling the spirit antlers beginning to sprout from his head where the Peacemaker laid his hands.

Always searching for weak points, the Entangled One strikes at Hiawatha's family. Hiawatha has remembered that he is a father, and he takes enormous pride in his daughters. The sorcerer mouths filthy charms over dolls, willing the girls to take him as their demon lover. He looses the monstrous snake that issues from his crotch to invade their bodies in the hollow of the night. The Entangled One may be huge, but his touch brings no pleasure. It is cold and sterile, and it tears. When the girls reject the sorcerer's advances, he sends evil birds to steal their sleep and their dreams and chant spells to drive them to madness and self-destruction.

Hiawatha lost his family before, when he forgot who he was. Now, remembering himself, he must suffer the further tragedy of seeing those he loves struck down by focused evil. One by one, Hiawatha's children are slaughtered by witchcraft.

The murder of Hiawatha's youngest and favorite daughter is the cruelest. People have gathered to try to lift Hiawatha's spirits; now, while fighting to restrain his rage for revenge, he risks sliding back into the condition of the down-minded, the toxically depressed. The Mohawks stage a lacrosse game, which usually gets everyone in a good mood, even if it is not an entirely safe outlet for the fighting instincts that might otherwise be vented on the warpath.*

Hiawatha's youngest daughter is sitting on the ground, half-watching the game—and maybe sizing up a player—when everyone is diverted by the appearance of an extraordinary bird whose brilliant and flashing plumage has never been seen before in these parts. The bird is a creature of the sorcerer. The lacrosse game is forgotten as players and spectators rush toward the falling bird, crazed with the desire to pluck out its feath-

---

*One of the great memorykeepers of the Iroquois, Chief John Arthur Gibson, was blinded in a lacrosse accident at the age of thirty-one.

ers. This feather lust grips them so violently that they trample Hiawatha's daughter to death without even noticing what they are doing.*

When people recover their senses, they are shamed and enraged by how their minds were turned. Mohawk warriors gather around Hiawatha, painted for slaughter. They urge him to take the path of the blood vendetta. "You are a man of power. You should use your power to kill your enemy. We will walk with you."

Through the pall of grief, Hiawatha remembers the shining face in the mirror and vows, *I will not become my enemy.*

"My children are all gone," he says quietly. "I will depart. I will split the sky."[6]

Carrying his grief, Hiawatha embarks on a journey to Oneida country to find himself again in the presence of the Peacemaker, who has been carrying the word of peace among the nations. Somewhere along his route, he discovers wampum and invents the great Iroquois condolence ceremony that heals minds and restores the soul to the body.

He comes to a lake that is entirely covered by waterfowl. As he watches, he sees that the ducks are changers. They shape-shift back and forth between the forms of humans and birds. He yearns for their wings, for their ability to soar and to dive, and to let life's burdens roll off their backs. He wishes for healing.

In a storm of beating wings, the waterbirds rise all at once from the lake, lifting its waters like a sheet of silk. Hiawatha is stunned to see that the floor of the lake is covered with glowing white shells. They shine like the face he saw in the mirror. Reverently, he walks along the lake bed, gathering shells and stowing them in a deerskin bag. When he finds shelter for the night, he is inspired to embed two branches of staghorn sumac in the ground and lay a straight stick between them. He shapes and bores holes in the shells, making cylindrical beads that he strings on lengths of

---

*This incident may be hard for a modern reader to believe, even if we are willing to accept that the Entangled One has a fantastic power to reach from afar and twist people's minds. A crowd kills a girl while fighting over a bunch of feathers? But perhaps this is not so remote from mob behavior in other places and situations—at a soccer game, for example, or at the opening of a big department store sale. And the Iroquois, then and now, do have a passion for both feathers and quills. I recall once driving at high speed on a road in northern Ontario with a Mohawk family in the car. One of the women suddenly screeched, "Stop the car!" I braked in a hurry, fearing some emergency—only to find that the Mohawks had spotted porcupine roadkill and were eager to collect the quills to use in jewelry.

deer sinew. He hangs the strings over the rod he has set up. Eventually there will be thirteen of these strings. He may not know it yet, but he is improvising a powerful ritual of healing that will release him—and many others—from grief and confusion and requicken in his heart and body the spirit and purpose of the shining ones.*

Hiawatha proceeds on his journey. When he nears the Oneida castle, he waits at the woods' edge for a new people to find him. The first Oneida to greet him carries a wolfskin quiver full of arrows; he will become known in legend and the roll call of the Iroquois chiefs as Odatshedeh, the Quiver Bearer.

The Peacekeeper has been very active among the Oneida, the People of the Standing Stone, walking through their dreams. They welcome Hiawatha as their kin. Instructed by him, they use the tools he has made from the shining shells of life to wipe the tears from his eyes, clear the obstruction from his throat, open his heart, and put the sun back in his sky.

In the night, the Peacemaker comes to talk with Hiawatha. The shining one appears outside the chief's lodge where Hiawatha is sleeping. The guards do not see him. When Hiawatha hears his whistle, he steps through the wall of the lodge and they converse under the stars. In the morning, the Peacemaker is with Hiawatha inside the lodge, and he speaks through him.

Over the wampum he has made, Hiawatha invites the Oneida to enter a family relationship with the Mohawks. The Mohawks will be "fathers" to the Oneida, because they were first to accept the Peacemaker's message—but the relationship will be that of equals. They will go forward together to bring the other Iroquois tribes—the Cayuga, the Seneca, and eventually the Onondaga—into their family, under the rafters of a longhouse where they can live together in harmony. The Oneida sing their response: "My father and I shall risk

---

*According to Joseph Brant, Hiawatha discovered shell wampum at Oquaga, an Iroquois settlement on the Susquehanna in the modern township of Windsor, New York, near the Pennsylvania line, when he ascended a branch to its source in a pond. He saw geese shedding feathers and changing into humans. When he called out, they all flew up, revealing the shells. See *Norton's Journal*. The lake shells are commonly believed to have been the shells of the uniosnail, which is related to the moon snail. In later times, wampum beads were manufactured from the shells of the quahog clam and the whelk, imported from the New England coast. Chief Gibson said that before the discovery of the lake shells, Hiawatha and the chiefs who received him experimented with other materials, crafting wampum from cored sumac (or basswood) sticks and cut-up eagle feathers.

together." But none of this can prosper unless the dark power at Onondaga can be broken.

With the Oneida on their side, the action quickens. The chiefs send for their best trackers to carry the message to other nations and to spy out the enemy's lair at Onondaga. The best scouts, of course, are those who can borrow the speed and sight and senses of animals and birds.[7]

Hawk-men fly off to talk to the Cayuga and the Seneca. Other bird-men volunteer for the dangerous reconnaissance at Onondaga. They are told to look for a hell's chimney of black smoke, rising from earth to sky. The heron-men are eager, but they fly too far and are seduced by a rich harvest of fish and groundnuts around the Genesee River. They feed so greedily they cannot get airborne, and they stay on in western New York, in human guise, to become the Heron Clan of the Seneca nation.

The crow-men are hungry, too, but they are better able to keep their eyes on the main event. They shake out their wings and fly toward the setting sun. From afar, they see the tower of black smoke and race toward it. They land under the cover of hemlocks and turn into men. They move cautiously toward the lodge on the hill—the one festooned with scalps and fetishes—and hardly need to ask whether this is the house of the Entangled One. When one of them does speak the name Thadodaho to a stooped, elderly woman, she skitters away as if she has been kicked, mumbling, "Tsk, tsk." To say the sorcerer's name aloud is to summon him.

The scouts are bold and quick as carrion birds on roadkill. They slip under a sheet of loose bark in the sorcerer's wall and get a good look at him. The Entangled One is no longer human. His hair is a mass of writhing, hissing snakes. His hands are like turtle claws and his feet are like bear claws, but they are "awry like those of a tortoise." The spies can't stop gaping at the sorcerer's penis. It is thick as a rattlesnake but much, much longer. It coils round and round his torso and loops around his neck. When flaccid, the upper part hangs down from his shoulder to his knees. He strokes the head casually as he studies the surface of his looking bowl, in which he can watch what is happening far away, and what may happen in the future.[8]

Thadodaho can kill with his voice; when he shouts, people fall dead. He can twist people's minds with the serpents of evil thoughts hissing from his head. He can kill and rape with the penis-snake, which is more than a Freudian nightmare: it is an exact description of shamanic power turned to the dark side.

The crow-men get out fast, sprout feathers again, and fly back to deliver their report.

The Peacemaker's word has spread through the nations. New Face, the Mary Magdalene of this story, has been visiting old boyfriends, cajoling and winning them round. The hawk-men impressed the senior chief of the Cayuga, landing and changing as he sat puffing on an enormous pipe. Mohawk and Oneida envoys have been running along the forest trails, toes turned inward to avoid protruding roots and boulders, issuing the new wampum strings of invitation to a great council. The shining one travels everywhere through the dreams of the people, calling the sleepers' dreamsouls from their bodies to remind them of what it means to be fully human, showing them the origin and the destiny of their souls. "Come to me, lost soul, I am calling to guide you." When a killer looks into those great shining eyes, he loses his appetite for slaughter.

The chiefs and elders the Peacemaker has chosen gather at the spot where he left his impossible ship. They will make a voyage together, to the place of the sorcerer. New Face is crucial to their mission, but she is late—it is a woman's prerogative—so Hiawatha goes ahead, accompanied by Mohawk and Oneida chiefs. (Some say that Cayuga and Seneca were there, too; others say that they came later.)

Watching them in his looking bowl, the sorcerer whips up a fierce storm to sink their boats. The waves in the lake rear like tsunamis. But the Peacemaker, through Hiawatha, orders the waters to be still. The Entangled One shouts out in wild fury, and the wind lashes even harder than before. Again the Peacemaker orders calm, and the elements obey. A third time, Thadodaho wages elemental war against the Peacemaker, plucking giant trees and boulders to hurl at the delegation on the lake. And again, the elements obey the Peacemaker when he commands them to be still.

The peace envoys approach the keep of darkness singing. The old ones will not allow us to forget this. Their voices swell and fall away like the wind in the forest. Their voices blow away the sorcerer's killing shouts and scatter the evil spirits Thadodaho has sent to oppose their passage. Their songs call up the beneficent forces of earth and sky. The ancestors walk with them as they chant the *haihai* chorus that honors those who have gone before and stay close to the earth to watch over those who share life upon it. Deepening voices call the benign spirits of woods and streams and rouse Great Turtle from his dreaming to shake the ground under the sorcerer's lodge.

Thadodaho sees ruin in his looking bowl. He tries to incant his blackest spells, but his tongue curls back on itself. He wills his great serpent to attack, but his penis won't rise; it flops like discarded snakeskin.

Hiawatha stands before him now, the light of the Peacemaker shining in his eyes. The Entangled One screams and writhes before that light. But his visitors are singing and laying strings of bright shells over his body. Each of the shells burns like fire. With hands and voices and shells, Hiawatha and the peace ambassadors are combing the sorcerer's hair, raking down through his energy field. The snakes of evil are falling away. The peace envoys are straightening his limbs, restoring his hands and legs to those of a human, naming each part as it is reformed.

"It is not intended that this should be thus," says the Peacemaker through his Speaker, indicating what was once Thadodaho's pride. They unwind the many fathoms of the sorcerer's penis from his body. They measure the span between a man's extended thumb and middle finger, a natural span. They cut away the rest of the sorcerer's organ. He has plenty left. But his exceptional power has not left him altogether. The old ones say, with a grin, that his organ grew back, but it had lost its poison and its power to kill from afar. New Face probably did not mind that at all.[9] They dress Thadodaho in the clothes of a man and place moccasins on his feet.

Then they do the most extraordinary thing of all. The Peacemaker has determined that this former enemy of humanity shall now be raised up as the first of the *rotiyaner,* or men of good minds, the lords of the Confederacy of the Longhouse that is about to be born.

This decision is almost inconceivable to us. Even if this bloody psychopath has been cured, how can he possibly be trusted to sit in the council of chiefs? We can only understand if we are able to grasp the depth of the spiritual operation that takes place in the primal condolence ceremony, and requickening. It will become the model for the celebrated Iroquois condolence ceremony that takes place when one chief passes on and another is raised up in his place.

"Yo-hay!" The Peacemaker's words burst into the air and fall away like birds exploding from a nest in a hollow tree and calling across the forest. The peace people lay strings of wampum to open the Entangled One's eyes and ears and mouth, to restore his heart and to cleanse his body with the water of mercy. They requicken the heart and soul of the compassionate man who checked out of this body when the Entangled One gave himself over to darkness. "Woh!" This is soul recovery, but it is more. It is spiritual enthronement. They are enthroning in Thadodaho's body a part of the shining one, the same great spirit that changed the cannibal into the Awakened One.[10]

They have a crown for Thadodaho, as for the others who will become the first lords of the Confederacy. But he cannot receive this from the hands of a man. New Face, the Peacemaker's first apostle, now reappears. She is bearing the living bones: a fine rack of antlers, set in a simple circlet that will later be decorated with a spray of feathers. Thadodaho receives the antlers of a chief from the hands of a woman. New Face proceeds to crown Hiawatha and the other chiefs who have been chosen by the Peacemaker. The deer horns rising above their heads are the sign that they have grown in understanding to tap into the spiritual plane. The central role of the Queen of Peace will be replicated, from generation to generation, by the clan mothers. The women will always choose the chiefs, and they may dehorn them if they fall short or betray their trust. The right to wear the antlers belongs only to those who will agree to be walking sticks for the people, and to rise above calumny and criticism as if they have skins seven thumbs thick, and will weigh the consequences of their actions down to the seventh generation beyond themselves. These are the requirements for a chief of men. Because men are forgetful, women will remind them and watch over their actions.

The first meeting of the Council of the League takes place right away. Seneca who have not yet accepted the peace message are now drawn in by the promise that they will be given special rank as guardians of the "western door." The Confederacy is organized as a family. Council procedures aimed at evolving consensus are defined and put into action.

The Peacemaker's tree, the great white pine, is planted at the heart of the Confederacy. Its white roots of peace will extend in all directions, to all peoples. An eagle perches at the top of the great tree, watching over the nations. The weapons of war are buried under the roots, falling into underground waters. A white mat is spread under the tree, with a large bird's wing for keeping the space clean and a rod for driving away creeping and crawling things.

The Peacemaker's mission has been concluded—for now. He withdraws from human sight, taking off in that strange vessel that glints like quartzite in the sun. He leaves the promise, "Say my name in the bushes, and I will stand here again."

PART THREE

THE
TEACHINGS
OF ISLAND
WOMAN

The soul of the Indians is much more independent of their bodies than ours is and takes much more liberty. It leaves the body whenever it deems it proper to do so to take flight and go to make excursions. . . . Long journeys are not difficult for it. It transports itself into the air, passes over the seas and penetrates the most tightly closed and inaccessible spaces.
JOSEPH-FRANÇOIS LAFITAU, *CUSTOMS OF THE AMERICAN INDIANS, COMPARED WITH THE CUSTOMS OF PRIMITIVE TIMES*, 1724

Ever since she has taken on her priesthood the gods have been appearing in visitations as never before, to the girls and women, but also to men and children. What does such a thing mean? Is it the sign of something good?
QUESTION OF ALEXANDRA TO THE ORACLE OF APOLLO AT MILETUS

If they cease to dream . . . they say their soul has left them.
FATHER PAUL LEJEUNE, 1639

The Wolfe never values how many the sheep are.
WILLIAM JOHNSON ON THE IROQUOIS, 1749

11

Dreaming in the Dark Times

*A nation is not conquered until the hearts of the women
are in the ground.*

CHEYENNE TRADITIONAL SONG

The Battle of the Twins is unending. The trials and challenges that can make or break a world do not only come in Noah's time, or Hiawatha's, or Churchill's; they come again and again.

When everything we hold dear and decent seems to be imperiled—when even the dreaming seems to have been hijacked by monsters—what are dreamers to do? Reach for the sky?

Well, yes. In the Iroquois mind, that is precisely what we can do: reach for, and hold on to, the Sky World—to the memory of the origin and destiny of our kind. Reach for the God we can talk to, who for the old ones of the Iroquois way is Tharonhiawakon, the Light Twin, or He Who Holds On to the Sky with Both Hands. He is the master of life, even when Earth seems to have fallen into the hands of the evil-minded.

Dreamers can not only reach into a deeper dimension; they can also reach to one another, to grow a web of soul healing and soul remembering. As timefolders, they can reach into the future, or the past, for paths and solutions beyond those that appear to be on offer in their moment of linear time.

The coming of the People from the Sunrise—the too-polite Mohawk name for the Europeans—menaced the survival of all the First Peoples of America in multiple ways. Some of the nations, as in New England, succumbed quickly to imperial rivalries, imported guns and alcohol, the intruders' land hunger, and alien diseases.

The Iroquois were remarkably quick and effective in responding to these new challenges. After Samuel de Champlain and his companions fired an arquebus or two at Mohawk chiefs to demonstrate the superiority of French arms to his Algonquian allies, the Mohawks learned that wooden armor had become outmoded, and that the French were not altogether friendly. So they made friends with the Dutch and later the English at Beverwyk (now known as Albany in honor of a forgotten duke), the hub of trade and navigation on the upper Hudson River. Next they moved very skillfully to ensure a constant supply of guns, powder, and manufactured goods—cooking pots, hatchets, and fabrics, for starters—by seizing and enforcing their control of the routes along which beaver furs (the "black gold" of the early colonies) traveled from interior America to Europe.

The Mohawks, and the Iroquois in general, were not only superlative warriors. They were also highly adept statesmen, orators, and diplomats. They taught successive colonial officials to fall in with their way of doing things: conducting conferences and making treaties; laying out belts and strings of wampum; burying the hatchet or taking it up ceremoniously; polishing up the silver Covenant Chain that was soon in force between the Confederacy of the Longhouse and the less unified English colonies; and traveling along the double road of the two-row wampum, Iroquois and English walking side by side on parallel paths.

Nonetheless, the Dark Times settled, and deepened, clotting the atmosphere, filling the mind with hissing snakes, the original Thadodaho's specialty. The Iroquois began to succumb to new appetites imported from the Old World, especially alcohol, never previously known in Iroquoia. *"Snekira!"* is the Mohawk way of saying "cheers" or "bottoms up." You can hear the hiss of a green serpent in the word. The Iroquois say that a man who has been drinking is not responsible for his actions because when the alcohol comes in, his mind leaves, and wild spirits take over the house of his body.

The truth of this was evident to me in a Canadian lounge frequented by Mohawk "high steel" men, renowned for their ability to walk fearlessly across the high girders of bridges and skyscrapers under construction. In this joint the tables and chairs were bolted to the floor and chicken wire protected the bottles behind the bar. Full of liquor, Iroquois elders ceased to be men of good minds. They signed away communal lands they had no authority to sell and agreed to go out as mercenary hit men against targets selected by the conniving merchant princes of Albany and New England. "In wartime," Mohawk Bear Clan elder Tom Porter told me, "my people became mercenaries."

From a traditional Iroquois viewpoint, what came into those hard-drinking warriors on the early frontier were the "burned bones," or hungry ghosts, of dead warriors and other earthbound entities lusting for blood and revenge. They drove the war parties not only to take scalps—for the time-honored reason that if you take the scalp (literally the spirit head, in Mohawk) of your enemy, you capture one of his souls—but also to eat the hearts and sometimes other body parts. The example of Hiawatha, who stopped being a cannibal when he was awakened by the vision of the shining one, was drowned in a tide of blood, alcohol, and evil thoughts.

The Tree of Peace creaks and complains. The Confederacy is at risk as its warriors become contract killers for white interests. The elders and clan mothers are no longer respected; they are seen as out of touch with the times, and unable to deliver the goods pouring out of English foundries and distilleries.

The Dark One's shadow thickens over the land. And darting everywhere, like a legion of demonic archers shooting poison arrows, are utterly foreign and inimical spirits of disease. They move like the whirlwind. They most love to strike in the shut-up times of midwinter, when the people lie close together around the fires of the longhouses, their pores clogged by soot and bear grease (which the Iroquois used to protect exposed skin from the cold). The Iroquois cannot even pronounce the white men's names for these disease spirits, names like smallpox and influenza. When the smallpox spirit flies into your lodge, you stop wanting to eat. You get listless and dull-eyed. Pretty soon you have a crashing pain over your eyes. Then you get chills, and you don't want to move, even to take a piss. The fever comes and goes until the pustules break out, and you get such a wild crazy itch you want to tear off your skin and some of the meat as well. You pale to the color of fading silver, and you die like a stinking, rotting sheep.

Successive epidemics of imported disease killed off huge numbers of American Indians on the first frontier, virtually eradicating several nations in New England.[1] The holocaust started as unintentional genocide, but white men hungry for land or easy victory over "hostile Indians" turned it into a strategy of deliberate genocide—when they came to understand what was going on—by distributing blankets infected with smallpox. But that part of the story is no longer the Iroquois story. There is no evidence, as far as I am aware, that the Iroquois or their Canadian cousins—and bitter enemies—the Hurons were deliberately infected by Europeans. The French and English killed them simply by coming into contact with them, and by giving or selling them dirty goods. The two Iroquoian peoples who lived closest to the Europeans, not surprisingly, died fastest. Influenza and smallpox very nearly exterminated both the Huron and the Mohawk nations.

In the Dark Times of early contact between the First Peoples of America and the Europeans, the ancient woman of power who had called me in my dreams was one of those who worked, through dreaming, to find a path for the preservation and healing of her people. Born a Huron, she was adopted into the Mohawk nation, so her life and her spiritual vocabulary span those two traditions. The name Island Woman will not be found in the history books, except as a generic description for a woman of Huron origin (in the colonial period, Mohawks referred to the Hurons as the Island People). Her grandchildren, on the other hand, loom larger in the histories than any other Mohawks, with the exception of Hiawatha. They are Molly Brant, the only woman who ever came close to domesticating Sir William Johnson— by matching his wildness, and through her gifts as a healer and counselor—and Joseph Brant, who became famous as the leader of Indian and Tory war parties during the American Revolution and led Mohawks into exile on the Grand River in Ontario after the defeat of the British cause. I am not going to turn this book into an extended history lesson, though the history professor inside of me would love to do that. Rather, I want to unfold Island Woman's story.

While I was working on this book, I taught a workshop in Los

Angeles at which I described Island Woman's belief that dreams show us the wishes of the soul and recall us to live from the soul's purpose. I felt impelled to speak over a string of wampum beads, as Island Woman had done when she first called me to her.

When I returned to the East Coast, I opened my e-mail and found a message from a Mohawk woman, previously unknown to me, who was now living in Southern California. Always alert to synchronicity, I was intrigued to see that she had sent her e-mail at the same time that I was speaking in her neighborhood over the wampum beads. She wrote:

> I read your two novels, *The Firekeeper* and *The Interpreter*. I have been searching for a teacher and now Island Woman is mine. I have 'flown' since I was seven in conscious awareness and always thought there was something wrong with me. When I came upon Island Woman I learned that it is very natural for me to fly and it probably comes from my bloodline. I am of Mohawk descent, of the Brants. Island Woman may be an ancestor of mine. I yearn for Island Woman and her teachings. Please bring her back. I pray she visits you in your dreams and you will bring her through again.

Island Woman has not only slipped through the veil of time; she has required me to drop the mask of fiction and present her life en clair. She has also made it clear that she wishes to speak in her own voice, as well as I can render it into English, to remind our world what it means to dream, and that through dreaming, we can reclaim the sky.

12

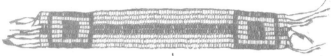

The Making of a Woman of Power

Nothing is more real than the women's superiority. It is they who really maintain the tribe, the nobility of blood, the order of generations and conservation of families. In them resides all the real authority. . . . The women choose their chiefs among their maternal brothers or their own children.
FATHER JOSEPH-FRANÇOIS LAFITAU, 1724

DREAM ARCHAEOLOGY

Island Woman called me after I went looking for William Johnson and found the Eyes of the Goddess, the double spiral incised on guardian stones at Newgrange, near his birthplace. As I struggled to reach a deeper understanding of my encounters with the ancient woman of power, it occurred to me that there might be a direct connection between Island Woman and that wild Irishman who never ceased to go Native, despite his English title of baronetcy and his status as king's superintendent of

Indians and one of the wealthiest men in the American colonies. But the connection was not obvious, until I learned—in a waking dream that played out like a holographic movie—that she was related to the one woman who came anywhere close to taming William Johnson.

That woman is known to history as Molly Brant, although she is Mary Brant in most of the documents, and Johnson called her *Tsitsa,* Flower, when they were alone together. Tsitsa (pronounced *chee-cha* but not to be confused with the South America brew) is a contraction of Molly's Longhouse name Konwatsitsaenni, which means They Are Sending Her Flowers. It probably relates to an important event in her life, or attending her life; in my vision, it related to a dream of her coming into this world.

I *knew,* as I stepped through timegates into Johnson's world, that Island Woman was Molly's grandmother. It so happens that *aksotha*— the Mohawk word for grandmother—is a term of respect for any older and wiser woman; the grandmother, used in this sense, need not be especially old, and she certainly does not need to be biologically related to the person addressing her. But I knew, or imagined I knew, that this connection flowed through the bloodlines. Island Woman gave birth to a daughter whose Mohawk name means Bright Meadow, because she came down the birth canal into a meadow full of flowers, near Sprakers, New York. (How do I know that? Johnson told me, in a lengthy conversation about his women and children.) And Bright Meadow gave birth to Molly and her famous brother Joseph.

Trust memory over history, Native Americans say. But the history professor in my left brain refused to accept this kind of direct knowing without documentary evidence. So I went looking. I discovered that Joseph Brant, Molly's brother, told a number of people, who wrote it down, that their grandmother was a Huron woman captured by a Mohawk raiding party from an "island" in Lake Ontario, and that she was adopted into the Mohawk nation. Joseph also liked to boast that his family had advanced psychic and magical abilities, inherited from their grandmother. The reminiscences of Joseph Brant recorded by a colorful frontier operator named Major John Norton—half-Cherokee and half-Scots, adopted into the Mohawk nation by Joseph—are full of Joseph's stories about the interplay between the spirits and the living, and how good the Brant family was at participating in that.[1]

The history professor inside me grumbled more softly now, and he even started to purr when my travels through the timegates revealed other things about Johnson, and Molly and Island Woman, that could be evidenced from the documents. For example, after I began writing the historical novel *The Firekeeper*, I wanted to see what had really happened in the Battle of Lake George in 1755, when a thoroughly nonconventional army of colonial militia and Iroquois commanded by Johnson and Mohawk ally Hendrick Tehayanoken routed crack French troops accompanied by a much larger host of Natives. I flew on the wings of Hawk over the battlefield—lost today among theme parks and resort developments—and watched the action unfold in its own time. One thing I noticed was that the officer in charge of Johnson's cannons was wearing a Scots bonnet (the polite Mohawk term for which translates as "piece of shit on his head"). When I returned from my time travel, the history professor in me muttered that this could not be correct. The English had just been slaughtering Scots highlanders at Culloden; surely no officer in the *English* army would be preening in a highlander's bonnet. So I took my history professor back to the books, and we turned up the interesting fact that Captain Eyres, the Englishman who was Johnson's gunnery commander in the Battle of Lake George, had actually been one of those responsible for mowing down highlanders with cannons at Culloden. We recognized that a certain kind of Englishman, proud of his superiority over a foe armed mostly with swords and pikes, might have sported a souvenir of his victory.[2]

I won't turn this into a lengthy disquisition on dream archaeology, although that is a discipline worth recognizing and practicing. Suffice it to say that I traveled across time intentionally and brought back accurate information going far beyond prior knowledge. I am satisfied that what I am about to report from Island Woman's life is true to her essential story, though I cannot footnote all of it.

DREAM TRACKER

She is born in the Peacemaker's country, in a northern land of lakes and islands and endless virgin forests where the earth is blanketed in snow and ice for half the year.

She comes into this world in a Dark Time when her birth people, the Hurons, are scattered and depleted, having been ravaged by imported diseases and having lost a bloody war with the Iroquois cousins—a war promoted by the white man's greed for control of the lucrative trade in furs, the "black gold" of the colonies.

She is only five years old, living with her family in a bark lodge in one of the few surviving settlements of the Island People, called Hurons by the French. In the depth of midwinter, after blizzards that have piled snowdrifts as high as the spikes of the palisades in the fortified village on the lake, her people feel safe from enemy raiders.

But in the night, the girl is brought suddenly awake by an urgent messenger. She has snuggled for warmth in the hollow of her mother's back, under a fur robe. She stirs into alertness when she feels a presence. The shiny black pupils of her visitor's eyes, hugely enlarged for night vision, stare into her own from very close. The sleek dark fur brushes her naked skin. She knows this night hunter: sheering teeth and swaying haunches, moonshadows dappling his black pelt, an edge of amber around those obsidian pupils. She is not afraid of the panther. He is an oyaron, a dream ally who has helped her in the past, showing her things she could not have seen without his keen vision.

She goes with him without question, leaving her body effortlessly as if she were merely slipping out from under the sleeping robe. She shape-shifts into something lithe and fast. She follows the panther, right through the bark walls of the Huron lodge, and shoots above the snow-drifts and frozen lake.

Panther shows her what she needs to see and report to her people. Along the lakeshore, enemy raiders have built shelters of skins and spruce boughs. The spoonlike prints of their snowshoes stretch far away, toward the lands of the Iroquois. The enemy warriors are already stirring, masking their faces with charcoal and grease. They have shaved their heads, leaving only a high ridge of hair in the center. They look to her like the Dark Twin, gouging his way out of the body of Earth Holder. They are Kanienkehaka, People of the Flint. Other nations call them Mohawks, or Cannibals.

The Mohawks have rested without making fires to hide their approach from the sleeping village. They will strike before sunrise, running like wolves up the snowbanks that have made the walls of the Huron village useless for defense.

The girl hears the panther's hiss on the wind as she rushes home to rouse her mother. She gets back in her body and shakes her mother awake. Her mother believes her and wakes the men. They are drowsy and sluggish. They do not want to leave the comfort of the fire. One of her uncles growls that the girl is too young to know the difference between true dreams and tall tales.

The girl sobs and shakes in frustration. Why won't they listen? She won't go back to the sleeping mat. Her mother takes her, swaddled in furs, to a hunting cabin outside the village so the men can sleep. The Mohawks come over the walls, undetected, in the hour before dawn—the twilight of the wolf. They find the girl later and take her back to their own country, to the village of Two Rivers.

BECOMING THE WOLF

The Mohawks survive, as a people, by adopting enemy captives. Their prisoners come from the Hurons, the Mahicans, the French, and frontier drifters of mixed identity. They make those they adopt their own so completely that captives adopted into the Mohawk nation never want to return to their original communities.

The Mohawks accomplish this identity change through a spiritual operation called a condolence ceremony, the origin of which lies with Hiawatha, the Awakened One. During the condolence, the spirit of a Mohawk who has passed on is requickened in the person who is adopted, or, in the case of a chief, raised up to take the place of the departed person.

So Island Woman now has more souls than she had before. In her body is the heart-soul and breath-soul of a Huron girl, but she also houses the breath-soul and mind of a Mohawk. She will have no trouble whatsoever in getting out of the body or sending a part of her energy and consciousness to do things at a distance. She is more than one person. And she is something besides human, because the Mohawks also make her Wolf.

The matriarch of her adoptive family is of the Wolf Clan; she may even be the clan mother. *"Sakkwaho,"* she informs the girl. "You now belong to Wolf."

Now that she is Wolf, her sense of smell really comes alive. In the woods, through the freshness of pine and spruce and the sweetness of fireweed, she can pick up the scent of deer scat from miles away. She can distinguish hundreds of different smells. Her hearing is also keen; she can hear deer mice scuffling under crusted snow.

She can read herds, animal or human. She knows who is weak and who is strong, who is weary or sick, who will be the first to run. She recognizes the stiff-legged approach of the dominant male—every woman can see that—and can decipher whether this one is a true alpha or a wannabe.

She travels well; she can really go the distance.

If she falls into a meat frenzy, she has no table manners whatsoever.

She knows to hunt into the wind so her quarry won't smell her coming. Her hunting style is to start with the easiest prey. If she has to take on a big guy, she'll try to gather a whole pack to help out and will bring down that bull moose by running him all over the place, slashing at his sides, not going at him head-on.

THE TEACHER

She is singled out early by a powerful ratetshents, or dream shaman, of the Mohawk people.* He generally lives apart from the Mohawk castles—the fortified villages that were reconstructed along the north side of the Mohawk River after a French invasion burned the castles on the south side—among the limestone caves in what is now Schoharie County, New York.

This shaman's personal name is never said out loud by the Mohawks, because they believe that to say his name aloud will bring him, or one of his oyaron, to that spot. They call him Longhair. He is renowned for his duels with enemy war magicians and self-serving witches.[3] Even the black-robed priests are impressed by secondhand accounts of how he detected and slew a lineage of evil sorcerers by tracking and killing their animal familiars.

Longhair, like all shamans of great power, works with many animal allies—predators and herbivores, burrowers and swimmers, fliers and creepers. He mentors Island Woman, as she grows, by sending her animal guides to show her what she needs to see.

She flies from her body to attend shaman school with him in the middle of the night, in his big cave under the Noses—where the river is pinched between limestone bluffs—in an area most people generally avoid because rattlesnakes abound in the high grass on top.

Longhair instructs the shaman-to-be: "You must visit the upper and lower worlds. You must journey to the land of souls and speak with your ancestors. You must know your spirit guides and your animal guardians, and how to summon and feed them.

---

* *Ateteshents* (feminine) or *ratetshents* (masculine) means literally "one who dreams"—that is, one who dreams profusely, embarks on conscious dream journeys, can travel across time and space in dreaming, and can enter the dreamspace of others to heal and to guide. The word can simply be translated as "dreamer." But it also means "shaman," "healer," and "doctor."

"You will be required to confront many powerful adversaries, because the dark always follows the light. You can only overcome these opponents if you refuse to *become* them. If you win by acting as they do, then you have lost everything.

"Never forget that the Real World cannot be seen with ordinary eyes, and that in the Real World there is only *now*. When you have done this, when your courage is proven, you will be an atetshents, one who dreams. When you awaken to *who you are*, you will be an arendiwanen, a woman of power."

RAISING A WOMAN

As she grows into womanhood, Island Woman is guided by women through the rites of passage. We'll jump forward to the time when Island Woman is grown and the mother of two girls, because I see her clearest later in life, above all as the wise woman who has survived countless winters and is fully at home outside time.

Among a people renowned for the ferocity of their warriors, the women rule the men. They raise up the chiefs and dehorn them when they neglect their duties.

Island Woman knows that women need to be strong. She makes her daughters run until they are exhausted, and beyond. She makes them run underwater, creek water lapping at their thighs. She makes them run backward. She makes them run through the woods without breaking a twig, without ruffling the fallen leaves.

When her favorite daughter is three, Island Woman takes her down to the river, ties her by the waist to a tree stump, and orders her to swim upstream, defying the mighty currents.

If her daughter disobeys, Island Woman might use her voice. She can yell hard enough to shake the bark roof off the lodge. Or she might take a swallow of water and blow it in a fine spray over her daughter's face, to cool her off, when she is small and a wild ball of energy, and, as her body grows straight and tall, to shame her.

But Island Woman also knows you must never set out to scare children more than is needed. You can frighten a child's soul right out of the body. If you scare or hurt a child badly enough, its soul might leave and go far away, and then that child will develop that dull look in the eyes, the soul-gone look of a person who is missing a vital part of his or her being. And then you will need an atetshents in a hurry, to go hunting that soul through the neverlands and try to put it back in the body.

In their moontime, in Island Woman's village, Mohawk women live apart from men, eating from sacred vessels. This is not because they are considered unclean, but because this is a time of overflowing power, when orenda must be carefully directed. It is the time when women return their blood to Earth Woman, whose blood fed the world when she gave birth to the Twins.

When her daughter Bright Meadow shows signs of her first period—when the cramping begins, low down in her belly, and she smells the blood—Island Woman takes her out to a cabin in the woods. She gives her a special bowl and shows her how to sit up straight, with her knees pressed up against her belly. She gives her soft strips of moss and a fat little clay pot with a bulge like a belly button.

Bright Meadow asks, "Why must we stay apart from the village for four whole nights? Is it because we are unclean?"

Island Woman laughs. "Men say such things, because they are afraid. This is our time of power. You now own the power that allows women to bring new life into the world. We give thanks to the Mother by returning our blood to the place from whence it comes.

"You will give your first blood to the Three Sisters* to thank them for supporting our life.

"This is the beginning of all sacrifice. This offering is sacred and acceptable to the Mother beyond all others, because it comes without killing. This power is something that belongs only to women. That is why men are afraid. Men can offer blood only by hunting and killing." She shows her daughter how to catch her blood in the rounded pot, and how to return it to the earth among the seeded rows of the Three Sisters.

During the night, Island Woman retells the stories that explain the nature of birth and why the bloodlines of the Real People are always traced on the mother's side. The stories draw the listener into the Real World.

"Woman is the life bringer. Man helps to make the path into the body for the soul that is coming here—but the true father is the spirit guide that escorts the incoming soul and introduces it into the body. *Tohsa sasa nikon'hren.* Do not forget this."

---

*Corn, beans, and squash

DREAM SCOUTS FOR THE COMMUNITY

People know Island Woman dreams true. When she tells a dream involving something that may happen in the future to another person, or may affect the well-being of the whole community, everyone listens very carefully. Then the elders and the grandmothers confer to clarify what action must be taken.

When Island Woman dreams the coming of a party of enemy raiders from the headwaters of the Susquehanna, the warriors are summoned. They question Island Woman to discover the exact path the enemies are following. Then they set up an ambush and destroy the raiders before they can ravage Mohawk land.

In the starving time in deep winter, Island Woman travels in the shape of a bird or on the racing legs of a timber wolf to find where the deer are yarding so she can give precise directions to the hunters on where they must go to bring back the meat and hides the people must have for their survival.

She has to get these things right. The Mohawks are a great people in power and reputation, but they are small in numbers. The loss of a single Mohawk life—as a Frenchman noted—is equivalent to the death of fifty members of a neighboring nation. Dreaming true is one of the things that keeps the Mohawks alive.

To ensure the survival of her people, Island Woman must dream bigger. Every day, white settlers are pushing deeper and deeper into Iroquois territory. Already the beaver has all but disappeared from the lands of the Six Nations. Bears are now seldom seen. Even the deer are fewer in number from year to year. And everywhere the Tiorhensaka—the People from the Sunrise—go, they carry axes and chains and torches to bring down the trees and make room for their cash crops and pastures.

Island Woman crosses dimensions to talk to a guide, a being even wiser than Longhair. She asks the great one, "Can a man be found among the newcomers who will defend our people as well as his own?"

"He will come."

"How will we know him?"

"He will know our ways as if born to them. *Rarenye's*—he spreads his energy around. You will feel the life force that is in him. It will make the earth tremble. He will dance with you, sing with you, run with you.

He will know your women. . . . When he comes, he will be like the other white men, except more powerful and more dangerous. Until you make him your own."

"How can we do this?"

"There is one who is the way."

She is dreaming of William Johnson. The Mohawks will make him their own. Before he ever holds an appointment with the British government, the Mohawks will adopt him and put a part of their own spirit inside him. He will never leave them to live in a tamer country and bask in his money and titles. And he will be joined to a beautiful young woman, Island Woman's granddaughter.

DREAMING BEYOND THE WHITE DEATH

Let's jump ahead to the time when Island Woman has become the mother of the Wolf Clan, and Molly Brant is charming William Johnson off his horse. He has won the Battle of Lake George, where his friend Hendrick fought and died, and for which victory a distant government will make him a baronet.

Kohseren—in the dead of winter, when the Dark Twin reigns— Johnson's best surviving friends among the Mohawks are dying of a white man's disease: smallpox. Hendrick's brother Abraham, the chief of the Mohawk castle at Canajoharie, and Seth, the chief at Schoharie, are both killed by smallpox that winter.[4] Wherever they look, Johnson and Island Woman see their friends and family swaying with fever, faltering, bursting into pustules and itching rotting flesh—and being carried off in old blankets or bark coffins. Grieving, Johnson is handing out black belts of wampum to cover the graves and strings of wampum to wipe away the tears, and clear the throats, and open the clouds in the day so the sun can shine again, and open the clouds at night so the moon and stars can be seen. But Mohawks go on dying—not only the chiefs and warriors Johnson has relied on, but the memorykeepers, the wise ones, the elders and grandmothers who remember the sky.

And the war goes on. It's a world war, between the British and French empires, known in the colonies as the French and Indian War. The British victory—to which Johnson and his Iroquois allies contribute mightily— will determine that North Americans (for the most part) will learn English rather than French, and it will clear the way for the American Revolution.

The French go away (until Lafayette comes to exact their revenge), but the Indians who sided with the French rather than the English are not inclined to lie down and let the English colonists take their lands. So a new frontier war erupts, which old guard historians call the Pontiac Rebellion. An English general, Sir Jeffery Amherst, allows his men to distribute hospital blankets infected with smallpox to kill off the "hostiles." This is a deliberate act of genocide, one that almost certainly spread the infection to "friendlies" as well, and probably to whites, too.[5]

Johnson is furious. The Mohawks tell him they are dreaming that the white death will return and carry off more of their people than before. Johnson looks at the beautiful Mohawk woman he has made his consort, now the mother of several of his children. He cannot stand to think of her lovely face disfigured by pockmarks, or of his children turning the color of faded silver and moaning their hearts out in the night.

He finds a way to protect his family, his Mohawk friends, and their neighbors in the Mohawk Valley. It is a way that was known to some men in the colonies but had been firmly rejected by most physicians as too dangerous.

I read in one history book after another that Molly Brant had been disfigured by smallpox. This claim was based on one document in the papers of Daniel Claus, Johnson's son-in-law and deputy in the department of Indian affairs. One of Johnson's biographers paraphrased the relevant passage as follows: "Claus wrote as an old man that Molly had been ugly and pitted with smallpox."[6]

I had a violent reaction to this statement. I knew it was simply not true—and that Claus would never have expressed himself along these lines. My friend Wanda Burch volunteered to check for Claus's remark in the original manuscript, available on microfilm from the National Archives of Canada in Ottawa. The handwriting was difficult to decipher, but as she puzzled over it Wanda realized it had been misread. Although a couple of words remained obscure, she was able to make a corrected transcription that revealed that Claus was actually saying that *he,* not Molly Brant, was the one who had contracted smallpox.[7] So Molly Brant's beautiful face did indeed stay unblemished.

Why did she, and many of the Mohawks, survive the terrible epidemics of the 1760s? Because William Johnson had them inoculated. Knowledge of inoculation came to the New World from Africa, not Europe. Cotton Mather and a doctor friend in Boston conducted experiments after they noticed a slave with inoculation scars. But, when a superstitious mob firebombed the doctor's house, the medical establishment in the colonies decided that inoculation was too dangerous to be tried.[8]

In my dreams, I felt Island Woman reaching beyond her time, scouting for the ways to help her people survive. I shared her grief as she watched a loved one die. She walked through my mind, telling me what it is to be the burden strap, to carry the weight of the nation, from the ancestors down to those whose faces are under the ground.

I dreamed of Johnson, too, trying to construct the apology for his life, trying to return the immense gifts he had received from the Iroquois, seeking to preserve his beloved Molly's unblemished face.

And I dreamed, again and again, of a black man walking into the valley, a black man who loved the spirits and was loved by them, a man who had been a babalao among his own Yoruba people in West Africa and knew something they did not yet know in the Valley of the Mohawks: how to tame the white death.

I saw Johnson, the war maker, and Island Woman, the healer, come together. I saw Johnson having himself inoculated in front of the Mohawks—most importantly in front of Island Woman—to demonstrate that this operation was to heal, not harm.[9] In that moment, the woman of power sees that William Johnson belongs to her people, as well as the people from whom he sprang on a small island across a great ocean.

Is this actually how inoculation came to the Mohawk country? The answer is not in the documents. And there is no record—because Johnson did not write such things down, and the Iroquois did not use writing as we know it—of dreamers folding time and bringing an answer to smallpox from the future. But we do have confirmation from Jesuit reports that the Iroquois regularly sent out their dream trackers to scout across time and space and provide vital information. It is not altogether wild speculation that this people of dreams might have applied their dreaming skills to taming the white death.

Maybe that is one reason Island Woman called to me: not because I have any great medical knowledge, but because I am capable of looking things up and making things up. Dream shamans know the value of making things up. Tell the body a story it can believe, and you can make it well. Come up with fresh words, and you can bring new creations sprouting and bursting into the physical world. Thoughts are things, even in the Earth-below-the-Sky.

13

The Dreamworld
Is the Real World

*The dream world is your home. Your spirit came here from
the dream world before you had a body, and it will return
to the dream world when you leave your body behind.*

ISLAND WOMAN

To interpret, in the Mohawk language, is to transplant something from
one bed of earth to another. You have to be careful not to damage the
roots, and you must make sure that the living plant has the water and
humus it needs to keep it strong. The teachings in this chapter are those
of Island Woman, but I have transplanted them into English. I have kept
some Mohawk and Huron terms that are an essential part of her spiritual
vocabulary, and I invite us to enlarge our own vocabulary to enter into
her world, which is not fixed in linear time. I am not channeling here;
these are some of the fruits of a very active collaboration in transplanting
things that Island Woman wants us to know. If I have misrepresented her
thoughts in any way, I am sure she will let me know.

You're Not Really Alive If You're Missing Your Animal Spirits

If we are not in touch with our animal spirits, we don't know how to be in our bodies or how to feed them.

Everybody is born with a soul in the wild, an animal double. That animal soul can move from one animal body to another, which is a good thing because animals usually have shorter lives than humans, or their lives are cut short. The needs of that animal are *your* needs. If that animal is a meat eater and you don't eat meat, you are going to get sick. If that animal is a runner and you never get off your butt, you are going to get sick.

As you grow in power, you will meet other animal guardians. A true person of power, an arendiwanen, has many animal guardians, and when they are not traveling around, they live in power objects and in power centers inside her body. I keep some pretty big packs and herds of animals in my solar plexus, because I need extra to give to people who have lost their own animal spirits, maybe because they forgot to feed them, maybe because they chose a tame life and the animal spirits became disgusted with them.

One of the quickest ways to boost people's orenda is to put an animal spirit inside them. I usually do this by blowing that animal power into a certain part of their body. If it's a hunting animal, I'll probably put it into the solar plexus. If it's a deer or a fish, I may put it down in the sex center; that will get things alive and juicy! If it's a hawk or an eagle, I'll put it into the third eye, because the gift of the great birds is vision. We say the Peacemaker put the eagle on top of the Tree of Peace because the eagle sees many looks away and can warn people of what is coming long before it gets to them.

Some of the kids still go vision questing to get an

oyaron. To go out in the wilderness by yourself, to fast and stay up all night and know fear are good things. A powerful oyaron won't bother with anyone who isn't brave enough to face him and claim his power, and we come into knowing by being alone with the spirits. But there are powerful callings that are announced when we are sleeping in our regular space. We may think we are hunting the spirits, but it's usually the other way round. They are hunting *us*, which is why they can always be found. Especially in dreams.

It's All About Soul

The most important thing to know about humans is that they have souls, and that everybody starts out with more than one soul or else they wouldn't be human.

The world is getting into trouble because a lot of people have lost one or more of their souls. Sometimes, when that happens, a dark spirit gets in—something that does not belong to you—and makes you do crazy things you would never do if you belonged to yourself. Most often the soul-gone just move into the endless procession of the walking dead. They don't feel anything truly anymore. They don't remember that their life has any meaning beyond the little pleasures and pains they experience from day to day.

There are hollow men all around us on this side of death and on the other. There are more and more lost souls that don't know where they are supposed to go or even that they are dead. They roost on the living, trying to hang on to what is familiar, trying to get another taste of whatever they craved when they had bodies.

This is making many people sick. It's not healthy to go around in the company of your dead all the time, especially if you are not even aware that they are there. They'll weigh you down. They'll confuse your thinking. You'll be stirred by feelings that are not your own. Your body can even take on the symptoms of a dead person who is traveling in your energy field.

Now, we believe in honoring the ancestors. We know that the ancestors are the true heads of the families, and we look for counsel from the great ones who chose to stay close to this earth when they died. But we never make the mistake of confusing the *ohskenrari* (the hungry ghost) with the *o'nikon:ra* (mind or higher spirit) of a great one who is trying to guide and protect.

Your world is in more danger than you know because you have lost the knowledge of soul. If you are going to make it through, you are going to have to recover the art of putting souls back in the bodies where they belong. And you are going to need to remember and work with the fact that when we die, more than one part of us survives, and those different parts need to be handled differently. Some of them need a safe place to be, close to this earth. Some of them need to be fed with the smoke of burning meat or tobacco. Some of them need to be guided to another body. Some of them need to be reminded of the path of strawberries that leads back to the Sky World.

You can't know these things just because someone tells you about them. You can only know by going there and experiencing the other side for yourself. That is why dreaming is so important. It shows us where the soul is, and it opens the road for the soul to come home.

There is more. Through dreaming, we recover the knowledge of our sacred purpose that belonged to us before we came into our present bodies. Then we can begin to live from our sacred purpose and unite ourselves to the powers of creation. We can also begin to get in touch with other members of our soul families who live in other places and times.

My teacher showed me a map of the soul's journey. It

doesn't end. You land in a womb, and you end up in the womb of rebirth. The challenge is to be conscious of what you are doing so you don't just go on repeating the same mistakes over and over.

Unless you dream, you'll never be fully awake. In the Shadow World, we go around like sleepwalkers. In big dreams, we wake up.

Big Dreams

Dreams that are wishes of the soul (when they are true dreams as well as wishes) can tell you that you need something you didn't know you needed, or something you denied wanting because you felt ashamed for wanting it.

Big dreams tell you more.

When you go walking in your dreambody, you can see things that are many looks away, things that can save your life. You can find where the deer are yarding in the starving time. You can see where your enemies are lying in ambush along the trail.

When your dreamsoul goes flying, it visits the future and brings back memories of things that haven't happened yet in the Shadow World. Sometimes you can stop those things from coming to pass. Sometimes you just have to live them out. Sometimes you can tame a future you don't want by acting out a little piece of it, enough to contain the event that is trying to come through.

Life is full of crossroads. Often you don't even notice them until they are behind you, unless you know how to dream. Through dreaming, you can scout out the different trails you might follow and see where they lead. Through dreaming, you are already choosing the events that will take place in your waking life.

The more conscious you are, the more practiced in hunting and catching dreams, the more you can accomplish. You can even find out who you are. Without a big dream, it is impossible to know this. During big dreams, your dreambody goes wandering and your oyaron—your spirit guide—can speak to you.

You might visit the great ones, or one of them might call on you, which is usually the way it happens the first time. Your guide might send you an animal or a bird to get you out of your body so you can begin to *see*. You might be called to a place of power, a place in the dreaming to which you can return, to receive initiation and training.

You will come to know that you have counterparts in the Real World. These beings appear in different forms. Some of them are people who are connected to you in other places and times. Some of them are your own greater self, as it becomes known to you.

When you have changed your eyes and your senses so you can see and experience the great ones as they truly are, they will give you songs of power so their energy can flow through you and touch and heal others.

When you start living with that power in the Shadow World, you are no longer like other people. You see their subtle bodies. You see the colors of their feelings. You see when a part of their soul is missing, or when something has been shot inside them that is causing pain and sickness. You see when the unhappy dead are roosting on their shoulders. You see when their beautiful child selves, lost through pain or abuse, go flitting through the air like lightning bugs.

And you want to help them. Although you are no longer like other people, your heart is open and your compassion streams to them. You know that everything is related, and that what harms another harms something everywhere in the world.

The life force, orenda, flows through everything. It

binds the universe. It gathers in some places that are natural accumulators: an old oak, a mountain, a stone. Some
people are charged with it; they light up a whole village.
You can feel their energy before you meet them. They
are not blocking themselves; their energy centers are all
connected. They can put the little day mind, with its
noise and clutter, on one side, and let the great ones
through. They can make themselves hollow bones for
spirit to work through.

Dreaming Is Traveling

If you can just remember a place beyond the Shadow
World—maybe a place you visited in a dream—you are
halfway there. If you can recall the place in vivid detail
and enter it fully, with your mind and your inner senses,
you *are* there.

The memory of a dream is the memory of a journey. It
may have been a short visit to a neighbor's place or a
date with the lover you will meet three years from now. It
may have been a journey to the spirits on the moon, or
into a universe inside a stone that is as big as the universe out there.

When you hold on to the dream, or let it gently return,
a road opens before you. Move toward the dreamspace,
and you travel between the worlds. Step fully inside the
dream, and you are there.

Dreams Require Action

There is limitless power and beauty and healing available
to us in the dreamworlds. To keep body and soul
together in the surface world—and to live from the pur-

poses of the soul—we need to bring that dream energy through. This requires action in the Shadow World.

The first part of that action may be speech, but not the chatter of idle birds or village gossips. The speech required is an *act* that brings something new into a world. Dreaming gives us the songs and the magic words that can bring something up from a soupy ocean of possibilities to take root in the earth. That is why real men and women of power are poets, singers, storytellers, performers. With skeins of song and dancing needles of magic words, they reweave the fabric of reality.

When we do this, we know that we are entertaining the spirits: our own vital spirits, the spirits of the ancestors, the great ones who reach to us from beyond space and time, the ancient and shining ones.

Nothing happens until it is dreamed. When we bring something good from the dreamworld into the surface world, we do the work of the Creator. We join in dancing a world into being, as Sky Woman danced on Turtle's back.

On Sorcery

Power can be used either way. You have to choose. The Dark Twin is a tempter, coming on to you like an elk in rutting season, telling you that you'll be the one everyone will fear and admire. And he'll touch something inside you, because there is nobody human who doesn't have something of the dark side within him or her. Try to deny that, and you'll find yourself fighting half the universe—and the dark side may swallow you while you are shouting that you are all about the light.

Like Longhair warned me, since I became a woman of power I've had to fight sorcery in many guises. The war magic of our enemies was not the worst of it. Jealous rage was behind the worst attacks. It's there at the beginning, in the battle between the Twins. The Dark Twin just can't stand it that it's his brother who has the power to create, to give life with his breath. There are people like that: if they can't do better than you, they are going to try to bring you down. If you let jealousy get away from you, it goes around like a hissing serpent, like an evil spirit. I knew a woman who always seemed sweet and mild, but the jealousy she was hiding grew so strong it got as big as Thadodaho's penis-snake. When she let it out, it could twist your mind and make you sick if you weren't protected.

Sorcerers might work with a little cornhusk doll or a rag doll, give it your name, put something of you inside it and around it, and do things to it to hurt you or control you. A love sorcerer will try to make you so hot for the man who has hired him that you've got to go to that man and present yourself like a bitch in season. A death sorcerer will try to pull your breath-soul out of your body and keep it captive or confused until you weaken and sicken and finally pass over.

But sorcery happens all the time, even when the people responsible aren't thinking about it and might never intend to intrude or do harm. You think of somebody and you touch them, unless they have shielded themselves so you can't get through. You feel for somebody and you can go right into their space, right inside their soul. Or you can call them to you. There is an energy cord between us and everyone who has ever entered our lives. Sometimes it's as wide as a road, and the two of you are traveling back and forth to visit each other all the time. That's how I knew what was going on with my daughters. I felt it right away, in my heart or my gut, and then I would *look* to see which of them was in trouble, or feeling something deeply, and whether they needed my help. The link was so strong I would know when one of them was having sex, because I would start having spasms in my own body.

When we wake up to the fact that our thoughts touch the people we are thinking about, we are again asked to choose which thoughts we send out. If we send out the thoughts of the heart, we can heal, even if the person who needs healing is far away. If we send out the thoughts of rage and envy, we can hurt that person just as if we were shooting nails or darts. I got a man I healed to puke up a bucketful of rusty nails that had been put into him by his enemies. Some of them came from the woman he once lived with. You couldn't see those nails unless you had the sight, but they were there, as real as the nails in a house.

Dreams often tell us when sorcery is going on. A woman dreamed that someone who pretended to be her friend was sending poisonous bugs to attack her. When she woke up, there was a hole in her skin where something had bitten her. She took the warning and closed herself so that person couldn't work on her mind.

A man dreamed he had amazing sex with a woman he found unattractive in waking life. He started following her around like a dog in season, and he started thinking about leaving his wife and kids. Then he dreamed that he was watching her strip, squeezing her breasts and shaking her ass like a trade woman, and he was chanting about how beautiful she was and how he would never be able to get it up with anyone but her. And the man saw that in the same room was the sorcerer we called Stump, directing the whole operation. They were trying to rule his mind, and his penis, and they might have succeeded—but for the dream.

True dreams warn us about problems like this, but false dreams can be part of the problem. Our best healers and our worst sorcerers are both dream senders. Someone who wants to harm you, or has been hired by someone to do that, will try to send evil thoughts into your head, the kind that fill you with fear and make you sick. If they can't get through to you, they may try to get at you through other people, putting out false dreams that they pass on to you, dreams in which you are sick or shamed or defeated, images that make you want to stay in bed all day.

The best way to protect yourself against evil intentions is to cut the link between you and the sender. There is always a link of some kind. It may be an object you have taken into your home, maybe a gift. It may be something of yours the sorcerer has taken. Or it might simply be a psychic connection that was established when you spent time together.

Then you are going to want to choose where you put the energy of your attention. In any of the challenges of life—not just if you are under psychic attack—you do *not* want to give energy to fear or unhappy images.

We must always remember that we are not alone: help is available if we ask for it. If you have a good relationship with the animal powers, they will take care of most energy intruders. But the animal guardians have to be fed and exercised. If you don't feed her the meat she needs, your Wolf may not be there when you need her. If you never let yourself fly, and look at the world from a higher perspective, you are not using the vision of Hawk, and she may fly off somewhere else.

The Burden Straps

When I was a kid, we never talked about them. It was all a secret, and the men were jealous because they wanted to run the big medicine societies.

The burden straps were the real women of power, the ones who put their gifts at the service of the people and weren't just about getting something for themselves or working a love charm or a witching spell for someone who hired them.

When I was initiated, they showed me an old-timer's *ahsha:ra*, a strap woven from the bark of slippery elm. Have you ever touched that bark? It's tough but soft at the same time, and it's not too hard to braid. The one I was shown was woven from twenty cords laid down lengthwise. There were fine, long moose hairs in the cross-weave, dyed in bright colors, making a sacred story.

We all knew what it meant. Any Mohawk woman could tell you, when we still knew how to make things the old way. A burden strap is passed around the forehead and lashed to a pack or litter. You use it to haul things that support life. Maybe you use it to carry life itself, in the shape of a baby in a cradle board used to carry all that was precious, all that supported life. Our Grandmother Ataensic, in the Sky World, pulled an impossible burden, with the aid of a burden strap, to feed all her people.

This is what is asked of a woman who becomes an ahsha:ra. You must be cleansed by fire and water, smudged and swept from the soles of the feet to the crown of your head. Your energy field must be combed with song. Your courage will be tested in places of fear, as you drop blindfolded into a tunnel in the earth. Your spirit supporters will be made to reveal themselves.

If you want to get in on this, you are crazy. Understand what waits for you if you are accepted. You will take up the burden. You will be poorer than all others, because the weight of their need will be on your back all your days and nights.

Calling the Dragon

I don't talk about my animal double, because it scares people. It doesn't live on the surface of the earth. It lives in deep waters, because its breath could set the world on fire. The night I came into this world, my mother saw it coming down from the sky, trailing a long tail of white flame. When the men talk about this being, they try to say that it is always male. They are scared of its power, and they want to get that power and keep it for themselves. The truth is there are very few men who can hold this power. It makes them crazy. It blows them apart. It darkens their minds and turns them to the dark side.

A man who can raise the Fire Dragon and hold its power does not come along very often, and when he does you had better get down and watch him very, very carefully. He could be a world destroyer or a world protector. He is going to shake the earth. You know him from far away because he spreads his energy. Women can't sit still when they feel the sexual force in him.

I called the Dragon, when our world was beginning to die, and he came in the shape of a man with laughing eyes from an island in a cold northern sea. When he entered the valley, I was afraid I had made a terrible mistake, because he was like the other newcomers, drinking and fucking and grabbing what he could get—except that his appetites were insatiable, and wherever they led him, people yielded to his will, because of his tremendous life force. Our women were in heat for him, fighting one another to get into his bed. When the war drums sounded, he called our warriors to follow him into battle on behalf of a distant king, and the hungry ghosts flocked to his colors, drawn by the smell of blood and firewater.

Call the Dragon, and you have to find a way to make him your own, so the world does not burn.

❧

14

Sisters of the Stones

Her eyes are spiral paths; the gyre of creation whirls
And sends me in green beauty to marry the worlds
"EYES OF THE GODDESS"

I was close to completing this book when Island Woman amazed me by stepping into my mind and telling me: "You came to me through the Eyes of the Goddess, through a portal you rediscovered in Ireland. This was no accident. The Sisters of the Stones are always watching, across time and space, seeking men who can be awakened and drawn to our purpose, which is to defend the body of Earth and the women who are its life bringers.

"We have tracked you across other lifetimes. You remember this in your dreams."

I wrote down the words as carefully as I could, and I backed them up on a disk, because I have noticed that when we get close to the big stuff, computers, and other electrical systems, can run amok.

And I sat stunned. *Of course.* I remembered the sequence better now. I dreamed of someone larger than human, a being "by whom the worlds are shaken." I found both William Johnson and myself—and others—in the coils of his story. I went to Ireland in quest of Johnson, and I found something more than the handsome stone house among the paddocks and weeping beeches, or even the lovely Boyne Valley with its memories of swanning Angus, the love-god, and the high holy hill of Tara, and the delight of bluebells under the greens of hedgerows. I found Newgrange, and the Eyes of the Goddess. And on the night Island Woman called me, unmistakably, into her dreaming, I was fooling around in the twilight zone and had just hit upon the idea of traveling through the portal of that double spiral I had seen on a guardian stone.

I went through a portal from the world of my European ancestors and into the realm of an ancient America. I had not understood, until Island Woman told me, the depth and currency of the connection. She had just announced to me not only that she was a Mohawk shaman and clan mother who had lived in Johnson's time, but also that she belonged to a sisterhood of seers and priestesses who operate in various times and places—and were taking an interest in me.

The rest of that story must wait for another book. The most important thing to be done in this book, now, is to provide tools for reclaiming the dreamways, and their paths to healing and soul remembering.

PART FOUR

RECLAIMING THE ANCIENT DREAMWAYS

In psychology one possesses nothing unless one has experienced its reality. A purely intellectual insight is not enough, because one knows only the words and not the substance of the thing from the inside.

C.G. JUNG, *AION*

If the soul is strong, the images are clear and the dream does not require interpretation...If a soul is so strong that sensible objects are powerless to turn it aside from the activity that corresponds to its proper nature...it perceives in the waking state what others perceive in dreams.

AVICENNA

It is safer to wander without a guide in unmapped country than to trust completely a map traced by men who came only as tourists and often with biased judgment.

MARIE-LOUISE SJOESTEDT, *GODS AND HEROES OF THE CELTS*

Western education predisposes us to think of knowledge in terms of factual information...By contrast, within the indigenous world the act of coming to know something involves a personal transformation.

F. DAVID PEAT, *BLACKFOOT PHYSICS: A JOURNEY INTO THE NATIVE AMERICAN UNIVERSE*

15

Turtle Woman Comes Looking for a Dreamer

*The Dunne-za assume that events can take place only after
people have known and experienced them in myths, dreams
and visions. . . . All persons continually bring the world
into being through the myths, dreams and visions they
share with one another.*
ROBIN RIDINGTON, *TRAIL TO HEAVEN: KNOWLEDGE
AND NARRATIVE IN A NORTHERN NATIVE COMMUNITY*

On a clear, bright day at the end of January 2001, when the snow lay
in huge drifts along the road and ice coated the hardwoods, I drove to
Still Point, a small retreat center near Saratoga Springs, New York, to
lead a program called Dreaming at Midwinter. For many years, it had
been my practice to come here, to a place of peace on traditional
Mohawk land, around the time of the Iroquois midwinter festival—
when dreams are played out and Sapling's energy is called back—to

honor the ancient ones and their dreamways. When I arrived, I set up a simple altar in the center of the meeting house, with objects representing the powers of the four elements and the powers of spirit.

In the middle of the altar cloth, next to the candle, I placed a large Iroquois rattle constructed from the shell of a snapping turtle. Through the magic of synchronicity, this turtle rattle had come into my keeping soon after I started dreaming in the Mohawk language. It is very large: the carapace is fourteen inches long and about ten inches wide, and the head and extended neck together measure ten inches. On the underside, the four-pointed star of the plastron is clearly visible. I had known, since I first held it, that this rattle—which was probably constructed in the early 1800s—is very powerful and should never be used in a casual way. I had taken it to a public gathering only once before. I had used it on that occasion only as a focus for meditation as we discussed the Iroquois belief that our world rests on Turtle's back.

I noticed that our group was quite large that morning. Thirty people were spreading cushions and rugs on the floor, forming a circle around the simple altar I had created. A large woodstove was crackling away. I fed a twist of tobacco to the coals, and as the smoke rose I thanked the ancient ones for their teachings and asked their blessing and protection. "*Aksothahi, raksothati*, grandmothers, grandfathers— we remember you. We honor you. We seek to walk in your paths of wisdom. We ask your blessing and protection on our journeys." The fire sighed and hissed. Just then, a group of four women, newcomers to the circle, walked in from the cold. I welcomed them and invited them to make themselves at home.

I began to drum for the group, inviting the participants to call up a dream—old or new, from sleep or waking or any place in between— that they might want to work with that day. I opened the circle with a statement of intention:

> *We come together in a sacred and loving way,*
> *to honor our dreams and the powers that speak to us in*
>   *dreams*
> *to honor our ancestors, and the First Peoples*
> *to defend earth and sea*
> *to walk the paths of soul and spirit in this lifetime*
> *with greater courage, clarity and compassion*
> *to be healed and to become healers*

> *to align ourselves with the Higher Self*
> *we come to remember*
> *who we are, where we come from*
> *and our sacred purpose in this life, and in other lives.*

With our hands joined, we called up earth energy from deep below, reaching down with our awareness through the foundations of the building, down through the frozen topsoil and rock, until we could feel the warmth and moisture of Mother Earth. We let the earth energy rise up through the soles of our feet, up through our legs and our lower energy centers. We let the energy pass hand to hand around the circle, growing a wheel of power. We sang songs to honor our Mother Earth— one of them came from my dreams—and a Mohawk song I had translated into English. The Mohawk song calls in the spirit of ohkwari, Medicine Bear, and with her all of the animal healers. It is a shaman song, and also a lullaby, used to comfort and bless troubled children in the night.

> *Don't cry little one*
> *Don't cry little one*
> *The bear is coming to dance for you*
> *The bear is coming to dance for you*

As we chanted the words together, we felt the delight of our inner children. We also became aware of the animal powers joining our circle.

The energy was coursing strong and deep around the circle. I asked people to park their energy for now and find comfortable places for their bodies while we shared our dreams and traveled into the dreamspace we would open. I held up my drum beater and announced that I was going to spin it and allow the play of synchronicity to show us who would be the first person to tell a dream to the circle.

I tossed the drumstick into the air. It whirled counterclockwise, the Iroquois path of creation. When it landed, it was pointing unmistakably at one of the newcomers who had arrived while I was offering tobacco to the spirits of the land.

She was a stocky woman of natural, unassuming dignity, wearing a dark blue long-sleeved dress that had a subdued floral pattern and was studded with silver brooches and pins. She introduced herself by saying, "I am a Mohawk grandmother and a healing woman. I am of the Turtle

Clan." I saw now that most of those silver brooches were turtles, and that she was also wearing a turtle necklace and turtle rings. Turtles all over.

"I come to you from Mohawk land, from the Six Nations reserve in Ontario. I have come to you with my friends because we have heard that you dream the way our ancient ones used to dream, and my people need to reclaim their dreaming. We have come to learn whether you can help us to bring back our dreaming."

I felt tremendous waves of energy streaming through my field, and I was moved almost to tears by her words.

"I have a dream to share," Turtle Woman continued. "It's a dream from thirty years ago in my life. I guess I'm a slow learner, because it took me fifteen years before I was ready to own that dream.

"In my dream, two Native guys knocked on the door of my place on the reserve. When I opened the door, they asked me if I had a turtle rattle. Sure, I told them. I'm Turtle Clan, I've got a turtle rattle. Get it for us, they told me. We want to use it while we teach you a healing song that will help your people.

"So I got my rattle and I gave it to them and they shook it while they danced around my house, singing a song of healing. When I woke, I could still hear that song vibrating in my room. It seemed like all the glass was shaking and chinking. But the dream began to fade, and the song went away. Pretty soon I couldn't remember it at all.

"Like I said, I'm a slow learner," she repeated modestly. "It took fifteen years before that dream was ready to come into my physical life. Fifteen years after the dream, two Native guys knocked on my door at the rez. They asked me if I had a turtle rattle. I guess I've been waiting for you, I told them. I guess you have, one of them said. So I fetched them my rattle, and they used it, and they taught me a healing song, and this time I remembered it."

She looked at me. With her eyes narrowed, and showing just the hint of a smile, she looked very much like a wise and ancient turtle. "Robert, I would like to give this song to you and your circle. Would it be okay if I used your turtle rattle?"

"Absolutely!" I hastily took it from the altar and placed it in her hands.

The Turtle Clan grandmother began to dance in a circle with amazing grace. As she snapped the huge rattle, it made a noise that sounded like thunderclaps inside our space. Her voice was shrill over us, chanting the song of healing, the song of orenda, the song of a woman of power. In that moment, the veil thinned, and even the least psychic person in the room felt and saw a gathering of the spirits of the land. Deer came to stand in the East, Hawk hovering above his antlers. Mountain Lion came prowling to the South, Raven and Wolf to the West, Bear to the North. Eagle watched over us from above, and from below rose the tremendous form of Great Turtle.

In telling her personal experience, and in sharing her dreamsong, Turtle Woman had given us a profound teaching about the nature of dreaming and its vital relationship to healing. She had reminded us not only that we dream things before they happen in waking life, but also that dreaming is part of the process of manifestation. In dreaming, we are present at the creation of the events that unfold in the surface world. She had also demonstrated, indelibly, that dreaming is real medicine and gives us tools for healing, of which one of the most powerful and practical is an authentic song of power.

Our whole day at Still Point was magical after that. Inspired by Turtle Woman's example, I asked the group to journey for their own songs of power, and many of our dreamers came back with songs in ancient languages—Gaelic, Hebrew, Ojibwa, Mohawk, and others—as well as wordless and primal chants that are sometimes the best wing songs (songs to journey by). Fueled by sound and story, on lent wings and with fleet legs and keener senses given us by the animal guardians, we embarked on many adventures in shared dreaming, crossing into one another's psychic space for adventure, guidance, and healing. Turtle Woman told us she herself received profound guidance and healing when she was able to travel back inside a dream and release some of her community she had seen trapped like deer with their legs frozen in the ice. She told us at the end of the day that one of the ways she intended to honor her dream experiences was to invite me to come to her healing center, on Mohawk land, to help her people to reclaim the ancient dreamways.

Around midwinter two years later, I drove through a blizzard in central New York and across the bridge at Niagara to the Six Nations reserve to teach the basic techniques of Active Dreaming to fifty Native Americans, many of them Mohawks. I was moved and honored to my core to be asked to reopen the ancient dreamways for the descendants of the dream shamans who had reopened them for me. My sense of an immense and beautiful time loop deepened as I sat in Turtle Woman's home over lunch with a lovely young woman who told me she was a direct descendant of Sir William Johnson and his Mohawk consort, Molly Brant. Inspired by my dreams of *them*—dreams so vivid I had little doubt that a timegate into an earlier life experience had opened—I had written about them, under the mask of fiction, in two historical novels. It seemed I was now well embarked on fulfilling a responsibility that had traveled with me from an earlier time.

I have a dream: that we will again become a society of dreamers. In a dreaming culture, dreams are valued and celebrated. The first business of the day for Island Woman and her people was to share their dreams and search them for guidance not only for the individual dreamers, but also for the community as a whole. They knew what modern people have forgotten: that the dreamworld is a *real* world, possibly more real than much of waking life, in which we often stumble about in the condition of sleepwalkers. They knew—and often owed their survival to this—that we dream the future, maybe all the time, and that nothing happens until it is dreamed. The following chapters offer some of the tools that can help us reclaim the powers of dream travel and dream healing.

16

The Shaman at the Breakfast Table

*A real dreamer is always hunting his power. He goes out
every night, like a hunter with a net, to stalk and catch
dreams. The more dreams he catches and brings home
alive, the more powerful he becomes.*

SHONNOUNKOUIRETSI, MOHAWK SHAMAN, IN *THE INTERPRETER*

Everyone who dreams is a little bit shaman. So say the Kagwahiv, a
dreaming people of Amazonia.[1] As we have seen, the Iroquois view is
more radical, from the perspective of our dream-deficient modern culture. The atetshents, the dreamer, *is* the shaman, and he or she may also
be the doctor and healer. To put it the other way around, a true shaman,
doctor, or healer is required to be a dreamer.

Think about what a tremendous invitation is contained in these
statements. If we tap into our dreams, and we find ways to bring their
guidance and magic into the waking world, we are on the path of the
shaman and healer. We have the material. It is there in the night—in the
dreams we may or may not remember—and it is all around us in waking

life, speaking to us in the manner of dreams when we pay attention.

Getting started is easy. We set the intention to seek dream guidance from the night *and* from the day. We make it our game to pay attention to what comes through in night dreams and in the symbols and synchronicities of waking life. We find a friend with whom we can share our experiences and who can help us devise an action plan to honor them. And we learn how to travel, wide awake and conscious, from the Shadow World to the Real World, through the gates opened by our dreams.

You say you don't have time for this in your stressed-out daily routine? Nonsense. You are about to learn a fresh and fun technique that will enable you to give or receive helpful feedback on dreams with just about anyone, anywhere, in ten minutes or less. You are about to be reminded that if you look at the incidents of everyday existence with fresh eyes, you may find that everything is alive with meaning, the gods are at play all around you, and you are being invited to recognize and navigate from a logic and order of events that is hidden from linear awareness.

LIGHTNING DREAMWORK FOR
EVERYDAY DREAM SHARING

As a society, we have been so estranged from dreaming that very few of us even know how to begin to talk about our dreams with other people. In telling our own dreams, we mix up the story, losing its power—and the attention of our audience—by bringing in unnecessary background information. In listening to other people's dreams, we often fail to give the undivided attention that dreams deserve—and when we comment on them, we often commit the error of trying to impose our own projections and associations, or we ask questions that violate the dreamer's privacy.

We need ways to make it easy, safe, and fun to share dreams with others. I have evolved a simple and powerful method for everyday dream sharing that I call Lightning Dreamwork. I chose this name because like lightning, this dreamwork is quick and also tends to focus extraordinary energy. You can do the whole process with a partner in ten minutes or less. This means that however busy our lives may be, we always have time to share our dreams.

The *way* we share our dreams is vitally important. Like Island Woman, we must not allow our dreams to be strangled by verbal analysis, losing their primal energy and magic. We must never presume to tell others what their dreams (or their lives) mean, and we must never use dream sharing as an excuse to pry into others' personal lives. We must always help one another celebrate our dreams and the powers that speak to us in dreams, and integrate their guidance into our relationships, choices, and life passages.

The Lightning Dreamwork process makes it possible to share dreams and receive helpful feedback just about anywhere: in the office, at the family breakfast table, or in the checkout line at the supermarket. You can share dreams with complete strangers or with that intimate stranger in your bed who may be the hardest person of all to speak with from the heart.

Let's assume you are going to do this with a single partner, and that the two of you will take turns playing dreamer and helper. The dreamer tells the dream; the helper guides the discussion and helps develop an action plan to honor the dream. Here are the four key steps in the process:

Step One: Tell the Dream as a Story with a Title

The dreamer tells the dream as simply and clearly as possible. The dreamer should always be encouraged to leave out his or her autobiography and simply tell the dream as a story, complete in itself. When we do this, we claim our power as storytellers and communicators. We also avoid the appearance of giving a license to others to probe into our personal lives, which must never be permitted in dream sharing.

The dreamer should always be encouraged to give the dream a title. It's amazing how the deeper meaning of dream experiences come into high relief when we do this.

Step Two: The Partner Asks Three Key Questions

If the dreamer has forgotten to give the dream a title, the partner should ask him or her to make one up. The next step is for the partner to ask three key questions:

Question 1. How did you feel when you woke up?

The dreamer's first emotional reactions to the dream are vital guidance on the basic quality of the dream and its relative urgency.

Question 2. Reality check

The reality check question is designed to establish whether the dream reflects situations in waking life, including things that might manifest in the future. Dreams often contain advisories it's important not to miss. By running a reality check, we help to clarify whether a dream is primarily (a) literal, (b) symbolic, or (c) an experience in a separate reality. In practice, the dreamer may need to ask several specific reality check questions focusing on specific elements in the dream. Here are a couple of broadbrush reality check questions that can be applied to just about any dream:

- Do you recognize any of the people or elements in the dream in waking life?
- Could any of the events in this dream possibly happen in the future?

Question 3. What would you like to know about this dream?

This simple question to the dreamer provides a clear focus for the next step.

Step Three: Playing the Game "If It Were My Dream"

Next the partner tells the dreamer, "If it were my dream, I would think about such-and-such." The partner is now free to bring in any associations, feelings, or memories the dream arouses, including dreams of his or her own that may contain similar themes. (Often we understand other people's dreams best when we can relate them to our own dream experiences.) For example, if the dreamer has told you a dream in which he or she is running away from a bear, you may recall a dream of your own in which you hid from a bear—before you discovered that the bear was an ally. Your own experience may lead you to say, "If it were my dream, I would like to go back into the dream and meet the bear again and see whether it might be an ally." In this way, you would be gently guiding the dreamer to take action on the dream.

It is very rewarding to receive a totally different perspective on a dream, so sharing in this way with strangers can be amazingly rewarding—as long as the rules of the game are respected.

Step Four: Taking Action to Honor the Dream

Finally the partner says to the dreamer, "How are you going to honor this dream?" or, "How are you going to act on the guidance of this dream?"

As I've said several times before, dreams require action. If we do not do something with our dreams in waking life, we miss out on the magic. Real magic consists of bringing something through from a deeper reality into our physical lives, which is why Active Dreaming is a way of natural magic—but only if we take the necessary action to bring the magic through. Keeping a dream journal and sharing dreams on a regular basis are important ways of honoring dreams and the powers that speak through dreams. But we need to do more. Here are some additional ways to honor dreams.

- *Write a bumper sticker from a dream experience.* This is always helpful. When we write a personal motto from a dream, we not only distill its teaching; we also begin to bring its energy through. I would love to see people driving around with dream bumper stickers on their fenders. Here are some bumper sticker examples from a dream-sharing session: Bring Kitty Home. Get to the Roots. Make Friends with Squirrels. The World Is Inside You. Unchained. Back to the Forest. I have a generic bumper sticker on my car: Wake Up and Dream.
- *Create from a dream.* Turn the dream into a story or poem. Draw from it, paint from it, turn it into a comic strip.
- *Take physical action.* Take physical action to celebrate an element in the dream, such as wearing the color that was featured in the dream, traveling to a place from the dream, or making a phone call to an old friend who showed up in the dream.
- *Create a dream talisman to hold the energy of the dream.* A stone or crystal may be a good place to hold the energy of a dream, and return to it.
- *Use the dream as a travel advisory.* If the dream appears to contain guidance on a future situation, carry it with you as a personal travel advisory. Summarize the dream information on an index card or hold it in an image you can physically carry.
- *Journey back inside the dream* to clarify details, begin a dialogue with a dream character, explore the larger reality—and have marvelous fun! See the section below, "The Dream Reentry Technique."
- *Share the dream with someone who may need the information.*

If you are sharing with a dreamer who can't come up with an action plan, you should suggest one.

Please note that this process is not meant to close out any of the multitude of other things you might want to do to explore and honor a dream. Some dreams require much longer and deeper exploration.

Some simply cannot be fathomed until a waking event catches up with the dream. But the Lightning Dreamwork gives you something fun you can do in a few minutes. And unlike so many analytical approaches, it alerts you to dream messages about the future that can support (and even save) your life, it orients you toward action, and it insists that the dreamer—and only the dreamer—is the final authority on his or her dreams.

When we have internalized the Lightning Dreamwork process and can guide people through it effortlessly, we are ready to operate as dream helpers and give something for which so many people hunger: a safe space in which to share and honor their sleep dreams and their life dreams.

NAVIGATING BY SYNCHRONICITY

Navigating by synchronicity—paying close attention to coincidence, chance encounters, the play of symbols all around us—is the dreamer's way of operating in waking life.

The epiphanies of life—those numinous moments when we glimpse the deeper reality behind the manifest world and derive insight into the larger meaning of our personal existence—come with the intersection of a hidden order of events with our seemingly linear progression through space and time. The grammar of epiphany is synchronicity, which Jung defined as "an acausal connecting principle."[2] Is there anyone who hasn't experienced a meaningful coincidence? If you become more closely attuned to these things, you will recognize in the workings of synchronicity a series of homing beacons.

The play of synchronicity can strengthen us in the determination to follow our deepest intuitions, even when they run counter to conventional wisdom and logic, and cannot be subjected to rational explanation. Like the exchange of handshakes between members of a secret fraternity, these signals alert us to the fact that we are not alone, that we have invisible sources of support, and that we are on the right course even when the whole world seems to be going the other way.

You can invite synchronicity to be your guide by putting your question to the world. Say there is a special theme on which you would like guidance, or a question in your life that needs an answer. You can carry that question or theme in your mind (and maybe on a piece of paper) and play this game: the first unusual or striking thing that enters your field of perception will be guidance to you from the world, or, if you like, a direct message from God to your soul. The message may come on a bumper sticker or logo on the truck in front of you, in the flight of a bird, in an overheard conversation, in the black dog that just happens to be boarding the same plane, or, as happened to me, in the amazing green-and-yellow bug that lands on your wrist at the moment you are talking about the day you put on a bracelet in exactly those colors.

But we really don't want to go around all the time looking for guidance on our conscious agendas. The universe may be putting questions to us that are bigger than all our questions. There's a great deal to be said for the Native American approach reflected in the behavior of the Navajo tracker in Tony Hillerman's novels. When a sheriff asks Joe Leaphorn what he is looking for, he says, "Nothing in particular."[3] If we are forever looking for something in particular, we are likely to miss what we are not expecting—and navigating by synchronicity is all about being open to the unexpected.

Let's remember to look out for negative, as well as positive, runs of synchronicity. These blocks and crosscurrents may be a caution to think again about the course we have chosen. Once, when I ran into a string of unexpected obstacles and setbacks, and could make no headway with a plan despite all my best efforts, I asked for guidance. Immediately a vivid scene opened in my inner sight. I saw myself beating on a huge iron-studded door until my knuckles were bleeding. Drawn into the scene, I felt the prickling of hairs on the back of my neck and turned to see a gatekeeper figure in a form I knew well. He was beckoning me toward a golden archway through which I saw limitless beauty and possibility. I ran through the archway, and I could already feel the patterns and roads of my life reforming into something far more interesting than the course I had been pursuing. At that moment, I looked back at the gatekeeper and noticed two things. With one hand he was beckoning me through the gateway of larger possibility, but with the other he was holding resolutely closed the door I had been trying to beat down. And behind that door was a space of confinement, something like a jail cell.

THE DREAM REENTRY TECHNIQUE

Fully remembered, the experience of a dream (as opposed to the often fragmentary and confused dream report) is its own interpretation. The best way to harvest the insight and energy of a dream, and to overcome nightmares, is to go back inside the dream through the technique of Dream Reentry.

Going back into a dream is like going back to a place you visited. Picture yourself returning to a friend's house or to a landscape you visited on vacation. Revisiting a dream is very similar.

You may want to get back inside a dream for any or all of the following reasons:

- to explore the dreamscape and gather helpful information
- to talk to dream characters, who may also be spiritual guides or visitors
- to go beyond nightmare terrors to healing and resolution
- to travel through personal doorways to other worlds
- to have fun and adventure in a deeper reality

To prepare for a Dream Reentry, you will want to do the following things:

1. *Pick a dream that has some real energy for you.* As long as it has juice, it doesn't matter whether it is a dream from last night or from twenty years ago. It can be a tiny fragment or a complex narrative. You can choose to work with a night dream, a vision, or a waking image. What's important is that the dream you choose to revisit has some charge—whether it is exciting, seductive, or challenging.
2. *Begin to relax.* Follow the flow of your breathing. If you are holding tension in any part of your body, tense and relax those muscle groups until you feel yourself becoming loose and comfy.
3. *Focus on a specific scene from your dream.* Let it become vivid on your mental screen. See if you can let all your senses become engaged, so you can touch it, smell it, hear it, taste it.
4. *Clarify your intention.* Come up with clear and simple answers to these two questions: (a) What do you want to know? (b) What do you intend to do, once you are back inside the dream?
5. *Call in guidance and protection.* If you have a connection with the animal spirits, you may wish to call for the help of your power animals. You may choose to invoke a sacred guardian by a familiar name, or you can simply ask for help in the name of Love and Light.
6. *Give yourself fuel for the journey.* Heartbeat shamanic drumming works for me, and it works well with my groups. I have recorded

my own shamanic drumming CD for dream travelers, *Wings for the Journey* (see appendix I for ordering information).

TRACKING DREAMS

You may find it easier to do a Dream Reentry if you go with a partner who can then become your tracker, your dream family, and, if required, your psychic bodyguard and lookout. You can invite this person to enter your dreamspace. Sometimes the tracker finds the assignment easier than the dreamer, because he or she is not as close to the dreamer's issues.

The task of the dream tracker is to enter the dreamer's psychic space, through the portal of a shared dream, in order to gather helpful information, support the dreamer in her own explorations, and perhaps assist her in moving beyond her fears to healing and resolution.

If you are going to track another person's dream, you'll want to start by getting a clear picture of the dream. Ask the dreamer to tell her dream as simply and clearly as possible. Then ask a few questions to clarify the details and bring the dream fully alive. You don't need personal history and you certainly don't want to get bogged down in analysis. If you are going to be a dream tracker, your assignment is not to interpret someone else's dream, but to put yourself inside it. You are preparing to make a journey, so the questions you want to ask are traveler's questions. You want to know what the weather is like in the dream, or what food is being served in the restaurant. You want to know the color of the dream lover's hair, the age of the children, and whether the dream house is in Chicago or on the fourth level of the astral realm. It's great if your sharing mobilizes all of your senses, so you can begin to smell and taste and feel the qualities of the dream place and the dream drama.

You'll want to clarify the dreamer's intentions in relation to the dream. What does she need to know? What does she intend to do, once she has reentered her dream?

You'll also want to establish the role the dreamer would like you to play. Does she simply want you to come inside her dream and share your impressions at the end of the journey? Or would she like you to play a more activist role—for example, by bringing your own energy (and perhaps your animal guardians) to support her in confronting a dream adversary, or opening that locked door, or in trying to bring home that beautiful child that may be an aspect of her own soul energy that was left behind through trauma.

After discussion, you'll probably want to have the dreamer tell her dream a second time, and as you listen you'll already be allowing yourself to flow beyond your physical space into the landscapes of the dream.

When I do dream reentry and tracking with a partner, I like to sit or lie down next to that person, holding hands or touching each other lightly—perhaps with the edge of an arm—so we have physical contact during the shared dream journey. I also like to use shamanic drumming to energize and focus the journey, although sometimes I substitute a "wing song," a song—often wordless, and usually the fruit of a personal vision—that helps to give us the power of dream flight.

The tracker's experience during the journey may range from a series of "pop-up" impressions to a strong and convincing experience of shared interactive dreaming. A couple in one of my workshops decided that they wanted to journey together inside the man's troubling dream of a situation in which he was summoned to a beach house he did not recognize in the midst of some crisis at the office. With the help of drumming, they succeeded in traveling together and explored the beach house room by room, almost as if they were doing a real estate tour. After the journey, they excitedly compared notes. Their descriptions were mutually confirming, though they had been drawn to different things in the dream house—the man, for example, had paid closer attention to the dock than the kitchen. They both identified the previously unknown beach house as a second home of one of the top executives at the man's corporation. As tracker, the woman was able to give the man some specific cautionary information about a possible future crisis at work that might cost him his job. This crisis was previewed in the original dream, but without the details he needed to take effective action to defend his position. He subsequently used the tracker's information to make certain prudent moves at the office—so that when the man was summoned six months later to a crisis meeting at the beach house he had dreamed, he was in good shape to survive a corporate meltdown, and did not need to ask directions to the restroom.

As in this example, the last phase of the process of dream reentry and tracking is for the partners to share their travel reports and for the dreamer to come up with an action plan to honor the experience (and maybe save his job!). The applications of this powerful technique are almost limitless. Beyond all else, conscious interactive dreaming of this kind is a magic carpet ride to wonderful fun and adventure, and experiential confirmation of the reality of dimensions beyond the physical.

17

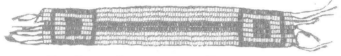

Bringing a Dream to Someone in Need of a Dream

The shamans and diviners called upon to know the inner workings of the soul...should be regarded as doctors of an order superior to the common laws of nature...It is their fancy, their imagination...that they consult.

FATHER JOSEPH-FRANÇOIS LAFITAU, 1724

A great many people around us are desperately in need of a dream. They find that much of their life is devoid of meaning and purpose. They are trapped in a box of self-limiting beliefs, maybe beliefs imposed on them by other people who too often tell us what we cannot do and what is not possible in the "real world." They have lost touch with their dreams and the part of themselves that is the beautiful dreamer. They may feel they have come to the edge of a precipice in their lives they can find no way to cross, and they cling to a crumbling ledge that cannot support them. They are in danger of doing untold harm to themselves and others, or of joining the wan procession of the walking dead. The Iroquois, like most Native peoples, say that if we are not in touch with our dreams, we have lost a part of our souls.

To bring a dream to people in need of one, we can invite them into a place of healing, courage, and vision by wrapping them inside a dream of our own, a dream of power we choose to share with them or grow for them, fresh and strong and new. This is actually an ancient practice of the dream shamans. They know, and modern physicians are just beginning to remember, that if we give the body the right image, it will believe it and move toward health. The dream shamans know that in sharing a dream of power, we may be sharing a guardian spirit—an oyaron—that can bring its blessing and protection into the life of the beneficiary. If we guide other people along the roads of our own dreaming, we may also be able to help them open their own roads through the thickets and obstacles of this life, and open a path for vital soul energy to come home. In this way, we can even help other people open a path to a happy situation in the afterlife, as in the moving "waterworld" story below, in which a dreamer gave her dream-less mother a dream that enabled her to meet a loving guide on the other side, and to embark on her own journey beyond death with grace and courage.

It is important to bring the *right* dream to the person in need. To do this, we may have to dream a new dream, call on the guidance of our spiritual allies, and trust the wisdom of the heart. Where do we find that dream? It may rise from our own wells of memory, from a life-empowering vision, or from an experience of healing. It may be inspired by a moment when we found our true north among the powers of nature. It may be the gift of an animal guardian that wants to share its energy with someone in need of healing, or of a spiritual guide that supports that person but that, until now, the person has been unable to hear or see.

This act, which I call dream transfer, is an immensely powerful tool for healing. And its applications are almost limitless. Let me briefly explain how I came to develop it as a conscious practice.

A dear friend approached me for guidance on behalf of her mother, who was in a horrible stuck place, scared of living and terrified of dying. The mother had been quite dependent on her husband, never learning to drive a car or balance a checkbook. After his death, she was very scared to leave the house. Her church had taught her that there was an afterlife, but she had no desire to see it for herself, not even if she could take on a beautiful new body, free of pain.

I suggested to my friend that she might want to ask for a dream for her mother, to write down that intention for the night and sleep on it. She did this, and in the morning she phoned me, bubbling with laughter, to tell me the dream that had flowed from her intention. In this dream, she and her mother were shooting down a slide into an enormous pool, whooping it up like happy kids in a theme park. Mom splashed into the water, shrieking with delight. At that point a barrier came down, preventing the dreamer from joining her, and a stentorian voice rumbled, "*You* may not enter at this time." The dreamer peeked over the barrier to see what was going on in the pool—and was amazed to see Mom fooling around with a well-endowed, much younger man in the water.

One of the curious things about the dream was that, in waking life, this woman's mother had never learned to swim and was terrified of the water. As we talked about the dream, we both realized that it would be an ideal vehicle for helping her mother move beyond her fear of a different element and get her ready for the big journey into the afterlife. The problem was that the dream was the daughter's, not the mom's.

I had a flash of inspiration. "Maybe we can *make* this your mother's dream."

"How could we do that?"

"Well, you could call her up and tell her the dream. Make sure you make the most of every sexy, sensory detail. I bet she'll want to hear it. Maybe, if you tell it well enough, you can bring her inside it."

My friend thought about it. Though her mother rarely shared dreams of her own, she had been willing to listen to her daughter's dreams before—and who is not interested, whatever their overt response, when we tell them, "I dreamed about you"?

The dreamer agreed to give it a try. She called her mom, who lived a thousand miles away, and told her the dream. When she was finished, there was a nervous titter at the end of the line, then, "Tell me again." After the second telling, her mom asked for a more explicit account of what exactly was going on with the hunk in the pool. The conversation dissolved into girlish giggles.

That might have been the end of the story, and that would have been fine. The dream gave my friend's mother a good laugh, lifted her pall of gloom and grief, and brought through some wonderful energy. But a sequel to the story made me aware of the full potential of the technique we were improvising.

A week later, the mom called the dreamer to report, "I know who the hunk in the pool was. Your father came to me in a dream last night. He knocked on the front door. He looked terrific. He appeared to be about thirty years old, strong and fit, and he reminded me of pleasures I haven't known for decades. He told me he lives in a country where it is always spring, and that he will be waiting to take me there when my time comes." As a result of this dream visitation, this woman lost her fear of death. When her time came, two years later, she was able to pass over with grace and confidence.

The dreamer produced a dream for her mother, who desperately needed one. She transferred that dream by telling it really well, making it an energy event that roused the senses as well as the brain. When her mother took that dream inside herself, she opened a dreamgate through which stepped a guide with a familiar face.

Since then, dream transfer has become an integral part of my practice, and I teach other dreamers to practice it in the cause of healing. It must never be abused in an effort to manipulate or control. We must always seek permission to share the dreams we grow for others, and we must encourage them to accept only what they want to take, and to make the dreams their own.

The stories that follow come from my personal practice. They unfold just a few of the many modes and applications of dream transfer. I think Island Woman would like them.

I was tired and potentially grouchy at an evening workshop in the Midwest, after a long drive through a wasteland of construction, auto plants, and fast-food restaurants. After my introduction and a demonstration of the technique, I invited participants to choose partners to do the Lightning Dreamwork process with one another. An older man asked if he could work with me. I asked him to tell me a dream.

"I don't think I have ever remembered a dream in my life."

"Okay, then pull up a life memory—anything that just comes to you now."

"Nothing is coming."

"Then go to a place in your body—the heart, the gut, wherever you are drawn—and tell me what you feel there."

"I don't feel anything. Just a kind of blur."

My grouchiness soared. I reminded myself that this man was here for a reason. Joe did not have a dream, or an image of any kind, but he was looking for something. Ignoring my fatigue and irritation, I half-closed my eyes and made it my intention to let something come to me we could work with.

A scene formed immediately in my inner sight. I saw Joe as a nine-year-old boy, playing at the edge of an ornamental pool in a park that reminded me of Ault Park in Cincinnati. He was having fun with a wooden sailboat that looked as if it had been put together from a model kit. The hull was brightly painted. Suddenly a huge, menacing shadow fell over the boy and the pool. A violent wind whipped up, capsizing the boat, which sank. The boy tried to retrieve it but could not reach deep enough. Then his adult self entered the scene and reached down and restored the sailboat to the surface. The boy laughed with joy as the sailboat glided across the pond, joined by many other model boats.

"I have a dream for you," I told Joe. "Would you like to hear it?"

He nodded eagerly. I told him the dream, and I invited him to make it his own and tell it back to me in his own way, changing the details as he pleased. He retold the dream vividly, and I noticed a wonderful lift in his energy as he claimed it as his own.

We then did the Lightning Dreamwork process as if the dream had always belonged to him. When we ran the reality check, I was fascinated to learn that he had not only loved and constructed model sailboats, but he had quite a collection of them, from his days in the merchant marine, at his home. Joe also told me that when he was nine, there had been a "tempest" in his life, involving a family member. He agreed he would take one of his sailboats to a pond in a park and float it in honor of his nine-year-old self.

There was an immediate sequel. Joe turned up the next morning for our weekend depth workshop. "You may think I'm not ready," he said. "But I really am. Last night I had the most incredible dream. It began with me looking down on my body in the bed, so I knew I was journeying beyond the body." It turned out to be a dream of soul recovery, of going back to the time of the tempest and reclaiming the vital energy of that boy who loved sailboats.

It's remarkable what can happen when we help another person reopen the dreamgates.

On the way to a waterfall in a redwood forest near Big Sur in California, I paused to look closely at a huge redwood that soared a hundred feet or more above my head. It was a miracle that that tree was alive. She had been charred and cored by fire. The hollow left inside the trunk was the size of a small room. On top of fire, the tree had been challenged by a landslide that left half its root system exposed, dangling down the cliffside. Yet above its fire-gutted core, the redwood towered healthy and strong, putting out fresh green shoots.

I stepped inside the tree chamber and sang a song that honored the earth and its endless power of renewal. I touched the blackened walls of this womblike space and thanked the tree for her ability to endure and to bring forth new life. I recalled the family motto of my father's Scottish clan: *Reviresco,* "I grow green again." The image on the Maxwell arms is the stump of a mighty oak putting forth new shoots. The presence of the redwood was even stronger. I knew I could come here, and bring others here, when there is need to rise from the ashes of a life.

That same day, I received an appeal for support from a wonderful woman whose doctors had just scheduled her for a hysterectomy. I invited her to step inside a waking dream of the redwood.

"You are stepping along a dappled path, into the redwood forest. You hear the gurgle of water splashing down a rocky ravine. You inhale the rich, fecund smell of warm earth after rain. You step off the path, and your feet sink into mosses and evergreen fronds, soft as deep-pile carpet.

"You enter the sacred space of a redwood that has been burned and hollowed near the base and yet stands immensely tall, raising a canopy of green branches to the sky. You are welcomed into the hallowed spaciousness of the redwood. Enveloped by the redwood, you know you can withstand the burning and hollowing of your own body and that whatever is removed from your body will be an offering that will allow new space for growth and creation. You marvel that ones who have been wounded so deeply can provide abundant life, a special mothering, a spaciousness for love.

"When your time comes, you feel your body heaving in childbirth. You squat down as waves of breathing and groaning move through you. You ease down onto the ground and lie with the soles of your feet on the earth, your knees rising like mountains toward the sky. You are panting, groaning, moaning, crying, and laughing all at once. From your body streams life, endless life, plants and animals, bright winged creatures of happiness and desire."

The transfer of the redwood dream went deep, and it helped the recipient to move swiftly and graciously through the surgery. She developed the imagery, making it her own, and she often placed herself inside the redwood womb in the course of her healing and recovery.

I invited a circle to enter the dream of the wounded redwood, drumming for the journey after sharing the initial meditation. We found that the womb of the redwood is a place of deep healing for all of us who have been wounded. "The tree gave me courage," Carol wrote to me afterward. "She showed me the beauty in my own life though I bore the wounding of abuse. I reveled in the experience of stepping into the hollow space of the burned-out redwood and gratefully, tenderly caressed the wood of my kin.

"When you led the meditation and then drummed, I was impelled to stand with her, the giant redwood, and to unite myself, body and soul, with life. Tears streamed down my face as I experienced both universal pain and joy and stood, rooted to the healing earth and opening to the expansive sky. My tears flowed from the ocean of love and compassion as I slowly began to rock in the healing winds, mercy branching out in all directions. The wound provides a place of spaciousness where all of us can find healing and compassion."

We can also grow a dream for someone who needs a dream for another person. A man I'll call Mark came to one of my dream healing workshops and told me he had come not only for himself but also to receive help for his three-year-old son, Luke, who was autistic. Moved by the depth of this young father's love and concern, I offered to grow a dream for him during one of the drumming journeys.

I found myself pulled immediately into my own solar plexus. Inside was a vast landscape, like an African savannah, teeming with animal life. I was drawn to a pride of lions. I noticed there were many, many lions of all ages, plenty to share. A magnificent maned lion spoke to me in his gravelly voice: "Bring *me* to the father," he instructed, "and I will bring his son back into conversation with the world." I recalled that part of the lion's power is in his voice.

I glimpsed the autistic boy, Luke, standing with his face turned to a wall, sad and alone and unreachable. I saw him turn, very slowly, as his father approached him with a lion that appeared to be only a stuffed toy. The boy turned away again before he accepted the lion. In his arms, the lion came alive. As he lay in bed with it, the lion entered his solar plexus and became part of him.

At the end of the drumming, I shared my dream with Mark, the father. Following my vision, I offered to put the lion energy in his solar plexus, quite literally, so he could carry that to his son. Mark accepted eagerly, and I blew the lion power into his third chakra with the breath of spirit. We both experienced a very strong energy transfer. We agreed that Mark would get a soft lion, a stuffed toy, for his son, and use this, as in the dream, as a vehicle for moving the energy to where it was most needed.

Mark wrote to me the following week to report on what transpired. Initially, Luke had rejected the toy. Then he accepted it and snuggled up with the lion in bed. A couple of days later, when his worried preschool teachers came calling—needing to assess whether they could take him on for a new term—Luke met them at the door, regaled them with stories, and was the life of the party for the whole visit.

The lion kept his promise to bring the autistic boy back into "conversation with the world." In this example, dream transfer extended to what Island Woman would regard as the sharing of an oyaron, in this case an animal guardian.

We enter the realm of the animal guardians again in the next story. We also confront the reality that if we are going to bring a dream to someone who is in a very dark place—in this case a place of life-threatening illness and crushing fear—we must acknowledge that darkness and fear and open a path beyond it.

We did not need any special powers to see that Chloe was severely ill. Her face was ashen under the head scarf she was wearing to cover the baldness caused by chemotherapy. She seemed to be walking very close to death, and when she introduced herself, she explained that her physicians—displaying that routine bedside manner of the black magicians of allopathic medicine—had given her just three months to live. "I have come to you," she announced in front of forty workshop participants, "because I do not intend to die the way my doctors have told me I am going to die." I asked for dream guidance for Chloe on the first night of the workshop, and Raven appeared and told me that she would be my guide.

On Sunday morning, after we had built the energy of the circle and called in spiritual helpers, I invited Chloe to join me in a demonstration of dream transfer in front of the whole group. We lay together on the floor, on my blanket, holding hands, and I covered my eyes with a bandanna while a vigorous drummer in the group laid down the rhythms for the journey.

Raven flew me through scenes of pain and darkness and immense challenge. It was very, very hard to move beyond these nightmare landscapes, but eventually I found a path that Chloe might be able to follow to healing, if she had the courage to go all the way. At the end of the drumming, I sat facing her, holding her hands.

"I have a dream for you. Are you willing to hear it?"

"Yes."

"I will invite you to take any part of this dream that you can use, and to make it your own. You should not accept any part of the dream that does not feel right, and you are free to take none of it. Is that understood?"

"Yes."

"In my dream, I see you under the shadow of an immense dark bird. You are running and stumbling through a dark wood, trying to get away. You are at the end of your strength. You trip and fall and cannot get up. And the great black bird is on you. You feel the stab of pain as its beak rips into the base of your neck and its talons tear into your flesh. You can't stand the pain. But in a while you realize that Raven is pecking out the cells of your disease, pecking them out and spitting them on the ground, where other birds come to carry them away."

Chloe was shaking violently. It was hard to hold her hands still. The tears streamed down her face so copiously that they made a dark patch on her blouse and on the blanket. But she stared, unflinching, into my eyes, ready to hear it all.

"At last the tearing is done. You are so very weak, but somehow you manage to haul yourself onto the back of the great dark bird. And she flies you to a terrible place. It is a bald mountain, where black-robed figures are gathered in a circle. You know that this is the council of your death. Your time is up. It's in the contract you agreed to before you came here.

"But you rage, and weep, and beg. You scream that you know all that, but you have important reasons to live. You promise that if you are given more time you will become an advocate for others, a helper in healing. You list six specific things you will do if you are given your life extension. One of the black-robed figures leaves the circle.

"After an aching delay, he returns. The good news is that you have been granted some more time. The bad news is you will now be required to honor each of the terms of your life extension." I added a little pendant scene in which Chloe is swimming, with her hair grown back again.

I watched to see what she would do. I reminded her that she must take only those elements from the dream that she felt would serve her.

"I accept all of it," she said, her fierce heart shining through the tears.

I asked her to tell the dream back to me, making it her own. She did this with spectacular artistry, weaving in the circumstances of her own life, listing the six specific things she chose to do to make her compact with death.

At the end of the workshop, Chloe stood in front of the circle and asked to speak. "I was in excruciating pain all day long," she told us. "But I knew this was Raven inside me, pecking out the cells of my disease. I do not know how I am going to die, but I am sure of one thing: I am *not* going to die the way my doctors prescribed."

In Chloe's case, dream transfer would not have worked had I offered a cute visualization that did not acknowledge the extremity of her fear and pain in the course of blazing a trail beyond the darkness. In this work, I had the benefit not only of the guidance of an animal guardian—Raven, who is adept at going into dark places—but also of a previous dream of power. My dream sister Wanda Burch was obliged to renegotiate her life contract, in a similar way, in an indelible experience of healing from breast cancer that I described in *Conscious Dreaming* and that she has since described in her own beautiful book *She Who Dreams: A Journey through Dreamwork into Healing*. I traveled with Wanda in some of her close encounters with death, and I learned, yet again, that profound healing is possible when we stop demonizing death. Because this is something our mainstream culture has yet to remember, one of the most important applications of dream transfer may well be to heal our relationship with death and claim the clarity and courage for *life* that come from receiving death as a teacher.

18

Medicine Dreaming

He walks with me like a faithful dog
though he's twice my size
and my ancestors feared and revered him so much
they never spoke his name out loud,
calling him Honey-mouth, or Sticky-paw
or the Matchless One. Upright, he seems man
more than animal, though on cold nights
men in the wild would envy his fine warm pelt.

We are going to the animal doctor
not the corner vet but the real thing
because the Bear is ready to give himself again.
He passes without pain, without blood.
The animal doctor explains we must use all of him,
every organ, wasting nothing, sharing with those in need.
We unwrap the Great One as a medicine bundle.
Everything inside his skin is clean and dry,
sorted for use. The gallbladder is prized above all.
It will go to one who has earned it.
When we have used all of him, Bear is reborn,

the same Honey-mouth, in a new body.
The animal doctor says we must remember this always:
When you take from the Bear with respect, wasting nothing
Bear always comes back, in a new pelt.

Now I walk with him in his new body
to help someone who has dreamed him,
padding softly down hospital halls.
The Master of Medicine gives himself over and over.
This is the most natural thing in the world.
There is no end to this, unless our love runs dry
and we forget what he is.

"BEAR GIVER"

Dreaming is medicine. A physician who has studied with me frequently prescribes dreams as well as medications for his patients: "Write down your intention to remember a dream or two before your next appointment, and then bring in descriptions of those dreams." Dr. Bob says that depressives benefit tremendously from the simple act of agreeing to make a connection with their dreams, and that when they do this, they can be weaned from their medications much faster than normal. Patients with physical complaints often receive dream help in many specific ways, ranging from advice on diet and complementary therapy to an introduction to an animal guardian that provides an energy boost and the thrill of tapping into a deeper dimension.

Another physician I know, a female doctor in Alaska who has some Athapaskan Indian heritage, came to a program I led because she dreamed that two of her grandmothers told her she needed to get herself to one of my workshops in order to "meet the bear." In that particular workshop, held in Oregon in February, I led the group on a journey deep into a cavernous space under the roots of an ancient tree. Our intention was to enter Bear's deep winter dreaming and discover what new creative life we could birth and release into the world in the spring, as ohkwari delivers the cub that grows inside her in the dark time of year. Donna entered the womb of Bear and then Bear entered her womb; she saw herself freeing her Bear-self to help and heal. Now the fortunate patients who find their way to her office get the best of modern medicine—and they also get the healing power of Bear.

Dreams help us to heal and integrate body, mind, and spirit in many ways. Dreams alert us to problems that may be developing inside the body before we develop symptoms, allowing us to choose whether we are going to move into a pattern of illness or out of it. Dreams frequently diagnose developing illness before physical symptoms are detected. By working with these diagnostic dreams, we can often deal with a problem before it has reached a critical phase, and sometimes avoid painful and costly medical interventions.

For example, Ellen, a woman in her late thirties, dreamed that a threatening intruder walked into her dream house and pointed a gun at her breast. Her feelings told her, in a way she could not brush aside, that the dream was a warning of breast cancer. She immediately sought medical help. As a result, Ellen's cancer was discovered in its earliest stages and the problem was contained by a simple lumpectomy.

A dream like Ellen's feels like a drama produced by the body itself. But sometimes dream diagnosis is the gift of dream visitors who have a better appreciation of what may be going on in our bodies than we do. Wanda was traveling abroad when her father, who had died several years before, turned up in a dream in a white medical coat and yelled at her, "Get to a doctor now! You have cancer!"

The warning propelled Wanda to go to her doctor's office as soon as she returned from her trip, and to insist on further testing when the initial scans were negative. The new tests revealed advanced and rapidly metastasizing breast cancer. Now that Wanda had embarked on a path of healing—combining medical intervention with dreamwork and visualization in what she later described as a healing cocktail—her father reappeared in a new guise, as a spiritual ally who presented her with an animal guardian, a black leopard.[1]

A New York woman, Cindy, suffered a series of health challenges, but because she disliked going to medical centers, she kept putting off making an appointment with a doctor. One morning, she woke from a dream in which her departed grandmother had urged her to have a medical checkup. She chose to disregard the dream, but she was then startled on the stairs by the sense of a strong, almost physical, visitation by her grandmother. "I swear my grandmother tripped me," she recalled. Cindy fell down the stairs and broke her leg, which forced her to go to her doctor. When she walked in, he told her he had scheduled her for a mammogram. "But I came in because my leg is broken!" she protested. Her physician told her that he had dreamed the night before that an elderly woman told him that his patient needed to get a mammogram. His visitor was presumably Cindy's grandmother. Between the incident on the stairs and her dream appearances, she managed not only to get a message across, but also to mobilize the necessary action. Cindy's tests revealed breast cancer.

As we see from Cindy's case, dreams can give counsel to doctors as well as patients. A physician I know told me he dreamed that a patient he had not seen in more than a year called for an emergency appointment. Someone told him in the dream that he had been mispronouncing the man's name. He was calling his patient Mr. Kees when his surname should actually be pronounced the Dutch way—Kays. Coached by his dream, the doctor was not altogether surprised when Mr. Kees called the next day for an emergency consultation. He remembered to check with his patient on how he wanted to be named—and discovered that Kays was indeed the correct and preferred pronunciation. The patient was glad to be treated as an individual, whose name mattered, and this laid the foundation for successful treatment.

Every night, if we will only pay attention, we receive the services of a personal physician, counselor, and therapist who makes house calls, can give us an impeccable diagnosis of our physical, emotional, and spiritual condition—and does everything pro bono. When we do get sick, our dreams provide us with customized imagery for healing and an invaluable resource for getting well, because the body believes in imagery and does not seem to distinguish between a vivid imaginal event and a physical one. Images communicate directly with the body, speaking to tissues and organs, skin and cells, to effect a change. As Jeanne Achterberg observes, "Images, indeed all thoughts, are electrochemical events, which are intricately woven into the fabric of the brain and body."[2]

Dreams are a wonderful source of fresh, spontaneous imagery for healing—imagery the body believes because it comes from deep within ourselves. Dream images are more powerful than prefabricated visualization scripts because they are our own material, produced especially for us.

Dreams show us our conditions in a different language from the medical profession (though they may also incorporate medical language and medical procedures). Like a dream shaman reweaving the body's template and the mind's web of possibilities by spreading energy and speaking magic words, our dreams offer us the power of visioning and naming our symptoms in ways that help us to become well.

A woman asked her dreams whether she should undergo surgery for a herniated disk. In the dream she had invited, she saw a zippy fifties roadster, painted red and white, with a huge, ultramodern sound system in the back. She was told in the dream that mechanical repairs were not necessary and would be excessively costly. Waking, she laughed when she recognized that her body was the fifties roadster, and that a sound system is also a disk player. She proceeded to experiment, with very healing results, with the power of toning and vibration to help with her back problem and keep the roadster humming along.

In dreams, we have direct access to sources of sacred healing, and we can connect with transpersonal allies who can help us raise our energy. As we connect with the bigger stories of our lives through dreaming, which is an inexhaustible well of living, personal myth, we find ways to move beyond suffering into myth, to paraphrase Joseph Campbell, who correctly perceived this to be the heart of healing.

HEALING GIFTS OF THE ANIMAL POWERS

Dreams introduce us to the realm of the animal powers and their healing gifts. This connection is especially prized in Iroquois and other Native traditions. The Lakota, for example, have many ways of seeking healing power and vision, some requiring tremendous sacrifice, courage, and stamina. But the most powerful healers of the Lakota are said to be the members of the Bear Dreamers Society, who are called by Bear in spontaneous dreams and visions. According to David Rockwell, "The Lakota said that any man who dreamed of the bear would be an expert in the use of plant medicines. They considered bear medicine men the most powerful of healers...Black Elk, the great Lakota holy man and medicine man, said that he received his power to cure from the bear spirit."[3]

To this day, many Native American girls and boys entering puberty undergo vision quests to discover and forge a close link with animal guardians. For the multitudes of people in modern society who have lost their dream connection with animal power, vision questing may be an *adult* necessity. It needs to involve a decisive break with our normal habits and consensual hallucinations about the real, but it may not require sweat lodges or fasting in the wilderness. Our animal guardians are hunting us in our dreams. If we will only stop running away, brave up, and *remember,* we can claim their power—though we will be required to feed them and honor them in our bodies and our lives.

Leslie dreamed she was back at her childhood home and was very upset that there was a horse on the porch that looked malnourished and abused. It seemed to be jammed half in and half out of the door of the family home. After working with her dream, she recognized that the condition of the horse very much represented the way she had handled her body. At her controlling mother's insistence, she had submitted to a series of diets and lifestyle rules that had left her hungry, physically and emotionally. Although she had long since left home, she saw now that she had internalized some of her mother's attitudes. She needed to get her horse out of the door of her mother's house and feed it what it wanted. When I work with dreams of horses like this (there is a very special connection between women and horses in dreams, as well as sometimes in physical life), I am reminded that the name for vital energy given by the Buryat—shamanic people of Mongolia—is windhorse.[4]

When shamans go dreaming, they usually operate under the protection and guidance of animal guardians. Forging a close relationship with one or more power animals is central to developing the arts of shamanic dream travel and tracking. It is invaluable in maintaining healthy boundaries and defending psychic space. A strong working connection with the animal powers brings the ability to shape-shift the energy body and project energy forms that can operate at a distance from the physical body.

Our ancestors believed that we are born with a connection to a particular totem animal. This was the foundation of the clan system. Some Australian Aborigines still believe that when a human is born, its "bush soul" is born in the form of an animal or bird. We may feel that we have a lifelong connection with a certain animal or bird. Others may observe this in our body type, our lifestyles, our modes of responding to challenges.

But in the course of a lifetime, we may develop many animal connections. Some of these may stem from our relations with the animals who share our homes and habitats, from family pets to wild animals encountered in nature and in our travels. Animals we have met in the physical world may reappear in our dreams, as allies and helpers.

To live strong, we need a vital working connection with the animal guardians. This should be an *energy* connection, not simply a matter of personal symbolism. We need to be able to borrow the senses and skills of the animal powers in order to track, establish psychic boundaries, and heal. One of the fastest ways I know to restore vitality, to improve the immune system, and to move beyond lethargy or depression is to bring through the animal spirits.

The best and simplest way to develop a strong connection with the animal powers is to build on a previous encounter—in a dream, a vision, or waking life—with the animal realm. Suppose you dreamed of running away from a bear, or swimming with the dolphins. You can go back inside that dream, using the Dream Reentry technique. If you find you are nervous or fearful, maybe you can find a friend who will accompany you on the journey, or at least hold your hand and watch over your physical space.

Dream Reentry works just as well with a life memory as with a sleep dream or vision. Maybe you remember watching a cormorant dive to get fish. You can make it your intention to take the plunge with the cormorant, just as you might go back inside a dream.

Many of us have close connections with animals that have shared our lives—a beloved dog or cat, a horse, a pet rabbit, a family of foxes that lived behind the barn. These familiar friends may prove to be real "familiars" in the other sense, as animal guardians and psychic allies—and we should not forget that it is quite shamanic to work with the energies of *any* animals we know well, including pets.

To claim a connection with an animal guardian that presents itself in a dream, we may have to "brave up." If you are meeting the lion or the bear for the first time, the encounter may not be cute and may not feel at all safe. As Rilke said, *"jeder engel ist schrecklich"* (every angel is terrifying), and this can be especially true when the angel appears as an animal power, at least on the first date. However, when we are able to move beyond fear and claim a gift in the realm of the animal powers, it opens up a world of healing. This is richly revealed in Peg's story.

"Bear Is My Very Best Friend"

Life had often seemed a long, hard road to Peg. She had suffered abuse and abandonment in childhood, and a good deal of heartbreak and disappointment before she reached her middle years. There were many times she felt a vital part of herself had gone missing, the part of her that could fully give and receive love and trust. She had made choices and compromises she had come to regret, and she came to suspect that parts of herself that resisted those choices had left her at these turnings in the road.

Many days, she felt she was simply going through the motions, doing what was required to keep food on the table and gas in the car and meet other people's demands and expectations. "Where's the rest of me?" was her frequent question. Or even, "Where am *I*?"

Her dreams began to answer her, though it took quite a long time before she recognized what the dreams were showing and offering. She dreamed of a happy, gurgling baby, loved and nourished in a dream nursery among the clouds. She dreamed of a sexy, vivacious young woman, courted by handsome, gentlemanly suitors. She dreamed of a woman of power, a medicine woman who lived closed to the earth and drew her strength from this deep earth connection. Over time, as she shared her dreams with sensitive friends and a caring therapist, Peg came to recognize that all these dream characters might be aspects of herself: the beautiful baby self who had gone missing because of family troubles, the lovely young woman who had been jilted and heartbroken, the medicine woman who was no stranger but was the part of her that stood with the earth and could draw on its energy and wisdom.

Through the window of her dreams, Peg came to understand something more. Dreams not only show us the many aspects of ourselves; they also issue an invitation for us to recall vital energy that may have been lost through pain or heartbreak, and to bring that energy into our bodies and our loves. Dreams also invite us to connect with larger aspects of our identity, with the part of us that knows the earth, or the animal powers, far better than our everyday personalities do. Dreams may even connect us with the god or goddess who wants to live in embodied life through us. When our dreams show us these things, they invite us to do more than expand our understanding: they call us to take action to move toward healing and wholeness, to mend the divided self by recovering soul.

Peg had been working with her dreams for several years and had experienced several levels of deep soul recovery when she dreamed that Bear was her very best friend. Here is her own telling:

"I am standing on a hillside. There are many other people around me. I don't recognize them to begin with. But as I look more closely, I realize that I know them. There is my baby self. There is my beautiful, lively nineteen-year-old self. There is my eleven-year-old self, standing apart from the others, and starting to drift away again. There is that powerful Earth Mother. I am in awe of her strength and majesty, but my Higher Self—whom I sense as a presence above and behind me— reminds me that she is also a part of me, the bigger me. Even the man who is on the hilltop, kicking his heels, is a part of me.

"I start drawing my many selves together, into a circle. We are join- ing hands. It feels really good, bringing all of myself together in this way. I feel loved and nourished and strong.

"Only my eleven-year-old doesn't seem to know where she belongs. She's taking off in a different direction. I'm sad she won't be part of the party. Without her, something is missing.

"I look down across the valley. There is an animal feeding down there. As I watch, it raises its head and I see it is a large black bear. It looks me straight in the eyes. It's shocking, the force and directness of that gaze. Now the bear is up on its legs and racing toward me. It moves amazingly fast up the slope, despite its great bulk. As it nears me, the bear stands up on its hind legs. Now it looks almost human.

"I am standing absolutely still. I have no fear. I am ready for what- ever the bear wants of me. The bear takes my hand in his great paw. He says to me, 'I am your very best friend.'"

Peg woke elated, charged with energy, feeling that her life was full of possibility. I shared her joy when she shared the dream in one of my circles, because it offered so many gifts and such profound and imme- diate healing. In her dream, Peg is able to recognize different aspects of herself—including younger selves who had been missing for many years through soul-loss—and bring them together. She is witnessing and acting in the presence of her Higher Self, from a deeper power and perspective than that of the ordinary personality or surface self. And she acquires a powerful ally: Bear announces that he is her very best friend.

Still, there was one element in the dream that troubled Peg. Her eleven-year-old self—a part of her that may have suffered traumatic domestic abuse—was still "out there." I asked her if she would be will- ing to go back inside her dream, meet Bear again, and see how he could help rescue her younger self and reclaim that energy in her life.

Peg readily agreed. I asked her to call up the dream scene and her feelings inside it as vividly as possible, until she could see the grass on the hilltop stirred by the breeze again and feel the shock of awe and recognition as the great bear raised its head and looked her full in the eyes. Powered by her intention to meet her Bear ally and heal her divided self, Peg moved back inside her dream as naturally as if she had walked into a literal landscape.

During her Dream Reentry, she found herself going right inside Bear. The space inside its rib cage was vast, a large and pleasant chamber where her various selves gathered with her, hugged her, and became one with her—all but the eleven-year-old, who was still out there somewhere. In her waking dream, Peg rose with Bear, *as* Bear, and went in search of her preteen self. When she found her lost kid, she reached for it, lovingly but firmly, and clasped it up in the strong arm of Bear. She brought it home, into her now-united self.

Peg's eyes were bright and tears of joy were flowing down her cheeks when she surfaced from this beautiful wide-awake dream. You might wonder, from the account so far, whether all that had taken place was creative fantasy. If that were all that was involved, I would celebrate the magic and joy that it brought through. But Peg and I are both convinced that more than fantasy was played out when she went to meet Bear. I saw from the light in her eyes and the lift in her spirits that deep soul recovery and a real infusion of energy had taken place.

We celebrated by singing together the Mohawk song that calls Medicine Bear:

> *Don't cry little one*
> *Don't cry little one*
> *The bear is coming to dance for you*
> *The bear is coming to dance for you*

I asked Peg what she would do now to honor Bear. She decided she would eat plenty of berries, and eat more fish in such a way that she—and the bear who lives with her—would feel the fish oil "exploding" in her mouth as she bit down.

I was thrilled by Peg's dream encounter with Bear and all that flowed from it. Peg's story is an inspiring example of what may come from accepting a conscious relationship not only with Medicine Bear, but with the whole realm of the animal powers.

Journey Exercise: Through the Tree Gate to the Animal Powers

Here is a way of entering the realm of the animal powers that works for almost everyone who is able to relax and set aside the chatter of the skeptic in the left brain.

1. Put yourself in a comfortable position, sitting or lying down, and shut out as much external light as possible. You may find your experience is accelerated and focused by using shamanic drumming. If you do not have a live drummer available, you may want to use a CD.
2. Call up the image of a tree you know, a tree that knows *you*. It's probably best if it's a tree you know in the natural world, but it may be a tree you have seen in dreaming, or indeed a Dreamtime tree like the many described in this book. Be with the tree with all of your inner senses.
3. Set your itinerary. You are going to travel, with your awareness, down through the roots of the tree into another realm. You may need to be prepared to pay the price of entry; for me, it was a song.
4. Set your intention. It is twofold. In a world beneath the roots of the tree, you are going to connect with spiritual allies who will appear to you as animals. You will receive direct healing and guidance in their realm. Then you will go deeper, into a space where you can find direction and creative inspiration on the major themes of your life.
5. Once you find an animal power, locate it in one of your energy centers. Where does it want to live within your energy system? In your solar plexus, in your second chakra, in your heart center?
6. Decide immediately what you will do to feed this energy in your body and your life. This involves *literal* feeding. If you make a connection with the Wolf or the Tiger, it is unlikely to prosper if you stay on a strict vegetarian diet. If you connect with a herbivore, on the other hand, you'll want to graze on leafy things. You'll also want to move your body—as far as is practicable!—in ways the animal moves, and let its senses and style come into play in your everyday circumstances.
7. Set an action plan to honor the deeper guidance and resonance of your journey.
8. Get physical. Move around, dance, walk outside and snack. You may want to put on some primal music and dance with your power animal. Don't think about whether you should slither or prowl or lope; just let your body direct you.

Testing your connection with the animal guardians as you go along will show you whether it is "real" and, if so, whether it is truly operational. Basically, if the animal guardians turn up when you need them—for example, for healing or psychic defense—then you will know you have made a working connection. Test what you can do with them, and they with you, in conscious dream journeying. Practice shape-shifting in your energy body. See whether one of your animal guardians is willing and able to perform tracking assignments or carry a message while your primary consciousness is engaged in something entirely different.

Notice how the unexpected appearance or movements of an animal helper can open you to perceive something you might otherwise have missed, even when you were closely focused on an issue. I was once tracking for a doctor friend and felt confident I had found everything I needed to find on his behalf. Then an animal I know well butted me so hard it was almost painful, directing me to look in a different direction. This resulted in a long and very rewarding exploration that enabled me to bring back far more than I could otherwise have done. It also assured me that my experience went beyond anything I could weave from my imagination.

Dreaming the Soul Back Home

I come here because I have fallen out of the sky

We are all here, in the generous kitchen
of the house where wings are mended.
Bird people are awkward on the ground
but we remember the high windy places
and we will reclaim the sky.

"HOUSE OF FOUR HAWKS"

The Iroquois teaching is that if we have lost our dreams, we have lost part of our soul, the part of us that is the dreamer. This is a serious condition, because soul-loss is held to be the primary source of illness, depression, and mental confusion. Lose your vital energy, and the magic goes out of life. Your immune system is shot, you are often fatigued for no good reason, you can't experience joy or love, and there is a gaping hole in you that you try to fill up with candy or booze or some other addiction. Soul-loss can kill you, even if Western doctors don't have a name for it. Worse, it can put you in the procession of the walking dead, shuffling from one meaningless milestone to the next, playing the roles that other people cast you for, clueless about who you are or why you are in this world.

WHY SOUL LEAVES THE BODY

In the course of a single lifetime, we may die many deaths. Some of these may be quite literal (i.e., physical) deaths, in the course of which we lose vital signs. This happens in crises of illness, on operating tables, in road accidents, in drownings and shootings, through drug overdose or attempted suicide, and in other extreme situations. Those who return from these brushes with death sometimes report fascinating and moving memories of episodes on the other side. These are widely described as near-death experiences, but they might more accurately be called temporary deaths, because they involve actually dying and coming back. Those who have encountered death in this intimate way and remember what they experienced on the other side frequently return with a deeper and more generous sense of what matters in life. Often they come back gifted with heightened psychic perception.

However, not everyone who survives temporary death returns intact. A part of them may still be "out there." The person who returns may be missing some part of their energy and identity, a piece of soul that remained on the other side. The panoply of modern technologies available for medical intervention contributes to this problem. We have many ways to revive a patient who has flatlined, even when the person who occupied that body does not want to come back.

We lose part of our vital soul because of pain and abuse and trauma, because of grief and heartbreak, because part of our vital energy is stolen or shut out of our body. We also lose part of our soul because we give up on our heart's desires, we agree to live inside a box others make for us, we won't take that leap of faith and trust ourselves to love, and to believe in the soul's purpose, and to hope that an answering power in the universe will provide. We may suffer soul-loss because of our life choices, as well as because of trauma. We make a certain choice—to be with one person rather than another, for example—and a part of us resists that choice, perhaps remaining "stuck" on a former partner.

One of my favorite writers on soul-loss is the Canadian magical realist Charles de Lint, whose depictions of the alternate realities where "lost girls" roam are both haunting and, in my experience, rather exact. A marvelous story by de Lint called "The Words That Remain" tells the tale of a writer on book tour arriving late and unexpectedly at a small, once-elegant hotel. The young woman with spiked punk hair at the desk tells him the hotel is haunted by a woman who made a deal with death to kill her bright spirit so she could fit in with her father's plans and take over from him as hotel manager instead of becoming an artist. The writer stops by the desk in the morning to leave a copy of his book for the girl. He finds a much older, hard-faced woman on duty. There is a vague family resemblance, and he is struck by the fact that the two women are both called Mary. When he remarks on this, the older woman snaps that there is only one Mary employed at the hotel—herself; she took over the management from her father. The writer realizes that this drab, weary husk-person is all that remained when her vibrant, artistic spirit moved out. The ghost that haunts the hotel is a ghost of the living. De Lint sows the thought that there are "people we leave behind when we make choices" and that the "ghosts of who we were" may be wandering around for anyone to see—except ourselves.[1]

I am strongly aware of the reality of soul-loss because I have been through it at several stages in my life, and probably in other instances I have not yet noticed. I lost some of my little Roberts when I was terribly ill and terribly alone as a boy. I suffered pneumonia in both lungs twelve times between the ages of three and eleven, and I went through what is now defined as a near-death experience—losing vital signs in the hospital—in the course of three medical crises. Many of my days were spent in the half-light and solitude of sickrooms. Some parts of my soul, pushed out of my body under general anesthesia, refused to come back because they did not want to be confined to a world of pain and isolation; they wanted to have fun and run and swim and find out about girls.

Later, when I was a teenager, I was separated by circumstances and family intervention from the first girl I loved, and another part of me went away—a hopelessly romantic poet. Enough of him stayed around to write a poem to heartbreak, a poem that on the night we were separated seemed like the antidote to self-destruction:

> *I love the bird with broken wings*
> *it is young and has no pride*
> *has no voice and yet it sings*

> *enchanted by its spiral dive*
> *and has the beak of hooded kings*
> *that broke the leash before they died*
> *cold goshawk at the heart of things*
> *that tears because it is alive*
> *and is remote from all that clings*
> *because the seasons claimed its bride*
> *falling through narrowing iron rings*
> *on talons bared like knives.*

Later, when I chose to end my first marriage and leave England for America, a part of me stayed behind, disapproving of my choices. Later still, when my encounters with the spirits led me to revalue everything I had considered important, and I made the decision to leave the life of a best-selling thriller writer for a different path, another part of me rebelled against my decision and broke away from me.

As life goes on, my dreams have alerted me to the need to accomplish soul recovery for each of these aspects of myself—which sometimes leads to interesting challenges in terms of integrating a family of selves! The alternative to calling our souls home is to go around with a gaping hole in our being, a hole we may try to fill or forget through addictive behaviors, or that may invite in things that do not belong with us at all.

Symptoms of Soul-Loss

1. inability to ground yourself: spaciness, tendency to drift off, "check out," or constantly try to escape from situations around you
2. chronic depression
3. chronic fatigue
4. dissociation and multiple personality disorder
5. addictive behaviors
6. low self-esteem
7. emotional numbness
8. inability to let go of past situations or people no longer in your life, for example, inability to move beyond a divorce or grief over the death of a loved one
9. obesity or unexplained serious weight gain (typical in women who are survivors of abuse)
10. abusive behaviors

11. absence of dream recall
12. recurring dreams of locations from earlier life, or of a younger self separate from yourself

DREAM TRACES OF OUR LOST GIRLS AND BOYS

Our dreams can tell us which parts of ourselves may be missing, and when it is time to bring them home. Recurring dreams in which we go back to a scene from our earlier lives may indicate that a part of us has remained there. Dreams in which we perceive a younger self as a separate individual may be nudging us to recognize and recover a part of ourselves we lost at that age. Sometimes we do not know who that beautiful child is, until we take a closer look. There is a marvelous story in my book *Dreamgates* about what happened when a woman went back into a dream of a beautiful five-year-old in a red coat and found herself fusing at the heart, in a blaze of light, with the part of herself she had lost at age five through family trauma.

A middle-aged woman approached me for help. She told me, "I feel I have lost the part of me that can give trust and know joy." As preparation for our meeting, I asked her to start a dream journal, although she said she hadn't remembered her dreams for many years. When she came to see me, she had succeeded in capturing just one tiny fragment from a dream. She remembered that she was standing over a table, looking at three large Post-it notes. Each had a typed message. But the ink had faded and she could not read the messages.

Slowly and carefully, I helped her to relax and encouraged her to try to go back inside her dream. Quite quickly, she found herself inside a room in the house where she had lived with her ex-husband prior to their divorce, almost twenty years before. Now she could read the typed messages. The first read, in bold capitals, YOU CAN DO IT. All the messages were about living with heart and trusting life.

She realized that she had left her ability to love and trust in that room nearly twenty years ago. I asked her what she needed to do. She told me, "I need to bring my heart out of that room and put it back in my body." She gathered up the messages and made the motion of bringing them into her heart. As her hands crossed over the place of her heart, we both saw a sweet and gentle light shine out from her heart center. She trembled, eyes shining, and told me, "Something just came back. Something that was missing for twenty years."

DREAM RECOVERY AS SOUL RECOVERY

The absence of dream recall is often a primary symptom of soul-loss—as if the part of the sufferer that knows how to dream and travel in deeper reality has gone away, out of pain or disgust. A Paiute song to heal soul-loss and depression is a call for dreams to return:

> *Now all my singing Dreams are gone,*
> *But none knows where they have fled*
> *Nor by what trails they have left me.*
>
> *Return, O Dreams of my heart,*
> *And sing in the Summer twilight.*
>
> *Return and sing, O my Dreams,*
> *In the dewy and palpitant pastures,*
> *Till the love of living awakes*
> *And the strength of the hills to uphold me.*[2]

The act of recalling dreams may be a vital act of soul recovery, as in Stephanie's story.

Stephanie was a very brave woman. On a breezy fall Saturday in Rhode Island, when I met several black dogs during a morning walk on the beach, she joined a two-day dream workshop with me, although she said the last sleep dream she remembered with clarity was one from thirty years ago. She was a veteran meditator and an advanced practitioner of several disciplines, as well as a caring mother and a humorous, all-around fun person to be with. But she was missing her dreams. "I haven't remembered a dream since I was sixteen years old," she told our circle.

I was delighted when she volunteered to reenter a dream and, impressively, was willing to invite the whole group to travel inside her dreamspace with her. Stephanie was not only brave enough to try to jump back into a dream from her teens, and thereby, in all likelihood, into the life and angst of her adolescent self; she was also ready to let a large group of both friends and strangers come deep inside her psychic space.

"You're on," I told her. "Can you give your dream a title?"

She thought for a moment, and then she told us the title was, "I Can't Stop Them."

In her dream, she is a slender sixteen-year-old girl, trying to stop male intruders who are attempting to break down the front door of her family home. She keeps calling for her father to help, but he doesn't come. She is simply not strong enough. The intruders smash through the door, and she wakes sobbing and terrified and "mad as hell" at her father.

Listening to this dream report, we might all have had various ideas about its meaning in the life of an adolescent girl—as indeed you might be having right now, reading it here. But our intention was not to analyze the dream, but to use it as the portal for a journey, one that would hopefully lead to healing and resolution and, in this case, to the breaking of a dream drought that had lasted for three decades.

Stephanie volunteered that she learned that her father had died of a massive heart attack the same night she dreamed this. Her dream and his death may have coincided. She felt guilty that she had not visited him in the hospital where he had been for several days, and she told us that she thought this guilt was part of the reason she had lost her dreams.

I asked Stephanie, "What do you want to know?"

"I want to know why Dad never came to me in the dream. I am still confused and angry about that."

I gently suggested that if it were my dream, I might want to identify the intruders, and also see whether Dream Reentry could provide access to my father and help settle any unresolved issues between us. She enthusiastically agreed that this was something she wanted to try.

I invited others in the circle to ask questions—not analytical questions, or probes into Stephanie's family history, but travelers' questions, like, "What did the front of the house look like?" or "Can you describe the men who were breaking down the door?"

When the members of the group had stretched out on the floor, making themselves comfortable with cushions and blankets and yoga mats, I had Stephanie tell her dream again. I restated the double intention: to identify and possibly interview the intruders, and to seek helpful contact with her departed father. Now we were all ready to travel into a different space, Stephanie's dreamspace, with the help of my heartbeat drumming.

I immediately encountered the intruders. They were not men, but radiant beings of light. They were the messengers of her father's death, and it was right for them to enter, because it was his time. In my dream, when the front door was smashed open, he suffered his fatal heart attack. I watched, in joy, as Stephanie found her father, embraced him, and exchanged mutual love and forgiveness.

After I sounded the recall from the journey, Stephanie was bursting to share her experiences with us. She now recognized that the intruders were indeed death angels. She described a beautiful reunion with her father that she felt had brought deep healing for both of them.

Like a true dreamer, Stephanie had explored beyond the maps and directions. She found herself reentering a memory from waking life of the night after the original dream, when she had tucked her mother into bed and curled up beside her, on top of the covers. In her workshop journey, she found herself dozing on that bed again, drifting into dreamspace—and watching, in wonder and rising excitement, as dream after dream flowed though her consciousness. "The lost dreams of thirty years were coming back to me," she said. As she spoke, we felt them streaming in. Stephanie described some of the lost dreams she had recovered. She could hold only so many in surface memory, but their energy was with her. And in that moment, we all saw the truth of the Native perception that when we lose our dreams, we lose parts of our soul—and that when we recover our dreams, we get that soul essence back.

Stephanie tripped out at the break, happy and glowing, to treat the beautiful sixteen-year-old who was now with her again to a few things her teen self would enjoy.

DREAMING THE PATHS OF SOUL AFTER DEATH

Island Woman is ferociously clear about our need to understand, through dreaming, what happens to the soul after death. She tells us that our psychic environment can be poisoned by the presence of the earthbound or vengeful dead, who can blight us with their cravings, confusion, and even bodily symptoms. She has absolute clarity about something that has been obfuscated, denied, or suppressed in mainstream Western religion and psychology: more than one aspect of energy and consciousness survives physical death, and we need to recognize and be prepared to deal with more than one aspect of the departed.

Island Woman's birth people, the Hurons, staged very elaborate "second burials" in an effort to contain and relocate an aspect of the soul that stays close to the Earth. We need a corresponding understanding and practice, because the problem of homeless souls just beyond the veil has become toxic.

I was given powerful experiential insight into the Iroquois understanding of the tripartite nature of soul when I was staying at a friend's retreat center in northern Ohio, on the banks of the Rocky River—a center she had founded because of her dreams.

Very late on my first night at Angel House, I walked down to the living room and found an elegant party taking place. I noticed from the clock that it was after three A.M. This was not crimping the style of the party people. The men were wearing black tie, with tuxedoes or smoking jackets. A distinguished older man with silver hair greeted me in a courtly way and introduced himself as Autochthon. The Greek-sounding word rang a distant bell, but I was diverted from puzzling over it because at this moment I noticed that the older man, and all of his companions, had the heads of wolves.

In the morning, I looked up the word *autochthon* in a dictionary and rediscovered that it meant native-born, indigenous. I had no doubt that the Wolf People at the party were indeed of the First Peoples. It was interesting that their leader used a Greek term in our dream encounter. Perhaps he was politely indicating that he, too, was willing to stretch his vocabulary—as Island Woman, the Mother of the Wolf Clan, had required me to do—in order to facilitate communication.

Carol Dombrose, my host, walked me up the hill to a circle of stones overlooking the river. At that moment, a blue heron winged by, looking very much like a flying serpent. Carol invited me to meditate with the stones. I held one and felt that it was an archive stone, holding the memory of a time when our planet was first visited by intelligent beings from a distant star, and the ongoing, but constantly embattled, experiment in the transfer of higher consciousness to a clumsy and slowly evolving life form was initiated.

Then my vision opened wider and I realized that the Wolf People were all around me. They were not dressed for a black-tie party now. They were in skins and tattoos and paint. The Wolf Clan mother watched me, stroking her wampum credentials. I followed the flow of her intention. She was telling me that it was vital for me to know, from the inside, what her people know about the destiny of the soul after death—above all, about the division of the soul after the body dies. This has been poorly explained, even by those who have labored valiantly to recover the secrets of death that mainstream Western religion has toiled so earnestly to suppress. When we are taught about soul and the after-life at all, in temples or churches, we are usually told that we are bodies and souls. The soul leaves when the body is used up, and it has a more or less pleasant experience, depending on a points chart maintained by someone higher up.

The idea that I could have a firsthand experience of the soul's transitions and possible divisions after death was in no way exotic to me. I had been through this several times. I remembered not only my near-death experiences in childhood, but also visions in which I had been able to study the ongoing situations of at least three spiritual bodies that survive physical death: the dense energy body, the astral body that is so active in dreams, and the subtle body that is a vehicle for higher consciousness—mind, *nous*, spirit.

The Wolf People—Island Woman's clan—beamed their intention. They were inviting me to enter the experience of one of their great ones as his energy and consciousness divided at the moment of death. It seemed that if I accepted, I would enter the life-in-death of the silver-headed elder who had introduced himself as Autochthon, the First Born. I thought of him now as Silver Wolf. It was a thrilling invitation, and a scary one.

Oh yes, I was there in my Australian white man's body, with the sun flashing on the river, and Carol poking around somewhere nearby in the woods, and the distant roar of commuter traffic on the highway. Yet I was also with the Wolf People, living in two worlds simultaneously, and of the two worlds, it was that of the Wolf People that seemed more real.

A part of me has a really hard time saying no, especially if what is being proposed has any entertainment value. My response flashed back: "Let's go for it."

I stepped into the center of the circle of stones, and it seemed that the veil had reformed behind me, screening me from the distractions of my contemporary world. I remembered an early dream, after Island Woman first contacted me, in which I was on sacred Iroquois land, setting up electrified fences and other barriers to prevent the unauthorized from getting in.

The Wolf People were chanting: "We fold you in the blanket of our Mother Earth." I felt my vital essence streaming into the earth.

Kia'tat. This word played over and over in my mind. I knew its double meaning: "I enter the womb" and "I am buried."

As I entered the womb of earth, I glimpsed, for a moment, the double spiral of the eyes of the Goddess. Birth and death, death and rebirth.

I gasped at the weight of the heavy stone that was placed over my torso. It stole my breath. It was asphyxiating. I felt, in the most literal way, that I was being buried alive. I fought back my desire to claw my way up. I knew, in my deeper mind, that what was being done was essential. Island Woman's people were burying and sealing one aspect of my energy in the earth, so that it would not wander about, troubling the living. This part of me was unreasoning, unfeeling, a thing of mere appetency and craving. I experienced its blind desperation without pity. This aspect of soul energy—which the Iroquois associate with the bones, or more specifically with bone marrow—must not be confused with the personality of the departed. It should be recycled into the earth as fast as possible. If this is not done, it can wander around seeking to feed on the energies of the living. It then becomes what the Iroquois call the *ohskenrari,* or burned bones—the "living dead" from the old horror flicks.

I was relieved when I was allowed to move from the grave and experience the transits of a second aspect of the soul. This one was lighter and could really get around. I enjoyed fast-traveling to visit old friends and neighborhoods, from a time long before highways and highrises. Then I felt a desire to settle down and rest, and I entered the deep dream of a tree. When I roused from my long nap—years later, perhaps—I felt myself gravitating toward something pink and juicy, delicious as a wet peach. I found myself being born a bear cub, small enough at birth to be held in the curl of my mother's paw. When I grew to full size, I realized I could go calling on people who were in need of healing. I was walking medicine.

I was now permitted to share in the experience of a third aspect of an ancient shaman's soul or spirit. I was lighter still. I could travel as fast as thought, without need of confining myself to any form. To travel up *there,* on the path to the Sky World I remembered and yearned for, I would put on another garment, which I saw as an animal skin lined with a sky full of stars. But I would not make that trip now. I was one of those called upon to stay close to the Earth, to watch over the people and guide them, and reach to dreamers to recall them to the memory of soul and the way of the Peacemaker.

I lived and died all of it intensely, this trisection of the spiritual energy of an ancient Iroquois elder. The vision gave me what Island Woman and Silver Wolf no doubt intended: clarity on how more than one piece of us survives physical death, and how understanding and working with this is central to rebirthing the true *ars moriendi*, or art of dying, that our society desperately needs.

If you are wondering, I do not consider that Silver Wolf is my counterpart in a different time and culture, at least not in the way I suspect that William Johnson may be, or others in other times. I *do* think we are now closely linked, as the result of ceremonies of burial, adoption, and requickening that were played out in a dreamspace very close to this world.

My vision in the stone circle left me deeply determined to help people in my time to heal their relationship with death and the departed. This involves separating the heavy energy of the dead from the living, finding satisfactory living arrangements for the dreamsoul in its astral body, and dialoguing with the higher consciousness of the departed and helping it to remember its multiple options.

Yeats said, "the living can assist the imaginations of the dead," and he was exactly right.[3] But to do that, we need firsthand experiences of the afterlife, and good working connections on the other side. We achieve this through dreaming.

20

Entertaining and Honoring the Spirits

Love and celebrate. The world is not your prison,
but your playground.
"Conversation with the Higher Self"

THANKING THE FRIENDS OF THE SOUL

How would you like to have a friend like this:

She shows up just when you need her. She always gives you the support and counsel you need, and she never judges you.

She is an amazing psychic advisor: she knows what the future holds for you, and she can tell you what to do and what not to do to avoid something bad or find the right job, or the right home, or the right partner.

She is a doctor and a healer who can help you to fix your body before you get sick, and who has the right medicine and nurturing to speed you into healing and recovery if you do. She makes house calls at any time, and she never charges you a cent.

She's fabulous fun and a great traveling companion. She makes you want to get up and dance, and sing, and play. She loves to fly off to exotic places, and she must be incredibly rich because sometimes she whisks you away on a private jet or a yacht. She has such powerful connections you never have to go through a security line or a customs check.

She has wonderful energy. An hour in her company gives you a boost for a whole week.

She'll mother you when you, and your beautiful child self, need mothering, hold you when you need holding, and give you a shove when you need to jump through a hole in the world.

She knows you better than you know yourself, in your everyday mind. When she holds up a mirror in front of you, you don't notice the blemishes. You see a being of radiant power and possibility, your ancient and shining self. And in that moment of recognition, you begin to remember and live from your soul's purpose, the sacred contract you signed before you came into your present body.

Let's suppose that you are blessed to have a friend who is all of these things, and more. And you never say thank you, or remember her birthday. You ignore her advice more often than not, and when you screw up you wail about how unfair life is, or how the world won't support you. You forget the songs you sang together, and those nights of love and beauty you did not have to pay for. If you find the moon through the smog and city lights, you do not recollect that she flew you there. You look in the bathroom mirror, and you do not see her looking back at you.

If she were a regular friend, she might dump you as a miserable ingrate. This friend is beyond the ordinary, and she has the patience of an angel—but even the patience of angels is not endless. So if you won't take her advice, she might make less of an effort to warn you that if you don't look out for that silver Subaru at that intersection next Tuesday, you'll wreck your car, or that if you won't speak from your heart, you will lose the love of your life. And if you are no fun to be around—because you are forever putting the poor mouth on life (as the Irish say), refusing the risk of birthing something new, and filling the hole in your world with drabness and addiction—your shining friend may begin to keep her distance. Then the magic begins to flicker in your world, and you are more alone than you ever need or want to be.

We now see the truth of the Iroquois insight that *dreams require action*. We must take action to honor the friend who visits and advises and travels with us in our dreams. We may discover that we have many allies in our dreams, but the most important is the one we find in the mirror—like Hiawatha—when our sight is clear: an ancient and shining self.

Taking the right action to honor dreams is practical magic of a high order. Real magic is the art of reaching into a deeper reality and bringing gifts from it into the physical world. This is what we do when we honor dreams, and the powers that speak through dreams.

The first part of the action we take to honor a dream may be speech, but it should be far more than rambling chitchat or left-brain analysis. The speech required is an act, a poetic movement, a moment of naming that brings something new into a world. Like the dream shamans, we must speak in the knowledge that dreaming gives us the songs and the magic words that can bring something—even a whole world—into manifestation from a soupy ocean of possibilities.

As Island Woman tells us, bringing something from the dreamworld into the surface world is not only a creative process; it is also a process of creation, a way of dancing a world into being, as Sky Woman danced on Turtle's back.

CREATING DREAM TALISMANS

Among the Iroquois, as among other cultures that value dreams, one of the important things we can do with the dream is to choose or construct an object that honors the dream and can hold its energy.

This is why stones are so prized by Island Woman and her sisters. A stone can not only hold the memory of a powerful dream; it can also hold its energy. Sometimes, a stone can also provide a space within which its holder can meet a dream guide again and continue a conversation. If there can be a universe inside a stone, there can most certainly be a place of encounter, whose architecture may be as simple or complex as the dreamer and the oyaron choose it to be.

For the Iroquois, certain stones and crystals already hold the energy and consciousness of sacred beings, in an animate universe, and you might select one of these for your personal "medicine bundle" if you have encountered one of those beings in your visionary life.

If you have dreamed of a certain animal or bird, you will want something that is of that creature. It may be a carving or artwork, but it will be most successful as a dream talisman if it embodies something of the bird or animal you dreamed: a feather, a piece of fur, a tooth or claw.

You may bring together elements of several dreams of power to fashion a shield or to fill a pouch with the vocabulary of your dreaming. I routinely travel with small objects representing the animal guardians of the cardinal directions in my personal dreaming, and some wampum strings and belts that hold the memory of Island Woman's teachings, one of which was crafted for me by a traditional wampum weaver to include codes for passing safely between different cultures, and over formidable mountains, and between dimensions.

CREATIVE DREAM JOURNALING

In *The Artist's Way*, Julia Cameron counsels aspiring writers to make time and space to write a few pages each morning, without worrying about content. This is excellent advice. But filling those pages with dreams—and reflections and associations from dreams—is even better. Stories and characters come spilling out. The narratives and dramas write themselves. And as we journal dreams and give them titles, we flex those writing muscles without needing to think about it. We can find ourselves moving deliciously into a flow state that can carry over into our other writing or other creative initiatives.

DRAWING AND PAINTING FROM DREAMS

We shouldn't just write our dreams and tell them; we should also draw them, paint them, turn them into art and artifact.

Drawing from dreams is easy, and there is really no reason not to make this a part of your daily play. Your inner child will love it if you have crayons, tempera paints, scratch paper, and collage supplies on your sometimes-so-boring desk or kitchen table, and the sparkling energy of your child will come to play in your life. If you are scared to draw or paint, start out by working with your nondominant hand, or try scribbling with your eyes closed. (Try this even if you are an accomplished artist; it's amazing what can come through.) I find it fun to make a series of drawings from dreams and visions. Sometimes the result looks like a page from a graphic novel, or a comic book.

TURNING DREAM REPORTS INTO POEMS

Many dreams are natural poems, and the experience of dream telling brings the poetry through as we adopt appropriate cadences and vocabulary.

Here's a fun assignment that will entertain the spirits: take a dream report and shape-shift it into poetry. You may find that all that is required, initially, is to write out the dream report again, with light editing, on a piece of paper in the form of free verse. Or you may prefer to take just a vignette, a phrase, a piece of the dream to make "sloppy haiku" or improvise something that takes off from the dream rather than remains bound to it.

Although I often turn dreams into free verse, I find that the spirit of the dream—or more accurately, perhaps, the spirit *in* the dream— requires me to craft a poem with more care and artifice. I have been meeting the poet and magus William Butler Yeats in various locales in the dreamworld for as much of my present life as I can remember. Sometimes we meet in a certain library; occasionally he receives me in a magical cottage in what he very precisely described as the fourth level of the astral plane. Close to the winter solstice in 2002, when I made a conscious dream journey from a drumming circle back to Newgrange where I had found the Eyes of the Goddess, he appeared as a guide along the way. I could not leave the poem I wrote from that journey in free verse. I had to borrow patterns of rhyme and rhythm akin to those of which Yeats was grand master:

Eyes of the Goddess
(from a journey to Newgrange)

The poet waits for me in his countryman's cape
And shows me the map in the gateway stone:
Twin spirals to get you in, and out, of the place of
*   bone;*
Wave paths to swim you from shadow to dreamscape;
A stairway of stars for when you are done with
*   earthing.*
I am here to practice the art of rebirthing.

She calls me, into the belly of the land that is She.
But I play, like the poet, with the shapes of time:
I am a swimming swan on the River Boyne;
I am a salmon, full with the knowing of the hazel tree;
I wander with Angus, and I know the girl I have
    visioned
In gold at the throat of a white swan, beating pinions.

Drawn by the old perfume of burned bones, I go down
And doze until solstice fire, bright and bountiful
Quickens me for the return of the Lady, lithe and
    beautiful
In the form she has taken, flowing as liquid bronze.
Her face is veiled, so the man-boy called to her side
Like the red deer in season will not die in her eyes.

I see beyond the veil, for I come from the Other.
Oh, I yearn for the smell of earth and the kiss of rain!
I leap with her on the hallowed bed, coming again.
She knows the deer-king, and I am child and lover.
Her eyes are spriral paths; the gyre of creation whirls
And sends me in green beauty to marry the worlds.

TURNING DREAMS INTO STORIES

When we tell a dream in a way that holds our audience, we are already claiming the story power that is one of the greatest gifts of dreams, and reviving the bardic power in our lives.

Stories and scripts can come streaming directly out of the dream experience. Some dream reports resemble a complete story, or the script for a movie or TV show; others can provide that script with minimal editing. Sometimes we need to travel back into the dreamspace to bring more of the story through.

Our dreams deliver the gift of story in a deeper sense: they put us in touch with the big story of our lives. They bring us into connection with the sacred drama that is playing beyond the veil of our daily dramas. They show us our counterparts in other times and other dimensions, and they bring us into the play of the gods. This opens channels to mythic healing, which flows from the power of rising beyond our symptoms and our daily grind to tap into the big story that wants to be lived through us.

The Dream Story–Swapping Game

Because I have a low boredom threshold, I am constantly in search of new games to play. I asked my dreams to give me a new one on the eve of a creativity workshop I was leading in Santa Fe. What I got was a scene in which my workshop participants were gathered around a deep lake. They were writing down summaries of the dreams that came to them from that well of vision. They mixed them up and passed them around at random, and then they took turns sitting in a very high wooden seat—the height of a lifeguard's chair, or a high throne—reading out the borrowed dream summary, and making up a story to go with it. As they did this, hosts of people, including creative writers and artists from the past, ancestors and Native spirits, thronged around the perimeter of the circle, listening with evident delight.

I introduced the game in my workshop the next day. A newcomer attending that program had been dragged out to the retreat center by well-meaning friends. She did not want to be there. She had no prior experience relevant to our work, and she rarely remembered her dreams. She was exhausted and literally sick to death, because her doctors—in the style of the black sorcerers of Western allopathic medicine—had told her she might only have a few months to live. She drew the card on which I had written a summary of a dream of my own, struggling to make my writing legible. This is the dream summary I put on the index card:

> I am in an army of warriors in leather armor who fight under the standard of the Bear Goddess. Tired of fighting, I abandon my weapons and walk into the wilderness until I can walk no more. A bear cub takes me by the hand and leads me to a place of healing.

The woman who drew my card read the words aloud, stumbling over a couple of my squiggles. She stopped, stared, read the report again— and then appeared to freeze. For an edgy moment, it seemed that our story game might become an embarrassing belly flop. Then the woman came alive—vibrantly, passionately alive. She got on her feet and put her whole body into her performance. Keening, shouting, whispering, groaning, she enthralled all of us as she spun a riveting epic from the scraps of my dream, a personal mythistory in which she found room for all her life struggles, and through which she opened a personal path to healing. She described how she had fought as a warrior woman under the banner of an environmental cause. She believed passionately in her cause, but she was sick of fighting. She described herself heading off into the desert badlands of her home territory, losing her strength, dying of thirst. She mimed herself gasping and dying—until the bear cub appeared and helped her to a healing shack, filled with herbs and natural remedies.

She listed the plants and talismans that were given to her. Three that she named were in my original dream, but not in my dream report, so one of the things that had happened spontaneously was that she had entered the dream reality I had discovered. In her story, she described how in the place of healing, dried lavender was placed as a protective garland around her neck—as it was placed around my neck in my original dream. With every line she spoke, she gained visibly in strength and courage. Moved to tears—and guided by synchronicity—her neighbor in the circle opened her journal and handed her a spring of dried lavender, to honor the dream.

TURNING DREAMS INTO THEATER

Performance and theater are central in the ancient and shamanic practices of dream healing. This is why the best theaters of ancient Greece were often built next to the dream temples of Asklepios. As we have seen, the Iroquois made it their practice to perform dreams, sometimes leaving out the ending so it could be guessed at in a community game, or changed for the better.

Of all the adventures we share in the workshops, dream theater may be my favorite. Spontaneous dream theater is the pinnacle of improvisation. It provides an immediate and powerful way to honor the dream. It brings all the elements and characters alive—to the point where the dreamer can run with the wolf or have a conversation with a doorknob. It deepens and binds the energy of the group, and it gives a lift to the session, any time of day. It is cathartic. It can open paths to healing and resolution, allowing the dreamer to move beyond a point of fear, interruption, or blockage in the original dream.

In the Dream School, we have developed a process that makes it possible to turn a dream into a play, choose the cast, set up the stage, choreograph the moves, rehearse the actors, hold a script conference and decide on any necessary changes, move into a finished production (with the dreamer as star), and have feedback from all the players, speaking from their own roles—in just thirty minutes.

Dreams are already dramas. When we do dream theater, we enact those dramas as actors perform from a script or a screenplay. But we have more leeway than actors working from a finished script, because we can improvise (with the dreamer's permission) and add additional scenes.

One of the most basic gifts of dream theater is the most obvious: we dramatize our dreams, and their messages. The characters and elements in the dream come alive, and can speak to us in body language as well as words. The dreamer can now interact, in the body, with personalities and energies from the dreamworld. Dream theater may also help to energize our lives, and mobilize us to make positive life choices, by bringing vitality and confidence from the dreamspace into our physical world.

A man who had been facing a number of challenges in his working environment dreamed that he was on the beach. Feeling hungry, he waded into the ocean, grabbed a large fish with his bare hands, and started eating it raw, enjoying his snack enormously. He carried the fish back to the beach to finish it as his leisure. In the dream, a hungry shark followed him onto the sand and tried to grab his food away from him. He bonked the shark on the nose, after which it lay down on the sand, docile as a puppy dog waiting for leftovers.

The dreamer enjoyed his dream, and he felt that it held the promise that he would be able to work out a way to handle the "sharks" in his work environment. That promise seemed to take physical form as we enacted his dream. The dreamer reveled in being able to contain and control the big man cast as the hungry shark. When he interviewed the players, they confirmed that what he has to offer (his fish snack in the dream) is "juicy" and appealing to others, and that he can find a way to bring the workplace "sharks" into a civilized situation where they can be taught to wait their turn. Energized by the dream theater, the dreamer came up with a practical action plan for dealing with the sharks at the office, centered on the clear understanding that he has something they want and value.

Dream theater may serve to constellate a power (to use a term Jung liked)—perhaps that of a goddess or an angel—that we have encountered in the dreamspace. The energy of an archetype or sacred being is embodied in a dream player, or perhaps the dance of all the dream players. I dreamed that the god Asklepios appeared as a figure of living gold and spun the form of the Medicine Bear from his solar plexus to bring healing to people in America. When the work was done, he drew the Bear back inside his body. As the dream was performed, we all felt an afflux of luminous healing energy joining us in the space. When this happens, the theater becomes a sacred ritual.

Dream theater also may enable us to act out what is otherwise difficult to express. This is one of the reasons it is so valuable to practice with children, who love acting anyway.

In the course of dream theater, we may be able to help the dreamer to dream the dream onward to healing and empowerment, moving beyond fear and blockage. A woman dreamed she was frozen in fear in an archway, unable to accept the invitation of a goddess to step into her precinct because she was terrified of a giant serpent that was writhing around the goddess. The dream performance was so powerful that for a moment, she was frozen again in the archway—but she was finally able to move beyond it. She was consumed by the serpent, but she was then born again from inside its form to dance with the goddess, who wished to live embodied life through her.

Another dreamer was terrified by armies of spiders moving over twin hills in her dream. She saw beautiful light shining through the cleft between the hills, and she knew she would find peace and healing if she could only enter that light—but she was paralyzed by her terror. When she bravely volunteered this dream for performance, she was terrified again by the players who gave a very convincing portrayal of the spiders. It took a great summoning of will for her to move through the valley between the hills of human spiders into a beautiful light burst (which was enacted by players standing on a window seat, unfurling bright scarves). In the course of the performance, the dreamer felt she had finally moved beyond her fear of breast cancer, and she resolved to carry that energy with her for further healing.

Mountain Lion Onstage

In the report that follows, we'll follow the performance of a dream step by step. The dream was my own, and the original title was "Mountain Lion Pulls Me Up to the Place of the Heart"; I told this dream in detail in part 1, chapter 6. Prior to the dream theater, I had done quite a lot of work with this dream, and I had even written about it in an article.

But the dream theater took me to a clearer level of awareness about one vital element: the need to get rid of some of my baggage. This mobilized me to remember the lesson and make sure I applied it at every turn in my life.

1. Telling the Dream as a Script

I told the group my dream, in which I am carrying a lot of stuff—a suitcase, a laptop bag, carrier bags, and other things—as I walk with a companion up a slope toward my car. I realize I have to put down some of my burdens. I give some things to my friend to carry and place others on the ground.

I find I have to scale a very steep cliff, and it's hard going even though now I am carrying only a small white box. I am grateful when a helper at the top of the cliff lowers a lifeline to me and helps pull me up. I discover that my helper is a mountain lion. When I get to the top, my helper tells me it's time to open the box. When I do, I find a strong, beating heart. I place it on the highest point of land and let the heartbeat sound. I feel it reaching people in all directions, across a great distance.

2. Casting the Dream

I picked members of the circle to play every role in the dream, starting with my dream self. I chose people to play my bags, my friend, the mountain lion, the lifeline, and the beating heart. I chose people to play the gentle slope and the near-vertical cliff. Everyone was given a role. If we had had more players, I would have cast them as trees on the hills, as the sea in the distance, as the people the heartbeat reaches when it is allowed to sound out.

3. Setting the Stage

We set up the room to accommodate the theater. I chose the side of the room with a heap of cushions along the wall as the place where we would set up the steep hill. We moved objects from the center out of the way so nothing would be knocked over, or trip up the players, during the performance.

4. Choreography

I told the dream again slowly, with many pauses, as I taught the players their lines and helped them find the places where they would stand or move. From the beginning, we were called on to improvise. It would have required complicated mechanics and some bodily pain to show the lifeline—played by a woman—hanging down vertically, so we had it move along a horizontal plane. This became part of the illumination that came with the theater.

5. Rehearsal
We were now ready for a full dress rehearsal. As the players portraying my baggage clustered around the woman I had cast to play me, I was shocked to see that she could hardly move! The idea of trying to get anywhere while carrying so much stuff was preposterous. I noticed that her companion seemed to be part of her burden, rather than a real source of help. While encumbered in this way, my dream self literally could not see the goal of her journey, or hope to find the lifeline that would help her to ascend the mountain. When she left her baggage behind, she also left her companion. All of this, as I watched the performance, was tremendously significant and moving for me.

6. Script Conference
We discussed whether changes or additions to the script were required. I invited the players to improvise. I especially encouraged my dream companion—silent in my dream report—to speak from her point of view. I invited the dream actor portraying the mountain lion to say more and to behave as a big cat might want to behave. The dream actor playing my beating heart asked whether he could borrow a drum to make the heartbeat reverberate more loudly. Naturally, I gave him a drum, and we encouraged him to make as much noise as he wanted to.

7. The Big Show
Now we were ready for the big production, in which I would play myself. I invited the friend who had played my dream self in the rehearsal to assume a new role, as one of those who would listen to the heartbeat from a distance.

From the moment I entered my own role in the play, I found the theater totally absorbing and immensely powerful. The players entered more deeply into their roles and became the forbidding cliff, the heavy suitcase covered with travel stickers, the friend who wanted to help but had herself become part of the burden.

I had felt blessed in the original dream. I felt doubly blessed this time as I seized hold of the lifeline and was carried up by the lion. I was awed, inside the animate world of the dream, as the heartbeat rode on the vibrations of the drum.

8. Applause
We applauded one another at the end of the show; any halfway-decent performance requires applause!

9. Feedback from the Dream Players
I asked the players to stay in their roles for a little while after the closing scene so they could talk to me from their perspective inside the dream theater. I told them, "If you were a bag, speak as a bag. If you were part of the cliff, speak as the cliff. Don't step outside your role. Tell me what you can say as a bag or a rock."

What was shared was fresh and full of valuable insights. The person playing my laptop bag was especially intuitive. She told me, "I'm a burden when you use me for e-mail, because that's taking too much of your time away from creative pursuits."

10. Action to Honor the Dream Theater
One thing I decided to do was to stop taking my laptop on trips because, as the player intuited, when I go around with my laptop I tend to spend too much time checking e-mail. By leaving my laptop behind, I made room for some big chunky journals in which I write stories by hand.

One of the most important and helpful communications I have ever received from my Higher Self was this: "Love and celebrate. Remember this world is not your prison; it is your playground." For me, that is a license to join in the constant pulse of creation, to birth something new every day, to improvise fresh games and fresh words to entertain the spirits—who are not so much out there as in here. If I want to say "I am alive" in the Mohawk language, I say *kia:tonte,* which basically means, "I am a spirit that has a body." I am one of the spirits that demand to be entertained, and so are you.

21

Becoming a Poet of Consciousness

I cannot be born
On solid ground,
Only where everything flows.
To enter my dawn
You must be unbound
From how the fixed world goes.

Leave behind
Your maps and losses
Let dreams be all your law.
Trust the wind
When the ocean tosses
Burn your boats on the farther shore.

Make new songs
And your floating island
Will be rooted beneath the waves.
Drink my sun

And you dance on the high land
Your heart, remembering, craves.

"BIRTH OF APOLLO"

Poets, said William Everson, are shamans of words.[1] True shamans, as we have learned, are dreamers and poets of consciousness. Journeying into a deeper reality with the aid of sung and spoken poetry, they bring back energy and healing through poetic acts. When we dream, we tap directly into the same creative source from which poets and shamans derive their gifts. When we create from our dreams, and enter dreamlike flow, we become poets and artists. When we *act* to bring the energy and imagery of dreams into physical reality, we become poets of consciousness, and we infuse our world with magic.

Across the centuries, many of our greatest poets have recognized their kinship with the shaman's way of shifting awareness and shapeshifting reality. As his name in a spiritual order, Goethe chose the name of a legendary shaman of antiquity, Abaris, who came flying out of the northern mists on an arrow from Apollo's bow.[2]

Our earliest poets were shamans. Today, as in the earliest times, true shamans know the power of song and story to teach and to heal. They understand that through the play of words, the magic of the Real World comes dancing into the surface world. The right words open pathways between the worlds. The poetry of consciousness delights the spirits. It draws in the gods and goddesses who wish to live through us.

Shamans use poetry, sung or spoken, to achieve ends that go deeper than our consensual world. They create poetic songs of power to invoke spiritual help, to journey into nonordinary reality, to open and maintain a space between the worlds where interaction between humans and multidimensional beings can take place, and to bring energy and healing through to the body and the physical world.

For the Iroquois, to sing is to "put forth your power."[3] As Turtle Woman taught me, a song may be the vehicle through which the healing and magic of the dreamworld is carried into the physical world. As I learned when I found the song that opened my way to the heart of Ancient Mother, a song may also be the key to opening the dreamworlds. Like the type of South American shaman called *payé*, skilled dream travelers take flight with the help of "wing songs."[4]

A young singer-songwriter I know composed a lovely song inspired by a single phrase from a dream: "Dreams are moonbabies." When she asked me to help her dream up new songs, and a path to a music publisher, I suggested that we should use the chorus of her song as our fuel and direction for a journey to a music academy in the realm of the moon. Lying on rugs on the floor, in silvery moonlight, we chanted and hummed together:

Dreams are moonbabies

We flew into the bright face of the moon. And we found, after skirting some initial diversions (the realm of Luna is full of distractions), a music school with a grand lobby of the kind that Mozart might have walked. To my surprise, my great-aunt, who was an opera singer and Dame Nellie Melba's close friend and understudy, as well as a gifted clairvoyant, met us and showed us around. The chanteuse was able to visit a studio where she played and memorized two songs she had not yet written or thought of composing. She was also able to examine the cover of a CD she had not yet recorded for guidance on where to go to have her new music recorded. And for good measure, my great-aunt gave both of us some exercises for strengthening the voice.

We have learned, from the beauty and power of the Iroquois mythistories, that the big stories stream directly to us from the Dreamtime, and that they want to be told in poetry more than prose. Like my Celtic ancestors, and my dream friend William Butler Yeats, indigenous peoples recognize the power of magic words and the fact that real poets are magicians by nature. Inuit shamans have a language of their own, which is often impenetrable to other Eskimos. It is a language that is never still. It bubbles and eddies, opening a whirlpool way to the deep bosom of the sea goddess, or a cavernous passage into the hidden fires of earth.

My favorite Inuit shaman-word is the one for *dream*. It looks like this: *kubsaitigisak*. It's pronounced koov-sigh-teegee-shakk, with a little click at the back of the throat when you come to the final consonant. It means "what makes me dive in headfirst."[5] Savor that for a moment, and all that flows with it. A dream, in Eskimo shaman-speech, is something that makes you dive in headfirst. Doesn't this wondrously evoke the kinesthetic energy of dreaming, the sense of plunging into a deeper world? Doesn't it also invite us to take the plunge, in the dream of life, and burst through the glass ceilings and paper barriers constructed by the daily trivial self?

Shamans know further uses for dream poetry. They call the soul back home, into the bodies of those who have lost vital energy through pain or trauma or heartbreak. And from their journeys, they bring back poetic imagery that can help to shape-shift the body's energy template in the direction of health. By bringing through the right images from the dreaming, the poets of consciousness explain dis-ease in ways that help the patient get well and that interact with the body and its immune system on multiple levels without invasive surgery.

After attending healing sessions of Cuna shamans in Panama, French anthropologist Claude Lévi-Strauss explained how the poetry of consciousness is a healing art. "The shaman provides the sick . . . with a language, by means of which unexpressed, and otherwise inexpressible, psychic states can immediately be expressed. And it is the transition to this verbal expression which induces the release of the physiological process."[6] Instead of giving an explanation of disease that leaves the sufferer powerless and "patient," the shaman explains disease through words and images that help the patient get well—just as our dreams do. This is healing through dream transfer, a poetic act.

Let's recall the Inuit wisdom, so closely corresponding to the wisdom of Island Woman's people, that with the poetic act, the worlds are joined and the sacred beings come dancing through. An old Inuit woman on Little Diomede Island explained to a Danish anthropologist that powerful spirits—like the spirit of the whale—must be summoned by "fresh words." "Worn-out songs" should never be used when you are trying to call on important spirits, she explained. In the fall, in a festival house, all the lights were extinguished and everyone sat in silence, waiting for a fresh song to burst forth that would entertain and draw the spirits. If you can find those fresh words—the right ones—you can call a whale.[7] Note that the poetry of consciousness feeds the soul on all levels. An Arctic shaman who can call a whale can supply his people with food and light for the winter.

And where do our fresh words and our poetic acts—in life as well as in art—have their genesis? In dreaming, and in dreamlike flow, and in synchronistic fugues, when we drop our left-brain inhibitions and get in touch with the source. As American poet William Everson observed, "There is no real creative process without mood. It is a losing of objectivity to another dimension, a further loss of self, and it is from this loss that all authentic work springs. . . . The great thing about the dream is that it takes us into that dimension of mood. Sometimes your finest poems come out of dreams, or out of your recording of a dream."[8]

My favorite poems flow from conscious dreaming, often from dream travel through the gateway of a dream image or memory, as I traveled through the Eyes of the Goddess or through the tree gate into the realm of Ancient Mother.

Here is a journey poem I wrote from a series of conscious dream journeys while I was leading a week-long retreat at Kripalu, a wonderful center for yoga and healing in Massachusetts. This poem reflects a collective experience of soul journeying and soul recovery in which I led a whole flight of dreamers on a journey beyond death to learn how to help souls on both sides of that swing door. The theme of the poem is the challenge of the final phase of the hero's or heroine's journey: bringing it all home.

The Return Journey

You found the courage
to turn on the tiger who pursued you
to fight with him hand to claw
to be swallowed and spat out
and to win through your losing
reforged in a shining body
worthy now to take his heart
and call him as your unswerving ally.
It is not enough.

Out of your yearning
you danced into worlds of enchantment
you drank from the breasts of the Goddess
where kisses flower into hyacinths
caresses stream into rivers of milk
every nerve ending is a partner in love
and hearts are never broken.
You discovered that dreaming is magic.
But it's not enough.

As a confident traveler, you learned
to shrug off your bodyshirt
and ride the World Tree
as your private elevator
to soar through the face of the moon
dance with the bear among the stars

to enter the sun behind the sun
and fly on wings of paradise over a fresh world.
You're out there, but it's not enough

Out of your calling
you braved the gates of the Underworld
and crossed the borderless river on your heartbeat
and tricked the Dark Angel in his own realm.
When you stood, defeated, before the impregnable walls
of death itself, you raised a song from your heart and
    belly
that called help from the highest heaven
to pluck a soul from the cold recreation yard
where nobody plays new games.
But you must make the return journey.

The way back is full of diversions.
Some will detain you with pink kisses;
some will drag on you as drowning men
You'll find the markers have been moved, or stolen.
Maybe you'll have gone so deep, or so high
you can't remember which world you left your body in.
Or you'll rebel against returning to a world
where hearts are broken, and the earth defiled.
You will return. This is your soul's agreement.

Now you have danced with the bear
you will bring healing to the world of pain.
Now you have traveled the roads of soul
you will help the soul-lost to bring their children home.
Now you have flown as Apollo on a shining arrow
you will bring light into the shadow world.
Now you know the gates and paths of the Real World
you will make bridges for others.
You will bring it all home.

Returning, you will remember your mission:
To serve the soul's remembering;
to go among people as dream ambassador

opening ways for soul to be heard and honored.
Let the world be your playground, not your prison.
Starchild, plunge with delight into the warm, loamy earth,
Renew the marriage of earth and sky,
Follow your heart-light, dance your dreams,
Commit poetry every day, in every way.
Now you are home.

When we turn our dreams into poems, we free our creative spirit, and our spirits come dancing. In one of my workshops, I was awed by a poem that came singing through a math major who had worked as a computer engineer for twenty-seven years and had never (to her recollection) written a poem until she received the gift of soul retrieval. Nancy's poem begins:

Wise child, joyful child,
dancing and laughing in the sun. Don't be afraid;
the cougar will protect you.
Your job is just to have fun.

Our dreams are calling us to use fresh words, to see the world with fresh eyes, to honor the secret wishes of the soul and commit poetry every day.

An Action Plan for Poets of Consciousness
1. Catch your dreams. Write them in a journal and give them titles.
2. Find a dream partner and tell dreams to each other every day, moving into the rhythms appropriate for the telling.
3. Make poetry, art, and creative decisions from your dreams.
4. Navigate by synchronicity; treat everything that enters your field of perception as a personal message from the Divine.
5. Withhold your consent from other people's limited definitions of reality.*
6. Avoid negative mantras and self-limiting beliefs.
7. Commit poetry, every day, in every way.

---

*When someone invites us to subscribe to the worldview that "Shit happens" or "There'll never be enough" or "You can't trust people" we don't need to argue; we can simply decline to give our endorsement. We should also withhold our consent from the belief that "reality" is the world of clock time and our everyday consensual hallucinations.

The Peril of Losing the Sky

*I know where we have come from. We have come from the
Sky, from the world above the Sky. I will never forget this.
I will continue to hold on with both hands to the place I
have come from.*

ATTRIBUTED TO THARONHIAWAKON, SKY HOLDER,
IN THE IROQUOIS CREATION STORY.

The sugar maples have burst into color, and I am driving through a world
of reds and golds. It's been two weeks since the mountain lion pulled me
up to the place of the heart, and I am on my way to lead a weekend workshop in a restored eighteenth-century house in the gentle woods of western Connecticut. The October light limns the edges of everything with the
precise beauty of a calligrapher's pen. Inspired by Normandi Ellis's lovely
poetic improvisations on Egyptian spells of rebirthing, I have crafted a
new workshop called Way of the Phoenix. I have dreamed up some rituals and journeys to help us rebirth ourselves from the ashes of our old
lives—like the legendary phoenix, the Benu bird of Egypt.

When I arrive at the house, set on a wilderness preserve of several
hundred acres, I am thrilled to hear that a great blue heron was sighted

on that land earlier in the day. The Egyptian phoenix looks very much like a heron, and shape-shifting into a heron, or another glorious bird, is a preferred Egyptian way of traveling from this world to other worlds, on either side of death. The heron is also a most important bird in the Iroquois Dreamtime. When Sky Woman falls from a world above the sky, pregnant with a new one, the herons lend her wings to come down safely.

At the house, I find that our generous Dream School helpers have set a huge bowl of strawberries among the snacks on the buffet table. I sink my teeth into a plump berry. As the sweet juice explodes in my mouth, I remember that for the Iroquois, strawberries are sacred food, and they line the path on which fortunate souls may return to the world above the sky.

In our meeting room, a fire is crackling in the great hearth. Opposite the fire, a man as tall and lean as a standing heron is laying his bundles on a red-striped blanket, like the Iroquois trade blankets of long ago. He is wearing a loose white linen shirt, a large shell gorget, silver armbands, and a necklace of claws and wampum beads, and his very long hair is tied back in a neat ponytail. He appears to have stepped out of another time, the time of Sir William Johnson and Island Woman.

He greets me with great courtesy and quiet intensity. He tells me he has come to me from the Mohawk community at Akwesasne, bearing two messages. He would like to give them to me privately, after our opening session that evening, if I am willing to smoke a pipe with him.

Later we sit outside, under an oak and a night full of stars. He lights up an old Cherokee pipe that he has filled with native tobacco from the Mohawk longhouse. The taste is harsh; you would not smoke this stuff without a powerful reason. The Iroquois say that the spirit rides to the heavens on a cloud of tobacco.

Ellis (who is not related to Normandi Ellis, though the echo is interesting, given our work that weekend) reminds me that we once met briefly at a lecture in New York. He explains that he is not Mohawk by birth, but spends several months of the year living with Mohawks and has been received into the Longhouse. Ellis astonishes me by telling me that I am regarded as an elder by Mohawks I have not yet met. He tells me that they believe I will help bring back the ancient dreamways and that they are grateful for my work.

Then he says that his more urgent message is from another Native people, with whom he also spends several months of the year. Shaman-priests of the Kogi have asked him to make contact with me. I am surprised and excited by the mention of the Kogi. I remember that I watched a British television documentary, many years before, about this dreaming people. The Kogi response to the European occupation of the Western hemisphere was to avoid the interlopers completely. Withdrawing to higher and higher levels of a remote and inaccessible mountain on the coast of Colombia, the Kogi preserved their old ways, which centered on dreaming.

I experienced a deep shock of recognition when I learned that the Kogi dream the coming of their shaman-priests before they are born, and they proceed to isolate the chosen from their own community, as well as the world outside, so that they will never confuse the physical world with the Real World. For the first fourteen years of his life, an apprentice Kogi shaman is not allowed to see the sunlit world, or to interact with anyone other than his teachers and appointed caregivers, who do not necessarily include his parents. During these fourteen years of darkness and isolation, the apprentice shaman essentially lives and travels in the dreamworld, which the Kogi call the Aluna. The Aluna is understood to be the energy domain that surrounds our physical reality and the principal plane of interaction between humans and beings other than human.

Until I heard about the Kogi, I had found no helpful analogy for my long childhood experience of solitude in the darkness of sickrooms, when my truest life was lived in the dreamworld. The elders of this extraordinary people subject their most gifted dreamers intentionally to what I had suffered spontaneously, without any context of meaning that my society could give me.

We pass the pipe back and forth and watch the smoke swirl upward through the branches of the spreading tree. Ellis talks about Kogi rituals for opening—and closing—portals between the worlds. He says he has a strong connection with a shaman-priest named Gabriel, whose special responsibility is to resist negative influences within the Aluna and stand guard over the worldgates. This task has become urgently important, because the Kogi believe that the Aluna is being poisoned by forces inimical to humanity. These forces—some generated by human hatred and evil over the millennia, others emanating from nonterrestrial sources—are the source of much of the violence and destructiveness on the Earth plane. The pollution has become so extreme that the Earth is now psychically "cloaked," and it is increasingly difficult for humans to receive clear communication from higher consciousness. The Kogi believe the Aluna has been breached by forces that could now destroy the Earth environment. Their shaman-priests are reaching out telepathically to powerful dreamers and teachers of other cultures who can help to reopen, and defend, the roads of dreaming.

Ellis tells me that the Kogi priests want to open a psychic link with me and my advanced circle so they can share their perceptions and build an alliance of dreamers. I agree without hesitation, promising that the following week I will invite a flight of gifted dreamers and healers to make a dream journey together from a mountain in the Adirondacks to meet the Kogi shamans on their mountain above the clouds. I take a last drag on the pipe, sending smoke from the Mohawk tobacco toward the south.

The Kogi do not waste any time after I agree to open the channel. Rising from sleep at dawn the next day, I feel the tug of their intention, benign but urgent. I am drawn into a vision that is vividly real.

I am airborne, flying at great speed on the wings of a red-tailed hawk. The ridges of the Appalachians slip away beneath me as I am drawn across bright blue waters. I see a lofty mountain draped in clouds. A huge bird—an eagle or condor—emerges from the clouds to meet me. We hang together in midair for a time, beating wings. Then the great bird becomes a nut-brown man with intense dark eyes. I have the impression of swinging bridges over deep mountain gorges, of people in conical hats, of a council of elders gathered by a fire. However, it is not their intention to give me a guided tour. Their need is pressing. To help me understand, the shaman-priests indicate that they are going to open a portal. I expect it will take me into an Otherworld environment.

Instead, I am surprised to find myself looking at a quite ordinary scene. Seemingly decent and respectable middle-class white people are going about their lives: going off to work, taking the kids to school, running errands, going here and there in the world. Everything about them seems normal, harmless, somewhat boring.

I am projected into the mind of one of them. I am horrified to discover the depth of his ignorance, and how dangerous this ignorance is. He's an ordinary guy, doing the best he can to fulfill his obligations the way he understands these things. But he does not have a clue about what matters. He does not know what is happening to the Earth. He does not know about the play of psychospiritual forces that are promoting war and destruction. He does not know how the trees and the oceans are being killed, or how the Aluna is being polluted.

He is not even aware that there are worlds beyond the physical on which life and soul depend. He is lost to soul. He has joined the procession of the soul-gone, the hollow men. What is most shocking to me is that this ignorance and estrangement from soul is profoundly *dangerous,* because it deprives us of an inner compass, a heart-centered way of knowing what is right for us, and the world we share. Ignorance and collective soul loss leave our kind defenseless against the rule of machine mentality and the psychic intrusion of forces that set us against each other, and apart from nature and the contact with higher intelligence.

Sadly, this condition is shared by so many, many people in our affluent Western culture. As Thomas Moore contends, "the great malady" of our times, "implicated in all of our troubles and affecting us individually and socially, is 'loss of soul'."[1] In the great mythistory of Hiawatha, it was this condition that brought on the Dark Times. This is what the Kogi shaman-priests want me to know—because reclaiming the ancient dreamways is the antidote to this dangerous ignorance.

I have encountered many shapes of terror, but this vision was one of the most terrifying experiences of my life. It filled me with crawling dread. It also mobilized me. I understood now, more strongly than ever, the urgent and vital necessity of bringing back the dreaming, to restore our connection with the origins and purpose of our lives.

I walked among the evergreens below the house where I was staying, in the early sunlight, and watched the light shine silver-bright on the underfeathers of a hawk flying above me. I remembered the great teaching of the Iroquois Dreamtime stories: the world falls into darkness when humans forget the sky. I felt tremendous, benign tremors of energy in my field as the ancient ones gathered close around me, speaking again in the old tongue. Truth comes with shivers.

Toward the end of our weekend program, we gathered around a fire pit on a wooded hill overlooking a waterfall and performed a Phoenix rite of rebirthing, rising from the ashes of our former lives.

> To know the fire, I become fire. Generation after generation, I create myself. I praise the moment I die in fire for the veils of illusion burn with me.[2]

Memories of other lives and other worlds streamed through my consciousness, flowing without confusion. I saw myself in a room of ancient mirrors, each one revealing a different face. A wind picked up and blew our ashes away across the gorge.

A red-tailed hawk circled low over our heads, singing sweeter than I have heard a hawk sing. At the fire, Ellis unknotted the deerskin ties of something wrapped in soft red cloth, a gift he brought to me from Mohawk country. I saw the feathers of a hawk, and I heard voices chanting in the old tongue from beyond our circle.

I honored my agreement with the Kogi. The next weekend, up on our mountain in Mohawk country, where Deer energy is strong and the Dragon and White Wolf are sometimes seen, I discussed the Kogi contact with thirty healers and dreamers who had traveled the dream roads with me over many years. We agreed to respond to the Kogi invitation by spreading our soul wings and flying together, as a group, to rendezvous with the Kogi shamans at their mountain. We made an initial journey to clarify the road we would take, and we were guided by the spirits of our mountain to travel through a tunnel they would open for us. We learned that there are direct paths between the sacred mountains of this world, although some of these roads have been blocked by malevolent forces, of human evil and of entities inimical to humans.

We called on our spiritual guides and our animal guardians to escort and protect us on the journey. I was grateful to see what looked like a whole Mohawk war party, led by an elder with long white hair, escorted by White Wolf, take up position around our perimeter. As I drummed for the big journey, our travelers shape-shifted into the forms of their bird allies.

Here is part of Sara's experience: "I take the form of the crow and my guides are right there with me. I fly through the tunnel. As I approach the opening at the other end, my guides tell me to change back. I do this and approach the opening with my hands extended, palms up, to let the man who is standing guard there know that I come in the spirit of peace. He is expecting us. We begin our exchange. All conversation is telepathic, a mixture of words and pictures. This was the first test, ensuring I could 'hear' and communicate in this manner. Next he asks if there are any dreams that I can share with him that will show my understanding of the purpose of the possible cooperation between our people. I tell him a dream in which I am shown the path of the souls of the departed, and a second dream in which the ancestors showed me the web of dreaming and how all the dreams are connected.

"He finds all of this very satisfactory, and it's clear I have passed another test. The gatekeeper seems almost excited. He instructs me to follow him. I enter a cave similar to the one our mountain people have shared with us. There is a fire and a circle of people waiting to accompany each of us. They shift back and forth in their forms and I note this. I'm invited to step through the fire and when I do this, an elder calls me Daughter of Fire. We talk about the purpose of this visit, comparing ways of life, the pros and cons of each lifestyle, and the dangers we are all facing for the world in the dreaming.

"I am taken to a place of darkness, a hut where a boy who is becoming a shaman has been kept for years. He will soon be coming out into the light. We exchange some thoughts and I understand why it's important for him to meet us. I feel him and his discretion is impeccable. He is one of their great ones coming at a time when his people and the people of the world will need great dreamers to shape what is to come.

"My Kogi guide takes me for a turn around the village and then tells me we're going to the top of their mountain. With this I know I passed the test in the hut of darkness. He takes his bird form and I take mine. We rapidly arrive at the top and resume our human forms. I can feel the rest of our group but we are shielded with our guides so there is no visual and little telepathic contact. I ask about this and he tells me it's being done for this first visit so that we can each focus completely on each other and have no interference in the exchange.

"The view from the top of the mountain is incredible. Then my deeper sight opens and I can see the energy grid they have set up to protect this space. Beyond that I can see the web of dreams and beyond that I can see the roads of soul. It's extraordinary and I am excited.

"My guide tells me we will go up to the web of dreams. When we do this and I get a better look, I can see there are tears in it. I can also see there are a number of Kogi and other people trying to repair the largest ones. I feel the urgency of this and now understand why we are here. The efforts being undertaken may not be enough and that is why we have been invited here, to explore how we can help. I also see the path of souls above us, and it is in danger as well. I now know I have passed another test, the test of sight.

"We go back down to the village and down to the cave. As I prepare to return, an elder steps forward. He is wearing a conical hat. I thank him and my guide and I give them permission to visit me in my dreams for further communication. I tell them all of us are dedicated to the dreaming, and that I will do whatever is necessary to help repair the tear in the web of dreaming and restore the path of souls."[3]

Every member of our circle returned with powerful experiences and highly specific messages from the Kogi. Each person was received and guided in a quite individual way, yet our experiences closely overlapped and were mutually confirming. All of us came back charged with an even deeper sense of the vital importance of bringing back the ancient dreamways.

I had already received the most urgent message in the Kogi-mediated vision of the ordinary man who has lost the sky. We have learned from the Iroquois, and we relearn from the Kogi, that the dark times come when humans cease to hold on to the sky.

To remember the origin and purpose of our lives, we must rebirth a dreaming society, a society where dreams are shared and honored every when, everywhere. We must do this *now*. We must not let our minds fall into forgetting that we are soul and spirit, and that our journeys and our obligations begin and continue in worlds beyond the surface world. We must heal the web of dreaming, and heal the wound between earth and sky.

Additional Resources Available from Author

WORKSHOPS AND COURSES IN ACTIVE DREAMING

Dreaming is daily practice. Active Dreaming is a discipline, to be studied and practiced on many levels.

To this end, I offer lectures, workshops, and trainings in Active Dreaming, creativity, shamanism, and imaginal healing in North America, Europe, and Australia. The format ranges from short evening programs to weekend and five-day depth workshops, advanced shamanic retreats, and my three-year training for teachers of Active Dreaming. In addition, graduates of my Dream Teacher Training offer evening classes in the core techniques of Active Dreaming at many locations.

For schedules and further information, please visit my website: www.mossdreams.com

AUDIO-VISUAL RESOURCES

Dream Gates: A Journey into Active Dreaming is a six-cassette audio training program (not to be confused with my book, *Dreamgates*). You may order the tapes from my website or direct from the publisher:

Sounds True
413 South Arthur Avenue
Louisville, CO 80027
Tel (800) 333-9185 or (303) 665-3151
e-mail: SoundsTrue@aol.com

The Way of the Dreamer is an eight-session video training course, available in both VCR and DVD. This series demonstrates core techniques of Active Dreaming including the processes of Lightning Dreamwork, Dream Reentry, and Tracking, There are also individual programs on themes such as Dreaming the Future, Dreaming with the Departed, Dream Guides and Guardians, and Healing through Dreams. You can order the videos from the producers:

Psyche Productions
PO Box 5414
Milford, CT 06460
(203) 877-9315
www.psycheproductions.net

Wings for the Journey: Shamanic Drumming for Dream Travelers is a CD I recorded in the Connecticut woods on my favorite drum. It also includes a group drumming track and a "bonus" track in which I recount a legend of the origin of the shaman's drum. Many users have found this CD quite effective in powering and focusing conscious dream travel and dream reentry, and I have been careful to guide journeyers safely home from their ecstatic flights. You can order the CD from the producers, Psyche Productions (see contact information above).

Building an Active Dream Circle in Your Community

We need to share our dreams—our dreams from the night and our life dreams—with caring and supportive partners who can help us to unlock their meanings and bring their energy to heal and empower our everyday lives. By practicing the Lightning Dreamwork technique whenever people are ready to share dreams with you, you will find others who might want to join you in sharing and working with dreams in a regular group. A dream-sharing circle develops a wonderful energy of its own.

The group may be as small as two people, or much larger. You need to start somewhere, and a good beginning is to get into the habit of sharing dreams on a regular basis, and receiving helpful feedback, from a caring friend. Since dreams are multi-layered and we dream in many different ways, it's good to have multiple viewpoints and many diverse life experiences reflected in a group. It is also important that everyone should commit to dreamwork methods that respect the privacy and authority of the dreamer, and bring through the energy and magic of the dreamworld instead of dissolving into verbal analysis.

If you are interested in a group where everyone can explore one of their dreams in depth every time you meet, the ideal group size is probably four to six people. However, in larger groups you will benefit from the vibrant circle energy you can generate, and—if you use the techniques of dream reentry and tracking, dream theater, and conscious dream travel explained in my books and tapes—everyone will be happily engaged in active dreaming throughout your session.

Here are some basic guidelines for getting a dream group off the ground and keeping it airborne:

1. **Commit to a regular schedule.** Decide how often you want to meet (once a month? once a week?) and for how long (two hours is probably long enough if you are meeting on a weekday evening). You may want to start with an exploratory meeting to which you'll invite new friends. You can announce your group through community bulletin boards, flyers, and networking. Once you have established your core group, you'll want to ask everyone to commit to attending at least six sessions.

2. **Homeplay assignments.** Everyone should be asked to start keeping a dream journal and give their dreams titles. Group members should be asked to dream with intention—writing down a theme or itinerary for a night of dreaming—and to monitor the play of synchronicity in everyday life.

3. **Open the circle with a simple ritual.** It's good to start each session with a short statement of intention (for example, "We come together in a sacred and loving way to honor and celebrate the wisdom of our dreams") and to spend a few moments building the energy of the group (simple relaxation exercise, "light energy" meditation, joining hands in a circle). Light a candle and invoke blessings for the circle from the sacred powers that speak to us in dreams.

4. **Share dream titles.** After opening the circle, give people a quiet moment to call up a dream they may want to share. Then have everyone take turns to share the *title* of a dream (and *only* the title) to start things rolling. This makes sure everyone is included from the word go. Next the group will choose one or more dreams to explore in depth.

5. **Practice the Lightning Dreamwork technique.** Ask the dreamer the three basic questions: (a) How did you feel? (b) How does this dream relate to your waking life, and could it be played out in some way in the future? (c) What do you need to know? Then play the "if it were my dream" game, which reaffirms that the dreamer is the final authority on his or her dreams. Finally, gently guide the dreamer to commit to an action plan to honor the dream and integrate its guidance in waking life. Dreams require action!

6. **Practice Dream Reentry and Tracking.** Use drumming, or a drumming CD, to help dreamers embark on conscious dream travel. You'll find that, with practice, the whole group will develop the ability to travel together into a shared dreamspace and bring through energy, guidance and healing—while having wonderful fun!

7. **Bring through energy as well as information!** Group dreamwork should always be devoted to bringing through *energy* as well as insight. Be sure you keep things moving in the group! *Dream theatre*—having the dreamer cast members of the group as figures in his or her dream, which they proceed to act out spontaneously—is a lovely, fun-filled way to honor a dream and bring through energy that is often deeply healing.

8. **Take it to the community!** We need to bring the gifts of dreaming to many people who many never sit with a dream group, but desperately need a dream in their lives. A fun assignment for your group is to ask your members to find a way—between each session—to bring dreaming into the life of someone who hasn't been in the habit of sharing dreams or drawing on their guidance. This person may be an intimate family member or a complete stranger, maybe someone you meet in a line at the post office or in the dentist's waiting room. Maybe you'll find a way to create a safe space where they can tell a dream, and receive some helpful feedback. Maybe you'll find yourself telling a simple story about a dream that came true, or a dream that brought healing, or how someone famous was guided by a dream—a story that might open up someone else's understanding of what dreaming might be. You'll find it vastly entertaining, and inspirational, to come back to your group with stories of how you brought dreams alive for others. In this way, through one encounter after another, you'll be making a beautiful contribution to the rebirth of a dreaming culture in our times.

Notes

ABBREVIATIONS FOR PRIMARY SOURCES

Colonial Documents: Edmund B. O'Callaghan, ed., *Documents Relative to the Colonial History of New York,* 15 vols. (Albany, NY: Weed, Parsons, 1853–87).

Gibson: Hanni Woodbury, ed. and trans., *Concerning the League: The Iroquois League Tradition as Dictated in Onondaga by John Arthur Gibson* (Winnipeg, MB: Algonquian and Iroquoian Linguistics Memoir 19, 1992).

Jesuit Relations: Reuben Gold Thwaites, ed., *Jesuit Relations and Allied Documents: Travels and Explorations of the Jesuit Missionaries in New France, 1610–1791,* 73 vols. (Cleveland, OH: Burrows Brothers, 1896–1901).

Johnson Papers: James Sullivan et al., eds., *The Papers of Sir William Johnson,* 14 vols. (Albany: State University of New York Press, 1921–65).

Lafitau: Joseph-François Lafitau, *Customs of the American Indians Compared with the Customs of Primitive Times,* ed. and trans. William N. Fenton and Elizabeth L. Moore, 2 vols. (Toronto: Champlain Society, 1974, 1977).

MM reports: Magic Mountain group journey reports, 1996–2004.

Norton's Journal: Carl F. Klinck and James J. Talman, eds., *The Journal of Major John Norton, 1809–1816* (Toronto: Champlain Society, 1970).

RM journal: Robert Moss dream journals, 1987–2004.

WB Journal: Wanda Easter Burch dream journals, 1987–2004

Introduction: Dreaming in Hawk

1. D. Kelcher, *Dreams in Old Norse Literature and their Affinities in Folklore* (Cambridge: Cambridge University Press, 1935), 66–72. See also Jean-Claude Schmitt, *Ghosts in the Middle Ages: The Living and the Dead in Medieval Society* (Chicago: University of Chicago Press, 1998).

Chapter 2: When the Ancestors Cross Into the Realm of the Living

1. Bougainville to Madame Hérault, April 21, 1758, in Louis Antoine de Bougainville, *Adventure in the Wilderness: The American Journals,* trans. and ed. Edward P. Hamilton (Norman: University of Oklahoma Press, 1964), 333. Bougainville's exact phrase was *lion Belgique,* the term *Belgique* being used to evoke the Belgae, the warrior Celts who fought Julius Caesar, not the modern political entity.

2. Writing in 1883, Horatio Hale—who left us invaluable transcriptions of Iroquois ritual chants and formulas in the original languages—gave the following evocative description of the Five Nations and their homelands: "When the five tribes or 'nations' of the Iroquois confederacy first became known to European explorers, they were found occupying the valleys and uplands of northern New York, in that picturesque and fruitful region which stretches westward from the head-waters of the Hudson to the Genesee. The Mohawks, or Caniengas—as they should properly be called—possessed the Mohawk River, and covered Lake George and Lake Champlain with their flotillas of large canoes, managed with the boldness and skill which, hereditary in their descendants, make them still the best boatmen of the North American rivers. West of the Caniengas the Oneidas held the small river and lake which bear their name . . . West of the Oneidas, the imperious Onondagas, the central and, in some respects, the ruling nation of the League, possessed the two lakes of Onondaga and Skaneateles, together with the common outlet of this inland lake system, the Oswego River, to its issue into Lake Ontario. Still proceeding westward, the lines of trail and river led to the long and winding stretch of Lake Cayuga, about which were clustered the towns of the people who gave their name to the lake; and beyond them, over the wide expanse of hills and dales surrounding Lakes Seneca and Canandaigua, were scattered the populous villages of the Senecas, more correctly styled Sonontowanas or Mountaineers. Such were the names and abodes of the allied nations . . . who were destined to become for a time the most notable and powerful community among the native tribes of North America." Horatio Hale, *The Iroquois Book of Rites* (Philadelphia: D. G. Brinton, 1883) 9–10.

3. The Six Nations Iroquois are related to a larger Iroquoian family identified by linguists as the Northern Iroquoians. At the time of first contact with the Europeans, this linguistic group also included the five nations of the Huron confederacy, the five nations of the Neutral confederacy, the Eries, and the Susquehannok. Some of these related nations were destroyed by the wars and epidemics of the seventeenth century. Languages and traditions of the Mohawk

and the Huron are closely connected, although historically these two peoples were often at war. The Cherokee are southern cousins of the Iroquois of New York and Canada, although the split between the Cherokee and the Northern Iroquoians occurred 3,500–4,000 years ago. See Dean R. Snow, *The Iroquois* (Oxford and Cambridge, Mass: Blackwell, 1994) 1, 9.)

4. Writing in 1644, the Dutch traveler Johannes Megapolensis made the following observations about the Mohawk use of wampum: "Their money consists of certain little bones, made of shells or cockle, which are found on the sea-beach; a hole is drilled through the middle of the little bones, and they string upon a thread, or they make of them belts as broad as a hand, or broader, and hang them upon their necks, or around their bodies. They also have several holes in their ears, and there they likewise hang some. They value these little bones as highly as many Christians do gold, silver and pearls; but they do not like our money." Reprinted in Dean R. Snow, Charles T. Gehring and William A. Starna (eds), *In Mohawk Country: Early Narratives about a Native People.* Syracuse: Syracuse University Press, 1996, 44.

Chapter 3: Meeting the Dream People

1. *Jesuit Relations*, 53:251–3.
2. *Jesuit Relations*, 6:159–61.
3. J. N. B. Hewitt, "The Iroquoian Concept of the Soul," *Journal of American Folk-Lore* 8 (1895): 107–16.
4. *Jesuit Relations*, 42:147.
5. *Jesuit Relations*, 33:191.
6. *Jesuit Relations*, 33:193.
7. *Jesuit Relations*, 17:155.
8. *Jesuit Relations*, 17:155–9.
9. Harriet Maxwell Converse, *Myths and Legends of the New York State Iroquois* (Albany, NY: New York State Museum Bulletin 125, 1908), 94.
10. *Jesuit Relations*, 33:191–3.
11. *Jesuit Relations*, 33:195.
12. *Jesuit Relations*, 17:179.
13. *Jesuit Relations*, 42:197–9.
14. *Jesuit Relations*, 42:153–5.
15. Robert Moss, *Dreaming True* (New York: Pocket Books, 2000).
16. Lafitau, 1:245.
17. *Jesuit Relations*, 53:161.
18. *Jesuit Relations*, 23:121–3.
19. *Jesuit Relations*, 39:19.
20. *Jesuit Relations*, 6:159–61.
21. The dreams and visions of Handsome Lake, or Ganiodaio, in 1799–1800 were the source of a religious revival among the Seneca that birthed a contemporary American Indian religion. After many bouts of excessive drinking, Handsome Lake fell into a coma. While he was out of his body, he encountered spiritual guides in traditional Iroquois dress who instructed him to give up alcohol and

revive the Strawberry Ceremony. In a subsequent vision, he embarked on a sky journey. As he told it, as he stood with the three "angels" from the previous vision and a fourth radiant being "a road [the Milky Way] slowly descended from the south sky and to where they were standing." This was a path to the afterlife. Traveling the path of the Milky Way, he proceeded to visit heavens and hells, encountered Jesus Christ and George Washington, and was inspired to construct a moral code called the Gai'wiio, or Good Word. In a third vision, Handsome Lake was instructed that the Midwinter Ceremony must be continued, or else the world would be destroyed by fire. He added four rites to the old Midwinter festival—the Feather Dance, the Thanksgiving Dance, the Rite of Personal Chant, and the Bowl Game. His visions also directed him to lead a witchhunt. See Anthony F. C. Wallace, *The Death and Rebirth of the Seneca* (New York: Knopf, 1970), 239–262.

22. *Jesuit Relations,* 17:151–3.

23. Lee Irwin, "Native American Dreaming," *Dreamtime* volume 19, numbers 2–3 (Summer-Fall 2002), 10–13, 37–38. *Dreamtime* is the magazine of the Association for the Study of Dreams.

24. Lafitau, 1:51.

Chapter 4: Living in Two Worlds

1. RM journal, October 18, 1993.

2. RM journal, December 15, 1993.

Chapter 5: Teachings of the Heart Shaman

1. Narration of "The Magic Lake" by Freeman Owle in Barbara R. Duncan, ed., *Living Stories of the Cherokee* (Chapel Hill: University of North Carolina Press, 1998), 207.

Chapter 6: Tree Gate to Ancient Mother

1. RM journal, September 16, 2002.

2. Henry Corbin, *The Man of Light in Iranian Sufism* (New Lebanon, NY: Omega, 1994), 21.

3. RM journal, September 20, 2002.

4. RM journal, October 7–8, 2002.

5. RM journal, December 4, 2002.

Chapter 7: Story Codes and Inner Songs

1. George Seferis, "Mythistorema," in *Collected Poems,* trans. and ed. Edmund Keeley and Philip Sherrard (London: Anvil Press Poetry, 1986).

2. Sam D. Gill, *Native American Religions: An Introduction* (Belmont, CA: Wordsworth, 1982), chap. 2.

3. J. N. B. Hewitt, "Iroquoian Cosmology, Part 2," *Annual Reports of the Bureau of American Ethnology* 43 (1928): 449–819.

4. Hewitt's essay in "Tawiskaron" was published in the *Handbook of American*

Indians North of Mexico. Edited by F. W. Hodge. vol. 2, pp. 707–11. Washington, DC: Smithsonian Institution Press, 1910.

5. *Gibson.*

6. Graham Townsley, "Song Paths: The Ways and Means of Yaminahua Shamanic Knowledge," *L'Homme* 33 (1993): 449–68. An excerpt of this article titled " 'Twisted Language': A Technique for Knowing" appears in Jeremy Narby and Francis Huxley, eds., *Shamans through Time* (New York: Tarcher/Putnam, 2001) 263–271.

7. Peter Ackroyd, *Blake: A Biography* (New York: Knopf, 1996), 47.

8. For Mary Austin's philosophy of releasing the inner song, see her book *The American Rhythm: Studies and Re-expressions of Amerindian Songs* (Boston: Houghton Mifflin, 1930). A fine example is her poem "A Song in Depression [from the Paiute]," first published in 1914, reprinted in *The American Rhythm* 96.

Chapter 8: Falling Woman Creates a World

1. Ataensic is the Huron name for Sky Woman, meaning She of the Ancient Body, or Ancient Mother. In the Seth Newhouse (Mohawk) version, she is not given a personal name; she is first called *eia'tase,* "the newly embodied one," and later *iakonwe,* "the she-being." (For some odd reason, Hewitt insisted on translating this as "she a man being" or "the female man-being.") J. N. B. Hewitt, "Iroquoian Cosmology, Part 1," *Annual Reports of the Bureau of American Ethnology* 21 (1903), 264, 284. In the Gibson (Onondaga) version, she is called Awenha'i, meaning Ripe Earth or Blossoming Flowers; Hewitt, "Iroquoian Cosmology, Part 2," 464. My retelling of her story is primarily based on the four recitations collected by Hewitt from John Buck (Onondaga), John Armstrong (Seneca), Seth Newhouse (Mohawk), and John Arthur Gibson (Onondaga) between 1889 and 1900 and printed in the two massive volumes of Hewitt's "Iroquoian Cosmology," supplemented by oral narratives and commentaries by contemporary Iroquois memory-keepers and some details from earlier accounts, including the Jesuit reports and the colorful version of Joseph Brant (Mohawk) preserved in *Norton's Journal.*

2. *Orato na'karonto'te*—"The Tree [in the Sky World] is such as the wild cherry" (Mohawk); Hewitt, "Iroquoian Cosmology, Part 1," 282.

3. Hewitt, "Iroquoian Cosmology, Part 2," 479.

4. The stem word in *Kahaseri'nes* is *ohasera',* the Mohawk term for something that emits light, such as a lamp, torch, or candle. Huron-Wyandot stories of White Lion are included in C. M. Barbeau, *Huron and Wyandot Mythology* (Ottawa: Department of Mines, Geological Survey Memoir 80, 1915). For a splendid scholarly discussion of the many forms of the Fire Dragon, see George R. Hamell, "Long-Tail: The Panther in Huron-Wyandot and Seneca Myth, Ritual and Material Culture," in *Icons of Power: Feline Symbolism in the Americas,* ed. Nicholas J. Saunders (New York: Routledge, 1998), 258–91.

5. Gibson version; Hewitt, "Iroquoian Cosmology, Part 2," 479–80.

6. Gibson version; Hewitt, "Iroquoian Cosmology, Part 2," 481.

7. Jesse J. Cornplanter, *Legends of the Longhouse* (Philadelphia: Lippincott, 1938). I have seen no evidence that the Iroquois and C. S. Lewis were aware of each other, but they may have been drinking from the same well of vision.

Chapter 9: The Battle of the Twins

1. Tom Porter, personal communication, July 9, 1988.
2. J. N. B. Hewitt, "Tawiskaron," in *Handbook of American Indians North of Mexico*, vol. 2, ed. Frederick Webb Hodge (Washington, DC: Bureau of American Ethnology Bulletin 30, Smithsonian Institution Press, 1910), 707.
3. Hewitt, "Tawiskaron," 2:708.
4. I have colloquialized this dialogue from Hewitt's interlinear translation of the 1900 Gibson version; Hewitt, "Iroquoian Cosmology, Part 2," 486–7. Tharonhiawakon is the Mohawk version of the Light Twin's name, and it literally means "He holds on to the sky with both hands."
5. In the Newhouse (Mohawk) version, Great Turtle says, *I nà konien'a,* "I am your parent." It is then specified, "This was said by him who stands there and who is the Great Turtle, Hania'ten'kowa." Hewitt, "Iroquoian Cosmology, Part 1," 299–300.
6. *Iote'hia'ron'tie,* "Let it increase in size," and *Oterontonni'a ion'kiats,* "They call me Sapling." The Newhouse (Mohawk) version is a marvelous evocation of an Amerindian Green Man. Hewitt, "Iroquoian Cosmology, Part 1," 301–2.
7. MM reports, April 28, 2004.
8. RM journal, October 11, 2003.
9. William N. Fenton, *The False Faces of the Iroquois* (Norman: University of Oklahoma Press, 1987), 95–7, 215–35. Fenton describes his first encounters with Chauncey Johnny John in *The Iroquois Eagle Dance: An Offshoot of the Calumet Dance.* (Bureau of American Ethnology Bulletin 156. Washington, D.C. 1953.)
10. Hewitt, "Tawiskaron," 2:711.

Chapter 10: Hiawatha's Mirror

1. William N. Fenton, *The Great Law and the Longhouse* (Norman: University of Oklahoma Press, 1998), 103.
2. These are the names as rendered in Chief Gibson's 1912 account. See *Gibson.*
3. "It is from the sky he came with his mission," agrees the first chief to recognize the shining one. *Gibson* 23.
4. In Tom Porter's contemporary Mohawk version, the Peacemaker's mother dreams that his father is one of the "Four Powers of Mystery, sent by the Creator to save mankind from its folly." The grandmother does not believe this, and she tries to kill the newborn baby by thrusting him down through a hole in the ice. Even after the baby miraculously survives, the grandmother continues to try to kill him, until a "beautiful being" appears in a dream and warns her that if she persists, she herself will die. (Tom Porter, personal communication, July 9, 1988.) Common elements in all versions of the Peacekeeper's birth are (a) this is a virgin birth, (b) he has been sent to Earth by a god who lives in another world, and (c) his identity and mission are revealed in dreams.
5. The most vivid account of Hiawatha's vision in the mirror is in Chief Gibson's 1899 version, elicited by Hewitt and translated as "Chief Gibson's Account" in Fenton, *The Great Law,* 85–97. The identity of the cannibal differs in successive versions of the legend. In his 1899 version (Fenton, *The Great Law,* 85–97)

Gibson gives the cannibal the name Hayenhwatha, translated as Early Riser. Seth Newhouse's Mohawk account (printed in Arthur C. Parker, Arthur C. *Parker on the Iroquois*. Edited by William N. Fenton. Syracuse, NY: Syracuse University Press, 1968, 14–60) equates the cannibal with Thadodaho. *Gibson* (the version transcribed in 1912) makes Hayenhwatha a different person, a Mohawk chief who stayed up at night after receiving word of the Peacemaker's coming.

6. *Gibson* 138.

7. Joseph Brant has left us the most striking account of the heron-men and crow-men. See *Norton's Journal*, 98–105. Brant was quite familiar with the abilities of shape-shifters as military scouts; he relied on them when leading war parties for the British in the American Revolution.

8. The most vivid account of the sorcerer and his sexual equipment is in the version by John Skanawati Buck, translated in J. N. B. Hewitt, "Legend of the Founding of the Iroquois League," *American Anthropologist* 5 (April 1892), 131–148. Hewitt's fellow ethnologist Jeremiah Curtin gave this account of the sorcerer's organ: "The great snake coiled around his body, which used to thrust its head over his right shoulder, was his *membrum virile;*" see Fenton, *The Great Law*, 79. In later public tellings, Iroquois memorykeepers have suppressed this vital detail. Fenton notes: "All later versions of the myth clean up this reference to the culture hero's sex organs, and some authorities have vehemently denied it, but Hewitt's 1892 paper represents his early and best period of fieldwork." *The Great Law*, 79.

9. Hewitt, "Founding of the Iroquois League," 140.

10. I have drawn on some of the oldest accounts of condolence ceremonies. These include the Jesuit description of the performance of the Mohawk Speaker Kiotsaeton, who arrived at Three Rivers in 1645 "almost entirely covered in porcelain beads" (*Jesuit Relations*, 27:24), and the report on the condolence ceremony held after Sir William Johnson's death in 1774 to mourn the great Indian agent and requicken his power in his nephew Guy (*Colonial Documents*, 8:471).

Chapter 11: Dreaming in the Dark Times

1. Samuel de Champlain, quoting Huron sources, estimated the population of Huronia in 1615–16 as 32,000. Fr Gabriel Sagard, in 1623, suggested a figure of 30,000–40,000. Though recent scholars have argued for slightly lower numbers, there can be no doubt about what had happened by 1639, when the Jesuits conducted a village-by-village census of the Hurons. The Huron population was about 9,000, less than a third of the lowest previous estimate. See Conrad Heidenreich, "Huron," in *Handbook of North American Indians*, vol. 15, *Northeast*, ed. Bruce G. Trigger, 369–70 (Washington, DC: Smithsonian Institution Press, 1978). The tragedy of the Hurons resembles that of many New England tribes, and it was replicated in Iroquois country. The demographic effects are analyzed in Russell Thornton, *American Indian Holocaust and Survival: A Population History Since 1492* (Norman: University of Oklahoma Press, 1987). On smallpox epidemics, see Henry F. Dobyns, *Their Number Became Thinned* (Knoxville: University of Tennessee Press, 1983).

Chapter 12: The Making of a Woman of Power

1. On Molly and Joseph Brant's descent from a Huron grandmother, see Isabel Thompson Kelsay, *Joseph Brant 1743–1807: Man of Two Worlds* (Syracuse, NY: Syracuse University Press, 1984), 7. For some of Joseph's stories of ghost and dreams, see *Norton's Journal*.

2. Johnson employed Iroquois dream scouts during his successful Lake George campaign and acted on their information. An Iroquois war chief's dream on September 6, 1755, which led Johnson to order that no man should go out to the left of the camp, is described by an English gunner in *Colonial Documents*, 6:1005. In his accounts for war expenses, Johnson made the following entry on September 3, 1755: "To Peter a Mohawk warrior to fulfill his dream a silver band"; see *Johnson Papers*, 2:593.

3. Lafitau has an account of a psychic battle between Longhair and a family of witches; Lafitau, 1:247–8.

4. On Abraham—or Canusta, as he was known by the Mohawks—see Conrad Weiser's account in *Colonial Documents*, 6:796.

5. Sir Jeffery Amherst wrote of the need "to stop the very being" of the Indians in a letter to Johnson dated August 27, 1763; *Colonial Documents*, 7:545. His correspondence with Colonel Bouquet on the desirability of deliberately infecting Native Americans with smallpox is in Sylvester K. Stevens and Donald H. Kent, eds., *The Papers of Col. Henry Bouquet* (Harrisburg, PA: Pennsylvania Historical Commission, 1940–3). Johnson and Amherst became bitter adversaries.

6. James Thomas Flexner, *Lord of the Mohawks* (Boston: Little, Brown, 1979), 234.

7. No. 2 Memoranda Book, Claus Papers, vol. 23 (in microfilm) National Archives of Canada, Ottawa. The entire passage, in Wanda's transcription, reads: "Mr. Claus return'd with King Henry by Esopus and Albany where Capt. St [?] [Thomas??] fell in Love with Ms Mary Brant who was then Likely *not as I* had the smallpox . . ."(emphasis added).

8. Kenneth Silverman, *The Life and Times of Cotton Mather* (New York: Harper & Row, 1984), 338–40.

9. Johnson was sponsoring widespread inoculation against smallpox among his family, his white neighbors, and the valley Mohawks by 1767, two years before another epidemic in the province of New York. *Johnson Papers*, 7:14, 874, 938; 12:763, 1019.

Chapter 16: The Shaman at the Breakfast Table

1. Waud Kracke, "Myths in Dreams, Thought in Images: An Amazonian Contribution to the Psychoanalytic Theory of Primary Process," in *Dreaming: Anthropological and Psychological Interpretations*, ed. Barbara Tedlock (Santa Fe, NM: School of American Research Press, 1992).

2. C. G. Jung, *Synchronicity: An Acausal Connecting Principle*. (Princeton, NJ: Princeton University Press, 1971).

3. Tony Hillerman, *Talking God* (New York: HarperTorch, 1991).

Chapter 18: Medicine Dreaming

1. Wanda Easter Burch, *She Who Dreams: A Journey into Healing through Dreamwork* (Novato, CA: New World Library, 2003).
2. Jeanne Achterberg, *Imagery in Healing: Shamanism and Modern Medicine* (Boston: Shambhala, 1985)9.
3. *Giving Voice to Bear: North American Indian Myths, Rituals and Images of the Bear* (Niwot, Colorado: Roberts Rinehart, 1991), 78.
4. Sarangerel, *Riding Windhorses: A Journey into the Heart of Mongolian Shamanism* (Rochester, VT: Destiny Books, 2000).

Chapter 19: Dreaming the Soul Back Home

1. Charles de Lint, "The Words That Remain," in *Tapping the Dream Tree* (New York: Tor, 2002). See also de Lint's marvelous novel *The Onion Girl*. New York: Tom Doherty Associates, 2001.
2. Mary Austin, "From the Paiute: A Song in Time of Depression," in *The American Rhythm: Studies and Reexpressions of Amerindian Songs* (Boston: Houghton Mifflin, 1930), 96.
3. W. B.Yeats, *A Vision*. New York: Collier Books, 1966, 221.

Chapter 21: Becoming a Poet of Consciousness

1. William Everson, *Birth of a Poet: The Santa Cruz Meditations,* ed. Lee Bartlett (Santa Barbara, CA: Black Sparrow Press, 1982), 41.
2. Gloria Flaherty, *Shamanism and the Eighteenth Century* (Princeton, NJ: Princeton University Press, 1992), 173.
3. J. N. B. Hewitt, "Orenda and a Definition of Religion," *American Anthropologist* 44, no. 1 (1902): 33–46.
4. Alfred Métraux, *Réligions et magies indiennes d'Amérique du Sud* (Indian Religion and Magic in South America) (Paris: Gallimard, 1967).
5. Knud Rasmussen, *The Netsilik Eskimos*, Report of the Fifth Thule Expedition (Copenhagen: Gyldendalske Boghandel, 1931), 309.
6. Claude Lévi-Strauss, "The Effectiveness of Symbols," in *Structural Anthropology,* vol. 1, trans. Claire Jacobson and Brooke Schoepf (New York: Basic Books, 1963). Reprinted in Jeremy Narby (ed.) *Shaman's through Time*, 108.
7. Peter Freuchen, *Peter Freuchen's Book of the Eskimos* (Cleveland, OH: World Publishing Company, 1961), 280–1.
8. (William Everson, 1982)

Epilogue: The Peril of Losing the Sky

1. Thomas Moore, *Care of the Soul*. New York: HarperCollins, 1992, xi.
2. Normandi Ellis, *Awakening Osiris: A New Translation of the Egyptian Book of the Dead* (Grand Rapids, MI: Phanes Press, 1988), 172.
3. MM Reports, November 2, 2002.

Glossary of Iroquois Words

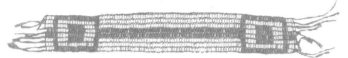

All words in this glossary are Mohawk unless otherwise noted. The Mohawk language is primarily oral, and as such it escapes easy transliteration. However, there is an agreed-upon modern orthography, based on phonetic principles, which I have generally followed in rendering most Native terms—with the exception of diacritical marks, for which I trust linguists and Mohawk teachers will not scalp me. My phonetic renderings generally correspond to those of David R. Maracle's pioneering *Mohawk Language Dictionary.* However, I have used the older, more familiar version of a few names and key terms, such as Hiawatha and *orenda.* I have preserved very ancient terms, like *ondinnonk,* in the form in which they appear in the early missionary accounts, or as they came to me in my dreams, or as they sounded to me when they were used by Iroquois dreamers who helped me find my way along the old paths.

The primary noun form in Iroquoian languages is always feminine, which is appropriate for a matriarchal people who trace their origins to a woman-being who fell from the sky. So, for example, in Mohawk, *ohkwari* (bear) literally means "she-bear"; to indicate a male bear, you add an *r* to make it *rohkwari.*

It is the misfortune of the Iroquois to be commonly known by names that were ascribed to them by their enemies. This is especially ironic for the Mohawk, whose own language does not include the letter *m.* The meanings of these "foreign" names—now in general use among the Iroquois themselves, at least when they are speaking English—are noted in this glossary, as well as the terms the Iroquois use for themselves.

The "on" and "en" forms in Mohawk should be pronounced as in French.

ahsha:ra. Burden strap
Ai'kon. Messenger who carries dreams to humans from Tharonhiawakon.
Akonwara. Mask, the man-being who dueled with Sapling at the mountain.
aksotha. Grandmother
a:kweks. Eagle

anokie. Muskrat

anonwara. Turtle

arendiwanen. "She has power." A woman of power, shaman, or healer.

ascwendics. Dream talisman. Of Huron origin. Ancient.

Ataensic. Ancient Mother. The Huron name for Sky Woman, the grandmother of the primal Twins who has a home in the moon.

atenenyarhon. Stone Giant, a monstrous being with a flint-covered body who is hostile to humans.

atetshensera. Dream

atetshents. "She who dreams." A shaman, healer, or doctor.

atonnhets. Soul or vital energy

Ato'wihtshera. Society of Faces. A fraternity of mask wearers who are usually called by their dreams to carve and use false face masks.

atsinahkon. "She uses white energy." Exorcist.

aweria'sa. The heart-soul or seat of the heart's desires

Cayuga. A Native people who are one of the Six Nations of the Iroquois Confederacy. From *Kayohkhono,* People of Oiogouen. The Mohawks call them the People of the Pipe.

erhar. Dog

Haudenosaunee. People of the Longhouse—that is, members of the Six Nations of the Iroquois Confederacy. This is the term preferred by the Iroquois. The spelling comes from Lewis Henry Morgan in his celebrated book *League of the Ho-De-No-Sau-Nee or Iroquois,* first published in 1851. The Mohawk version of this name is Rotinonhsonni.

Hiawatha. The best-known rendering of a name that in one version of the Hiawatha legend means He Combs It and in another means He Is Awake (hence the Awakened One). In the legend, Hiawatha is the fallen man whose life is transformed when he sees the radiant face of the Peacemaker in the mirror of a cooking pot. Today, Hiawatha (Ayonwatha) is the title of a Mohawk Turtle Clan chief.

Hi'no. Thunder, a guardian against evil spirits and serpents

Huron. The French name for the northern Iroquois people who called themselves Wen:dat. It translates as "bristly head."

Iroquois. Long used as a name for the Six Nations of the Iroquois Confederacy, this is a non-Iroquoian term whose etymology is uncertain and does not exist in its current form in any American Indian language. Champlain heard the word used by Algonquian Indians on the St. Lawrence in 1603; he spelled it Irocois and Yrocois. It was probably pronounced ir-o-kwe, and it may have been inspired by the shouts traditionally raised in an Iroquois council. See P. Bakker, "A Basque Etymology for the Word 'Iroquois'" in *Man in the Northeast* 40 (1990), 89-93.

Kahaseri'nes. "Light traveling constantly." A powerful spiritual being, known to the Wyandot as White Lion, who is associated with the comet, the coming of a new aeon, times of world change, and times of immense danger and opportunity.

kahnekowa. Primal ocean where Sky Woman makes a world

kahsto:wa. Iroquois feathered headdress

Kaianere'ko:wa. Great Law of the Iroquois

kaion:ni. Wampum belt

kakonsa. Iroquois mask; commonly called false face. The original mask-being was a sorcerer—possibly an aspect of Tawiskaron—with whom Tharonhiawakon fought a magical duel near the western rim of the world. Some early Iroquois masks may represent dead shamans. Others represent disease spirits. They are regarded as alive and needing to be fed, especially with tobacco and corn mush.

ka'nahkon. Deerskin drum

kana:ta. Village. The origin of the word *Canada*, literally, "the [country-sized] village."

Kanienkehaka. Mohawks, or People of the Flint

kano:nawe. Pipe

karen:na. "Putting forth power." A song or chant.

Karhakonha. Hawk

Karihwi:io. The good message or the good word

ka'shatstenhsera. Strength, power, health, or vitality; having and using necessary force

katatkens. "I look in a mirror" or "I see myself"

katera'swas. "I bring myself good luck" or "I dream"

kenra:ken. "It is white"

kenreks. Lion

kenreksaken. White lion

keriwahontha. "I put the matter into the fire" or "I see as a clairvoyant"

khenoronkhwa. "I want your soul" or "I love you"

kia'tat. "I am in my mother's womb" or "I am buried"

kia:tonte. "I have a body" or "I am alive"

Mahicans. A Native people who were rivals of the Mohawks for control of the upper Hudson River Valley. One of their names for themselves was Muhheakunneuw, "from the place of tidal water," which was pronounced ma-hi-can by Dutch interpreters. It was translated as "wolf" by the Algonquians because it sounded like their word for wolf.

Mohawk. "Man-eater." The easternmost people of the Six Nations of the Iroquois Confederacy. *Mohawk* was borrowed by New England settlers from the Narragansett word *Mohowawogs*. The Mohawks call themselves the People of the Flint, or Kanienkehaka.

ohkiwe. Ritual for the dead or ghost dance

ohkwari. Bear

ohseron. Midwinter festival

ohskenonton. Deer

ohskenrari. "Burned bones." An earthbound ghost. Ancient.

ohstawen. Rattle

ohwachira. Matrilineal family

ohwako. Wolf

onakara. Antlers

ondinnonk. "Secret wish of the soul." An object of desire seen in dreams. Of Huron origin. Ancient.

Oneida. People of the Standing Stone. A Native people who are one of the Six Nations of the Iroquois Confederacy.

o'neko:rha. Wampum string

onen'ki'wahi. "That's it for now" or "good-bye"

o'nikon:ra. Mind, spirit (in the sense of the higher, enduring consciousness).

Onkwehonwe. Real People. The First Peoples of America.

Onondaga. People of the Hill. A Native people who are one of the Six Nations of the Iroquois Confederacy. In Mohawk, the word for them is *Ononta'kehaka.*

ononhkwa. Medicine

ononhouroia. "Overturning of heads." The Feast of Dreams. The word is of Huron origin and very ancient. A key feature of the sacred rites of Midwinter, when dream-guessing games are played—recalling the dream-guessing game introduced by Earth Holder in the Sky World—and actions are taken to honor the "secret wishes of the soul" as revealed in dreams.

onononra. "Spirit head." Scalp.

orato. Wild cherry or dogwood. *Orato na'karonto'te* means "The Tree [in the Sky World] is such as the wild cherry."

orenda. Vital energy or magical power

oterontonni'a. Sapling, which is another name for Tharonhiawakon

otkon. Spirit, usually a malign or mischievous one. *Rotkon* means "dark side sorcerer."

otsienha. Council fire

owha:ra. The hollow of a tree; a tunnel or passage. In my dreaming, it's a doorway between the worlds.

oyaron. Power animal—a bird or animal whose form a shape-shifter assumes

raksotha. Grandfather

raniatekowa. Great Turtle, father of the primal Twins

rarenye's. "He spreads himself." A charismatic person.

ratetshents. "He who dreams." Male shaman, healer or doctor.

Ratiwera's. The Thunderers—elemental powers armed with lightning, the bane of evil sorcerers.

roterennote. "He is putting out his power" or "he is singing." Archaic.

Rotinonhsonni. People of the Longhouse; the Six Nations of the Iroquois Confederacy

royaner. "Man of good mind." A traditional lord of the Iroquois Confederacy, chosen by the clan mothers to wear the antlers of office. *Rotiyaner* is the plural form.

sakowennakarahtats. "He sets up the words." An interpreter.

Seneca. One of the Six Nations of the Iroquois Confederacy and the Keepers of its Western Door. The etymology of the word *Seneca* is obscure. The Seneca call themselves Nowataka, People of the Great Hill. Their Cayuga name means the Bird People.

Shonnounkouiretsi. "He has very long hair." A Mohawk shaman who's featured in Father Lafitau's account of the Mohawks.

Skahnehtati. "Through the pines." Albany, New York (not the modern Schenectady, which from the Mohawk viewpoint is on the near side of the pine bush).

sken'nen. Peace

Sonkwaiathison. "He created us." The Creator.

Tawiskaron. Dark Twin. The stem of his name means "ice" in Mohawk; J. N. B. Hewitt speculated that his name means "he is arrayed in ice to a double degree." In this aspect, he is the winter god or frost giant. But his Trickster aspect—his tendency to shake things up and twist things around—can also be detected in his name. Because the stem *wiskar* can also give us the word for slippery, I guess his name means something like "twice as slippery as ice." The Onondaga call him Ohaa and his Seneca name is Otha'kwenda. I sometimes call him Twisty Man because that's his style.

Thadodaho. The Entangled One. In the legend, Thadodaho is the sorcerer-tyrant of Onondaga whose malign power was broken when his mind was cleansed by Hiawatha and the Peacemaker. Today, Thadodaho is the title of an Onondaga chief.

Tharonhiawakon. He Holds on to the Sky with Both Hands. Sky Holder, the Light Twin. He is also called Sapling. He is an embodiment of the life force and the power of insemination, germination, budding, and growth. He creates the good things of the earth, but his creative process is constantly checked and changed by his Dark Twin.

Tuscaroras. People of the Hemp. A Native people who are one of the Six Nations of the Iroquois Confederacy. They migrated north from coastal North Carolina and were adopted into the Confederacy after their disastrous losses in the Tuscarora Wars of 1711–13. With their adoption, the Five Nations of the Confederacy became the Six Nations.

wakaterion'tare. "I know this matter"

wata'enneras. "She shoots arrows." Witch.

watera'swo. "It brings good luck." Dream.

Wyandot. "Speaks the same language." A common rendition of Wen:dat, the Huron name for themselves. It designates the Hurons who fled west after their defeat by the Iroquois in 1649–50.

Bibliography

Achterberg, Jeanne. *Imagery in Healing: Shamanism and Modern Medicine.* Boston: Shambhala, 1985.

Altman, Nathaniel. *Sacred Trees.* San Francisco: Sierra Club, 1994.

Aristides, P. Aelius. *Complete Works.* Vol. 2, *Orations XVII-LIII* and *Sacred Tales.* Leiden, The Netherlands: E. J. Brill, 1981.

Armstrong, William E. *Warrior in Two Camps: Ely S. Parker, Union General and Seneca Chief.* Syracuse, NY: Syracuse University Press, 1978.

Bakker, P. "A Basque Etymology for the Word 'Iroquois.'" *Man in the Northeast* 40 (1990): 89–93.

Barbeau, C. M. *Huron and Wyandot Mythology.* Ottawa: Department of Mines, Geological Survey Memoir 80, 1915.

Beauchamp, William M. *A History of the New York Iroquois.* Albany: New York State Museum Bulletin 78, 1905.

———. *Iroquois Folk Lore Gathered from the Six Nations of New York.* Syracuse, NY: Onondaga Historical Association, 1922.

———. "Iroquois Notes." *Journal of American Folk-Lore* 4 (1891): 39–46.

Becker, Raymond de. *The Understanding of Dreams and Their Influence on the History of Man.* New York: Bell, 1968.

Bierhorst, John, ed. *The Sacred Path: Spells, Prayers & Power Songs of the American Indians.* New York: Quill, 1984.

Bogaert, Harmen Meydertsz van den, *A Journey into Mohawk and Oneida Country, 1634-1635.* Trans. and ed. Charles T. Gehring and William A. Starna. Syracuse: Syracuse University Press, 1988.

Bolgiano, Chris. *Mountain Lion: An Unnatural History of Pumas and People.* Mechanicsburg, PA: Stackpole, 2001.

Bougainville, Louis Antoine de, *Adventures in the Wilderness: The American Journals of Louis Antoine de Bougainville.* Trans. and ed. Edward P. Hamilton. Norman: University of Oklahoma Press, 1964.

264

Bruchac, Joseph, ed. *New Voices from the Longhouse: An Anthology of Contemporary Iroquois Writing.* Greenfield Center, NY: Greenfield Review Press, 1989.

Bruyas, Jacques, *Radices verborum iroquaeorum* (Radical Words of the Mohawk Language, with Their Derivatives). New York: Cramoisy Press, 1863.

Burch, Wanda Easter. *She Who Dreams: A Journey into Healing through Dreamwork.* Novato, CA: New World Library, 2003.

———. "Sir William Johnson's Cabinet of Curiosities." *New York History* 73 (July 1990): 261–82.

Caillois, Roger, ed. *The Dream Adventure.* New York: Orion Press, 1963.

Caillois, Roger, and G. E. von Grünebaum, eds. *Le rêve et les sociétés humaines.* (Dreams and Human Societies) Paris: Gallimard, 1967.

Campbell, Joseph. *The Way of the Animal Powers.* San Francisco: Alfred van der Marck/Harper & Row, 1983.

Campbell, Lyle. *American Indian Languages: The Historical Linguistics of Native America.* New York: Oxford University Press, 1997.

Cashford, Jules. *The Moon: Myth and Image.* New York: Four Walls Eight Windows, 2003.

Colden, Cadwallader. *The History of the Five Indian Nations Depending on the Province of New-York in America.* Ithaca, NY: Cornell University Press, 1964.

Converse, Harriet Maxwell. *Myths and Legends of the New York State Iroquois.* Albany: New York State Museum Bulletin 125, 1908.

Cornplanter, Jesse J. *Legends of the Longhouse.* Philadelphia: Lippincott, 1938.

Couliano, I. P. *Out of this World: Otherworld Journeys from Gilgamesh to Einstein.* Boston: Shambhala, 1991.

Deering, Nora, and Helga Harries Delisle. *Mohawk: A Teaching Grammar.* Ecowi, Quebec: Thunderbird Press, 1976.

Densmore, Frances. *Chippewa Customs.* Washington, DC: Bureau of American Ethnology Bulletin 86, 1929.

Dossey, Larry. *Reinventing Medicine: Beyond Mind-Body to a New Era of Healing.* San Francisco: Harper San Francisco, 1999.

Duncan, Barbara R., ed. *Living Stories of the Cherokee.* Chapel Hill: University of North Carolina Press, 1998.

Durdin-Robertson, Lawrence, *The Cult of the Goddess.* Enniscorthy, Eire: Cesara Publications, 1974.

Eliade, Mircea. *Shamanism: Archaic Techniques of Ecstasy.* Princeton, NJ: Princeton University Press, 1974.

Ellis, Normandi. *Awakening Osiris: A New Translation of the Egyptian Book of the Dead.* Grand Rapids, MI: Phanes Press, 1988.

Ereira, Alan. *The Elder Brothers.* New York: Knopf, 1992.

Everson, William. *Birth of a Poet: The Santa Cruz Meditations.* Santa Barbara, CA: Black Sparrow Press, 1982.

Faraone, Christopher A., and Dirk Obbink, eds. *Magika Hiera: Ancient Greek Magic and Religion.* New York: Oxford University Press, 1997.

Fenton, William N. *The False Faces of the Iroquois.* Norman: University of Oklahoma Press, 1987.

————. *The Great Law and the Longhouse.* Norman: University of Oklahoma Press, 1998.

————. *The Iroquois Eagle Dance, An Offshoot of the Calumet Dance.* Washington, DC: Bureau of American Ethnology Bulletin 156, 1953.

Foster, Michael K., Jack Campisi, and Marianne Mithun, eds. *Extending the Rafters: Interdisciplinary Approaches to Iroquois Studies.* Albany: State University of New York Press, 1984.

Freuchen, Peter. *Peter Freuchen's Book of the Eskimos.* Cleveland, OH: World Publishing Company, 1961.

Garfield, Patricia. *Creative Dreaming.* New York: Ballantine, 1976.

Gill, Sam D. *Native American Religions: An Introduction.* Belmont, CA: Wadsworth, 1982.

Gimbutas, Marija, *The Living Goddesses.* Ed. Miriam Robbins Dexter. Berkeley: University of California Press, 2001.

Graymont, Barbara. *The Iroquois in the American Revolution.* Syracuse, NY: Syracuse University Press, 1972.

Greene, Alma. *Tales of the Mohawks.* Toronto: J. M. Dent, 1975.

Greer, Mary K. *Women of the Golden Dawn.* Rochester, VT: Park Street Press, 1995.

Grim, John A. *The Shaman: Patterns of Religious Healing among the Ojibway Indians.* Norman: University of Oklahoma Press, 1983.

Guldenzopf, David B., "The Colonial Transformation of Mohawk Iroquois Society." PhD Dissertation. Albany: State University of New York, 1986.

Guss, David M. *Language of the Birds: Tales, Text & Poems of Interspecies Communication.* San Francisco: North Point Press, 1985.

Hale, Horatio. *The Iroquois Book of Rites.* Philadelphia: D. G. Brinton, 1883.

Hamell, George R. "The Iroquois and the World's Rim: Speculations on Color, Culture and Contact." *American Indian Quarterly* 26 (Fall 1992): 451–69.

————. "Long-Tail: The Panther in Huron-Wyandot and Seneca Myth, Ritual and Material Culture" In *Icons of Power: Feline Symbolism in the Americas,* edited by Nicholas J. Saunders, 258–91. New York: Routledge, 1998.

Harner, Michael. *The Jivaro: People of the Sacred Waterfalls.* Berkeley: University of California Press, 1984.

————. *The Way of the Shaman.* New York: Harper San Francisco, 1990

Heckewelder, John. *History, Manners and Customs of the Indian Nations who Once Inhabited Pennsylvania and the Neighboring States.* New York: Arno Press, 1971.

Hewitt, J. N. B. "The Iroquoian Concept of the Soul." *Journal of American Folk-Lore* 8 (1895): 107–16.

————. "Iroquoian Cosmology, Part 1." *Annual Reports of the Bureau of American Ethnology* 21 (1903): 127–339.

————. "Iroquoian Cosmology, Part 2." *Annual Reports of the Bureau of American Ethnology* 43 (1928): 449–819.

————. "Kaahastinens or the Fire-dragon." *American Anthropologist* IV, vol. 4 (1891): 384.

———. "Legend of the Founding of the Iroquois League." *American Anthropologist* 5, vol. 2 (1892): 131–48.

———. "Orenda and a Definition of Religion." *American Anthropologist* 44, vol. 1 (1902): 33–46.

———. "Tawiskaron." In *Handbook of American Indians North of Mexico*, edited by F. W. Hodge, vol. 2, 707–11. Washington, DC: Smithsonian Institution Press, 1910.

———. "White Dog Sacrifice." In *Handbook of American Indians North of Mexico*, edited by F. W. Hodge, vol. 2, 939–44. Washington, DC: Smithsonian Institution Press, 1910.

Hewitt, J. N. B., and Jeremiah Curtin, eds. "Seneca Fiction, Legends and Myths," in Annual Reports of the Bureau of American Ethnology 32:37–813. Washington, D.C., 1918.

Hodge, Frederick Webb, ed. *Handbook of American Indians North of Mexico*, vol. 2. Washington, DC: Bureau of American Ethnology Bulletin 30, Smithsonian Institution Press, 1910.

Hoffman, W. J. "The Midewiwin or 'Grand Medicine Society' of the Ojibwa." *Annual Reports of the Bureau of American Ethnology* 7 (1891): 143–300.

Hultkrantz, Ake. *Conceptions of the Soul among North American Indians.* Stockholm: Statens Etnografiska Museum, 1953.

———. *The North American Indian Orpheus Tradition.* Stockholm: Statens Etnografiska Museum, 1957.

———. *The Religions of the American Indians.* Berkeley: University of California Press, 1980.

Hunt, Harry T. *The Multiplicity of Dreams.* New Haven, CT: Yale University Press, 1989.

Ingerman, Sandra. *Soul Retrieval.* San Francisco: Harper San Francisco, 1991.

James, Edwin, ed. *A Narrative of the Captivity and Adventures of John Tanner.* New York: Garland, 1975.

Jennings, Francis, *The Ambiguous Iroquois Empire.* New York: Norton, 1984.

Johansen, Bruce E. *Forgotten Founders: Benjamin Franklin, the Iroquois and the Rationale for the American Revolution.* Ipswich, MA: Gambit, 1982.

Johnson, Sir William. *The Papers of Sir William Johnson.* Edited by James Sullivan et al. 14 vols. Albany: State University of New York Press, 1921–65.

Jung, C. G. *Dreams.* Translated by R. F. C. Hull. Princeton, NJ: Princeton University Press, 1974.

———. *Memories, Dreams, Reflections.* Edited by Aniela Jaffe. New York: Vintage, 1965.

Kalweit, Holger. *Dreamtime & Inner Space: The World of the Shaman.* Boston: Shambhala, 1988.

Kelcher, G. D. *Dreams in Old Norse Literature and their Affinities in Folklore.* Cambridge: Cambridge University Press, 1935.

Kelsay, Isabel Thompson. *Joseph Brant 1743–1807: Man of Two Worlds.* Syracuse, NY: Syracuse University Press, 1984.

Kelsey, Morton P. *God, Dreams and Revelation.* Mahwah, NJ: Paulist Press, 1991.

Krippner, Stanley, and Patrick Welch. *Spiritual Dimensions of Healing.* New York: Irvington, 1992.

Kurath, Gertrude. "The Iroquois Bear Society Ritual Drama." *American Indian Tradition* 8 (1962) no. 2: 84–5.

Lafitau, Joseph-François. *Customs of the American Indians Compared with the Customs of Primitive Times*. Edited and translated by William N. Fenton and Elizabeth L. Moore. 2 vols. Toronto: Champlain Society, 1974, 1977.

———. *Moeurs des sauvages ameriquains, comparés aux moeurs des premiers temps*. 2 vols. Paris: Saugrain l'ainé, 1724. (The original French edition of the work cited above)

Lake, Medicine Grizzlybear. *Native Healer: Initiation into an Ancient Art*. Wheaton, IL: Quest Books, 1991.

Lang, Andrew. *Dreams and Ghosts*. Hollywood, CA: Newcastle Publishing, 1972.

Larsen, Stephen. *The Shaman's Doorway*. Barrytown, NY: Station Hill Press, 1988.

Lawlor, Robert. *Voices of the First Day: Awakening in the Aboriginal Dreamtime*. Rochester, VT: Inner Traditions, 1991.

Le Goff, Jacques. *The Birth of Purgatory*. Chicago: University of Chicago Press, 1984.

———. *L'imaginaire médiéval*. (The Medieval Imaginal Realm) Paris: Gallimard, 1985.

Lohmann, Roger Ivar. *Dream Travelers: Sleep Experiences and Culture in the Western Pacific*. New York: Palgrave Macmillan, 2003.

Long, Max Freedom. *The Secret Science behind Miracles*. Marina del Rey, CA: DeVorss, 1976.

Lopez, Barry. *Of Wolves and Men*. New York: Scribners, 1978.

Lounsbury, Floyd G. *Iroquois Place-Names in the Champlain Valley*. Albany: New York State Education Department, 1960.

Loyola, Ignatius. *The Spiritual Exercises: A Literal Translation and a Contemporary Reading*. Edited by David J. Heming. St. Louis, MO: The Institute of Jesuit Sources, 1978.

Mails, Thomas E. *Fools Crow: Wisdom and Power*. Tulsa, OK: Council Oaks, 1991.

Maracle, David R., *Iontewennaweienhstahkwa: Mohawk Language Dictionary* (Xerox copy) Bay of Quinte, Ontario: 1985

Matthews, Caitlin. *Singing the Soul Back Home*. Shaftesbury, Dorset and Rockport, Mass: Element, 1995.

Matthews, Caitlin and John. *The Encyclopedia of Celtic Wisdom*. Shaftesbury, Dorset and Rockport, Mass: Element, 1997.

McTaggart, Lynne. *The Field: The Quest for the Secret Force of the Universe*. New York: Harper Collins, 2002.

Megapolensis, Johannes, "A Short Account of the Mohawk Indians" in J.F. Jameson, ed., *Narratives of New Netherland*. New York: Barnes and Noble, 1909, 163-180.

Mellick, Jill. *The Natural Artistry of Dreams*. Berkeley, CA: Conari Press, 1996.

Métraux, Alfred. *Réligions et magies indiennes d'Amérique du Sud*. (Indian Religion and Magic in South America) Paris: Gallimard, 1967.

Michelson, Gunther. *A Thousand Words of Mohawk*. Ottawa: National Museum of Man, 1973.

Miller, Patricia Cox. *Dreams in Late Antiquity*. Princeton, NJ: Princeton University Press, 1994.

Modesto, Ruby, and Guy Mount. *Not for Innocent Ears: Spiritual Traditions of a Desert Cahuilla Medicine Woman.* Arcata, CA: Sweetlight Books, 2000.

Morgan, Lewis Henry. *League of the Ho-De-No-Sau-Nee or Iroquois.* 2 vols. New York: Dodd, Mead, 1901.

Moss, Robert. "Blackrobes and Dreamers: Jesuit Reports on the Shamanic Dream Practices of the Northern Iroquoians." *Shaman's Drum* 28 (1992): 30–9.

———. *Conscious Dreaming.* New York: Crown, 1996.

———. *Dreamgates: An Explorer's Guide to the Worlds of Soul, Imagination and Life beyond Death.* New York: Three Rivers Press, 1998.

———. *Dreaming True.* New York: Pocket Books, 2000.

———. *Fire Along the Sky.* Revised and expanded edition containing the love letters of Valerie D'Arcy, complete and unexpurgated. New York: Tom Doherty Associates, 1995.

———. *The Firekeeper: A Narrative of the Eastern Frontier.* New York: Tom Doherty Associates, 1995.

———. "The Healing Power of Ancient Iroquoian Dreamways." *Shaman's Drum* 64 (2003): 54–65.

———*The Interpreter: A Story of Two Worlds.* New York: Tom Doherty Associates, 1997.

———. "Missionaries and Magicians." In *Wonders of the Invisible World: 1600–1900,* edited by Peter Benes. Boston: Boston University Press, 1995.

Narby, Jeremy, and Francis Huxley, eds. *Shamans through Time.* New York: Tarcher/Putnam, 2001.

Needleman, Jacob. *The American Soul: Rediscovering the Wisdom of the Founders.* New York: Tarcher/Putnam, 2003.

Neihardt, John G. *Black Elk Speaks.* New York: Washington Square Press, 1992.

Noel, Daniel C., *The Soul of Shamanism: Western Fatnasies, Imaginal Realities.* New York: Continuum, 1997.

Norton, John. *The Journal of Major John Norton, 1809–1816.* Edited by Carl F. Klinck and James J. Talman. Toronto: Champlain Society, 1970.

O'Callaghan, Edmund B., ed. *Documents Relative to the Colonial History of New York.* 15 vols. Albany, NY: Weed, Parsons, 1853–87.

O'Flaherty, Wendy Doniger. *Dreams, Illusion and Other Realities.* Chicago: University of Chicago Press, 1984.

O'Kelly, Michael J., *Newgrange: Archeology, Art and Legend.* London: Thames and Hudson, 1982.

Oppenheim, A. Leo. *The Interpretation of Dreams in the Ancient Near East.* Philadelphia: American Philosophical Society, 1956.

Parker, Arthur C. *Parker on the Iroquois.* Edited by William N. Fenton. Syracuse, NY: Syracuse University Press, 1968.

———. *Seneca Myths and Folk Tales.* Lincoln: University of Nebraska Press, 1989.

Parkman, Francis, *The Jesuits in North America in the Seventeenth Century.* 2 vols. Boston: Little, Brown, 1902.

Peat, F. David, *Blackfoot Physics: A Journey into the Native American Universe.* Grand Rapids, Michigan: Phanes Press, 2002.

Perkins, John. *The World Is as You Dream It: Shamanic Teachings from the Amazon and Andes.* Rochester, VT: Destiny Books, 1994.

Plato. *Collected Dialogues.* Edited by Edith Hamilton and Huntington Cairns. Princeton, NJ: Bollingen, 1989.

Plutarch. "Concerning the Face Which Appears in the Orb of the Moon." In *Moralia,* vol. 12. Translated by Harold Cherniss and William Helmbold. Cambridge, MA: Harvard University Press, 1995.

Poortman, J. J. *Vehicles of Consciousness.* 4 vols. Utrecht, The Netherlands: Theosophical Society, 1978.

Prechtel, Martin. *Secrets of the Talking Jaguar.* New York: Tarcher/Putnam, 1998.

Radin, Paul. *The Autobiography of a Winnebago Indian.* New York: Dover, 1973.

———. *The Winnebago Tribe.* Lincoln: University of Nebraska Press, 1973.

Richelieu, Peter. *A Soul's Journey.* Wellingborough, Northamptonshire, U.K.: Aquarian Press, 1989.

Ridington, Robin. *Trail to Heaven: Knowledge and Narrative in a Northern Native Community.* Iowa City: University of Iowa Press, 1988.

Rockwell, David. *Giving Voice to Bear: North American Indian Myths, Rituals and Images of the Bear.* Niwot, CO: Roberts Rinehart, 1991.

Rothenberg, Jerome, ed. *Shaking the Pumpkin: Traditional Poetry of the Indian North Americas.* New York: Alfred van der Marck, 1986.

———, ed. *Technicians of the Sacred: A Range of Poetries from Africa, Asia, Europe & Oceania.* Berkeley: University of California Press, 1985.

Russell, Mary Doria. *The Sparrow.* New York: Fawcett Columbine, 1996.

Ryan, Robert E. *The Strong Eye of Shamanism: A Journey into the Caves of Consciousness.* Rochester, VT: Inner Traditions, 1999.

Sagard, Gabriel. *The Long Journey to the Country of the Hurons.* Edited by George M. Wrong. Toronto: Champlain Society, 1939.

Sarangerel. *Riding Windhorses: A Journey into the Heart of Mongolian Shamanism.* Rochester, VT: Destiny Books, 2000.

Schmitt, Jean-Claude. *Ghosts in the Middle Ages: The Living and the Dead in Medieval Society.* Chicago: University of Chicago Press, 1998.

Shulman, David, and Guy G. Stroumsa, eds. *Dream Cultures: Explorations in the Comparative History of Dreaming.* New York: Oxford University Press, 1999.

Silverman, Kenneth. *The Life and Times of Cotton Mather.* New York: Harper & Row, 1984.

Snow, Dean R. *The Iroquois.* Oxford and Cambridge, MA: Blackwell, 1994.

Snow, Dean R., Charles T. Gehring, and William A. Starna. *In Mohawk Country: Early Narratives about a Native People.* Syracuse, NY: Syracuse University Press, 1996.

Stephen, Michele. *A'isa's Gifts: A Study of Magic and the Self.* Berkeley: University of California Press, 1995.

Stevens, Paul Lawrence. "His Majesty's Savage Allies: British Policy and the Northern Indians During the Revolutionary War." 4 vols. PhD diss., State University of New York at Buffalo, 1984.

Sullivan, Lawrence E. *Icanchu's Drum: An Orientation to Meaning in South American Traditions.* New York: Macmillan, 1988.

Szpakowska, Kasia Maria. "The Perception of Dreams and Nightmares in Ancient Egypt: Old Kingdom to Third Intermediate Period." PhD diss., University of California at Los Angeles, 2000.

Tedlock, Barbara, ed. *Dreaming: Anthropological and Psychological Interpretations.* Santa Fe, NM: School of American Research Press, 1992.

Tehanetorens. *Tales of the Iroquois.* Rooseveltown, NY (Mohawk Nation): Akwesasne Notes, 1976.

———. *Wampum Belts of the Iroquois.* Summertown, TN: Book Publishing Company, 1999.

Thompson, Stith. *Tales of the North American Indians.* Bloomington: Indiana University Press, 1966.

Thwaites, Reuben Gold, ed. *Jesuit Relations and Allied Documents: Travels and Explorations of the Jesuit Missionaries in New France, 1610–1791.* 73 vols. Cleveland, OH: Burrows Brothers, 1896–1901.

Tooker, Elizabeth. *The Iroquois Ceremonial of Midwinter.* Syracuse, NY: Syracuse University Press, 1970.

———, ed. *Native North American Spirituality of the Eastern Woodlands.* Mahwah, NJ: Paulist Press, 1979.

Trigger, Bruce G. *The Children of Ataensic: A History of the Huron People to 1660.* Montreal, QC, and Kingston, ON: McGill-Queens University Press, 1987.

———, ed. *Handbook of North American Indians.* Vol. 15, *Northeast.* Washington, DC: Smithsonian Institution Press, 1978.

Tylor, Edward B. *Primitive Culture: Researches into the Development of Mythology, Philosophy, Religion, Language, Art and Custom.* 2 vols. New York: Henry Holt, 1871.

Ullman, Montague, Stanley Krippner, and Alan Vaughan. *Dream Telepathy.* London: Turnstone Books, 1973.

University of Toronto Press. *Dictionary of Canadian Biography.* Vol. 1, *1000 to 1700.* Toronto: University of Toronto Press, 1966.

Wallace, Anthony F. C. *The Death and Rebirth of the Seneca.* New York: Knopf, 1970.

———. "Dreams and the Wishes of the Soul: A Type of Psychoanalytic Theory among the Seventeenth Century Iroquois." *American Anthropologist* 60 (1958): 234–48.

Wallace, Paul A. W. *The White Roots of Peace.* Philadelphia: University of Pennsylvania Press, 1946.

Walsh, Roger N. *The Spirit of Shamanism.* New York: Jeremy P. Tarcher/Perigee, 1990.

Watkins, Susan M. *Dreaming Myself, Dreaming a Town.* New York: Kendall Enterprises, 1989.

Weslager, C. A. *The Delaware Indians: A History.* New Brunswick, NJ: Rutgers University Press, 1972.

Wilber, Ken. *Up From Eden: A Transpersonal View of Human Evolution.* Wheaton, IL: Theosophical Publishing House, 1996.

Wolf, Fred. *The Eagle's Quest: A Physicist Finds Scientific Truth at the Heart of the Shamanic World.* New York: Touchstone, 1991.

Wolf, Morris. *Iroquois Religion and its Relation to their Morals*. New York: Columbia University Press, 1919.

Woodbury, Hanni, ed. and trans. *Concerning the League: The Iroquois League Tradition as Dictated in Onondaga by John Arthur Gibson*. Winnipeg, MB: Algonquian and Iroquoian Linguistics Memoir 19, 1992.

Index